W9-DGS-704

Food Safety

Recent Titles in the
CONTEMPORARY WORLD ISSUES
Series

Books in the **Contemporary World Issues** series address vital issues in today's society such as genetic engineering, pollution, and biodiversity. Written by professional writers, scholars, and nonacademic experts, these books are authoritative, clearly written, up-to-date, and objective. They provide a good starting point for research by high school and college students, scholars, and general readers as well as by legislators, businesspeople, activists, and others.

Each book, carefully organized and easy to use, contains an overview of the subject, a detailed chronology, biographical sketches, facts and data and/or documents and other primary source material, a forum of authoritative perspective essays, annotated lists of print and nonprint resources, and an index.

Readers of books in the Contemporary World Issues series will find the information they need in order to have a better understanding of the social, political, environmental, and economic issues facing the world today.

Food Safety

A REFERENCE HANDBOOK

Third Edition

Nina E. Redman and Michele Morrone

ABC-CLIO™

An Imprint of ABC-CLIO, LLC
Santa Barbara, California • Denver, Colorado

Kishwaukee College Library
21193 Malta Rd.
Malta, IL 60150-9699

Copyright © 2017 by ABC-CLIO, LLC

All rights reserved. No part of this publication may be reproduced, stored in a retrieval system, or transmitted, in any form or by any means, electronic, mechanical, photocopying, recording, or otherwise, except for the inclusion of brief quotations in a review, without prior permission in writing from the publisher.

Library of Congress Cataloging-in-Publication Data

Names: Redman, Nina, author. | Morrone, Michele, 1962– author.
Title: Food safety : a reference handbook / Nina E. Redman
    and Michele Morrone.
Description: Third edition. | Santa Barbara, California :
    ABC-CLIO, 2017. | Series: Contemporary world issues |
    Includes bibliographical references and index.
Identifiers: LCCN 2016042042 (print) | LCCN 2016044841
    (ebook) | ISBN 9781440852626 (alk. paper) |
    ISBN 9781440852633 (ebook)
Subjects: LCSH: Food adulteration and inspection—Handbooks,
    manuals, etc. | Food industry and trade—Safety measures—
    Handbooks, manuals, etc.
Classification: LCC TX531 .R44 2017 (print) | LCC TX531
    (ebook) | DDC 363.19/26—dc23
LC record available at https://lccn.loc.gov/2016042042

ISBN: 978-1-4408-5262-6
EISBN: 978-1-4408-5263-3

21 20 19 18 17   1 2 3 4 5

This book is also available as an eBook.

ABC-CLIO
An Imprint of ABC-CLIO, LLC

ABC-CLIO, LLC
130 Cremona Drive, P.O. Box 1911
Santa Barbara, California 93116-1911
www.abc-clio.com

This book is printed on acid-free paper ∞

Manufactured in the United States of America

Contents

Ten years have passed since the second edition of this book, and many new food safety trends, opportunities, and threats have emerged. For example, the local foods movement enhances fresh ingredients for some but also increases the regulatory burden to ensure these foods are safe. Genetically modified organism are increasingly viewed as endangering public health even though much evidence suggests otherwise. The first revision to federal food safety legislation in more than 70 years was signed into law in 2011, but the number of multistate foodborne outbreak investigations continues unabated. Each section of this new edition has been completely revised with the most current information as of late 2016.

Chapter 1 briefly outlines the regulatory history of the food industry, providing some background information about the most common foodborne illnesses with an emphasis on microbes. Additionally, food safety management systems, outbreak investigations, international food safety, and consumer's roles in food safety are discussed. Chapter 2 examines other food safety threats, including the additives and contaminants aspartame, olestra, acrylamide, benzene, mercury in fish, and polychlorinated biphenyls in salmon. Additional problems and controversies, including pesticides, growth hormones in cattle, genetically modified organisms, irradiation, antibiotic resistance, pink slime, and raw milk, are included in this chapter.

The food industry has a great impact on the environment and human health, and people face increasing threats from diseases that both humans and animals can contract, such as avian flu, and from increased air and water pollution.

Chapter 3 is a new feature of the third edition, consisting of perspectives from a variety of individuals with experience in food safety issues. These perspectives bring together key voices from diverse disciplinary contexts and raise some compelling questions about the state of food safety in the United States.

Chapter 4 has biographical sketches of prominent people who have influenced food safety. Improving food safety is a result of the combined efforts of food safety activists, legislators, food technologists, epidemiologists who track the sources of disease, scientists who discover better ways to process food, and companies that dedicate themselves to producing and serving safe food. The people discussed in this chapter are representative of the kinds of people working on food safety both today and in the past. A directory of food safety organizations and agencies, including industry trade groups, activist organizations, and federal, state, and international governmental organizations concerned with food safety, is also included in Chapter 4.

Chapter 5 contains facts and statistics about food safety issues, passages from significant writings that have influenced food safety, and excerpts from food safety reports, laws, and guidance documents, including a portion of the Food Safety Modernization Act of 2010. Chapter 6 includes an annotated bibliography of books, journals, databases, training resources, data visualization tools, and consumer resources. Chapter 7 presents a chronology of important events in food safety history from ancient times to the present. A glossary of frequently used terms is included at the end of the book.

Food Safety

Experts disagree about whether food is safer today than in the past, but they agree that ensuring safe food is more complex now than at any other point in history. Although we have solved many historical food safety challenges, new problems continually emerge. We farm, live, and eat differently now, creating new niches for foodborne illnesses. This chapter provides a brief history of food safety, including background on the U.S. regulatory structure, information about causes of major foodborne illnesses, and consumer tips for illness prevention.

Legislative and Regulatory Overview

"Safer and healthier foods" is considered one of the ten great public health achievements in the 20th century (CDC, 2013a). From 1900 to 1999, food safety practices changed dramatically as a result of advances in refrigeration, food processing, and regulatory protocols. Food safety issues have evolved from major

---

Meat inspectors at the Swift & Company packing house in Chicago, ca. 1906. Both hygiene and labor conditions within the meatpacking industry came under close scrutiny by so-called muckraking journalists at the turn of the century. Upton Sinclair's seminal work *The Jungle* was a fictionalized account of working conditions in a packing house, but it created public outrage about the safety and sanitation of the food supply. Sinclair's work helped bring about the passage of the first laws dedicated to food safety in 1906, the Federal Meat Inspection Act and Pure Food and Drug Act. (Library of Congress)

epidemics of typhoid fever and tuberculosis to those involving pathogens such as *Salmonella, Escherichia coli,* and noroviruses. As food safety issues have changed, so have society's methods for making food as safe as possible. Before contemporary food processing, traditional farming practices and preserving techniques ensured safe food as people ate fresh produce and local meats. Today, much of the American diet is reliant on food technologies and processed foods that can contribute to widespread outbreaks involving thousands of people.

Food technology expanded during the Industrial Revolution in the mid to late 1800s in response to multiple factors, including improvements in transportation systems. As consumers moved further from their food supply and many settled in more urban areas, the need to preserve food for long-distance travel created concerns over the quality of food. Questions were raised about the safety of adulterating foods by adding substances to preserve them or maximize profits. This was during a time when there was no oversight and food manufacturers were essentially unregulated.

The start of the "pure foods movement" is often attributed to women activists in the 1880s who were protesting the conditions at slaughterhouses in New York City and adulterated foods in other parts of the country. The movement gained momentum in 1883, when Harvey W. Wiley, chief chemist of the Bureau of Chemistry in the U.S. Department of Agriculture, began experimenting with food and drug adulteration. He enlisted volunteers to take small doses of toxic chemicals and other substances in foods to determine possible health effects. This group of volunteers was known as the "poison squad," and the experiments went on for many years. Wiley, who is referred to as the "father of the Pure Food and Drugs Act," was instrumental in passing legislation to regulate what could go into food; by the turn of the century, most states has passed pure foods laws (Law, 2003).

Even with the work of Wiley and the pure foods movement, lawmakers may not have acted to legislate food safety if it wasn't for public outcry resulting from a popular book that was intended to highlight poor working conditions. Author Upton Sinclair spent several weeks in a Chicago meat-packing plant investigating labor conditions and turned his discoveries into a book, *The Jungle*, published in 1906. Although the book's focus was on conditions experienced by immigrants in the early 20th century, Sinclair also provided graphic descriptions of the filth and poor hygiene in the packing plants. These descriptions of packing plants—not the poor working conditions of immigrants—caught the public's attention. People complained to Congress and President Theodore Roosevelt, and led to pressure from foreign governments wanting some assurances that food imported from the United States was pure and wholesome. Combined with these factors were concerns raised by food manufacturers who were forced to comply with varying laws that were being implemented in individual states. The result of public, manufacturing, and political outcry was the passage of two seminal laws in 1906: the Pure Food and Drugs Act and the Federal Meat Inspection Act.

Throughout history, food safety laws and regulations have mostly been reactionary rather than preventive, coming about in response to outbreaks and public concern about specific health hazards. The very brief discussion below of some of the major food safety legislation underscores a federal government approach that relies on congressional appropriations of adequate resources for inspections, voluntary compliance, and training and education. It also highlights some of the challenges in regulating food safety in the United States based on the convoluted governmental approach.

Legislation

The Pure Food and Drugs Act of 1906 made it illegal to adulterate or misbrand food by threatening fines and imprisonment of anyone caught doing so. It required the U.S. Department of Agriculture (USDA) to test food products to ensure that they did not contain poisonous or putrid substances. The act also established protocols for importing and exporting foods and essentially laid the foundation for inspection services provided by the government.

Twenty years after the Pure Food and Drugs Act of 1906, the Bureau of Chemistry was reorganized and enforcing the law was separated from research activities. The Food, Drug, and Insecticide Administration was created in 1927, and its name was shortened to the Food and Drug Administration (FDA) in 1930. After more than 100 people died from ingesting a contaminated elixir in 1937, it was clear that the penalties in the Pure Food and Drug Act were not a deterrent to adulterating food products. In 1938, the Federal Food, Drug, and Cosmetics Act (FFDCA) replaced the 1906 Act, authorizing inspections of factories and setting tolerance levels for poisonous substances. The FFDCA remained one cornerstone of food safety legislation for more than 70 years.

After several years of implementation, weaknesses with the FFDCA emerged, specifically in the FDA's ability to establish and enforce levels of chemicals in foods. During this time, the public was becoming more aware of chemicals and pesticides and concerned about connections to cancer. Congress responded with several amendments to the FFDCA, including the adoption of the Food Additives Amendments in 1958 and the Color Additive Amendments in 1960, which included a stipulation known as the "Delaney Clause," named for Congressman James Delaney of New York. The Delaney Clause expanded the FDA's regulatory powers and required manufacturers to prove additives and pesticides are safe before they could be used. This law specifically focused on substances that were determined to be carcinogenic, and the burden of proof was on manufacturers to ensure substances such as chemicals, colors, and preservatives were safe for human consumption.

Food product labeling has been part of the legislative landscape since the early 1900s. In addition to the misbranding components of the Pure Food and Drugs Act, the 1913 Gould Amendment to the 1906 law led to regulations focused mainly on weights and numerical counts of packaged foods rather than nutrition. The 1930 McNary-Mapes Amendments to the Pure Food and Drugs Act specifically authorized the Secretary of Agriculture to establish labeling standards for canned foods. It wasn't until 1967, with the passage of the Fair Packaging and Labeling Act, that labels became standardized and were required to provide honest information. This act was jointly administered by the FDA and the Federal Trade Commission and required labels to include ingredient information in addition to weights and measures.

The FDA has been directly responsible in ensuring food products are labeled accurately for decades; historically, this mainly involved safeguarding consumers from unsubstantiated health claims. In 1990, the Nutrition Labeling and Education Act expanded labeling requirements so that all packaged foods identified nutrition information, health claims, and ingredients. Today, labeling has become a greater challenge because of public concerns over safety rather than health claims. For example, calls for foods to be labeled if they are irradiated, contain genetically modified organisms, or are allergen-free come from individuals and organizations who are worried about food safety.

The FFDCA and the Federal Insecticide, Fungicide, and Rodenticide Acts (FIFRA) were amended by the Food Quality Protection Act (FQPA) of 1996. The FQPA changed the way acceptable pesticide amounts are calculated so that total exposure from all sources must be assessed for tolerance levels. This meant that cumulative impacts of using more than one pesticide or chemical in food must be evaluated and remain under acceptable levels. This law also focused on minimizing exposures in children by mandating a safety margin for quantities of pesticide in foods. It would be the last significant federal legislation related to food safety until 2011.

After a series of multistate outbreaks involving everything from frozen pizza to fresh tomatoes, the U.S. Congress passed the Food Safety Modernization Act (FSMA) in 2010, and

President Obama signed it into law in January 2011. The FSMA mandates a preventive approach to food safety and addresses capacity to prevent, detect, and respond to food safety problems. The first rules from the FSMA were proposed in 2013, and final rules were codified in 2016 for several key issues including produce safety, food product transportation, and adulteration. One key feature of the FSMA is that it strengthens the government's authority to require recalls of potentially unsafe food products. In addition, the FSMA specifically focuses on strengthening the safety of imported foods, which are becoming an increasingly important component of the American diet.

There have been other federal laws that either directly or indirectly impact food safety. However, the most important federal legislation that addresses food safety is the annual budget. Even with comprehensive laws in place with stringent requirements, if there are no or limited resources to craft regulations to enforce these laws, little progress will be made in food safety. One of the main criticisms of the FSMA is that it will not be as effective as it could be due to resource constraints. In addition, it does little to address the fragmented nature of the food safety regulatory system in the United States, which involves multiple players, all with significant, mostly unmet, resource needs (Tai, 2015).

Regulatory System

There are currently at least 15 different agencies in several federal government departments responsible for food safety in the United States (Government Accountability Office, 2014; Johnson, 2014). Each of these agencies is authorized to act under specific statutes and with specific roles and responsibilities, leading to a fragmented regulatory system at the federal level (Government Accountability Office, 2011). The FDA and the USDA are two components of this system with the longest history, dating back to the 1800s. While the FDA was originally part of the USDA and the Public Health Service, it is now housed in the Department of Health and Human Services. The USDA is a stand-alone cabinet department that includes the Food Safety Inspection Service (FSIS) and the Animal and Plant Health Inspection Service, among others.

Generally responsible for the safety of most animal products, the USDA celebrated its 150th anniversary in 2012 (U.S. Department of Agriculture, 2015). President Lincoln created the USDA in 1862, but it wasn't until the 1890s, when some European governments raised questions about the safety of U.S. beef, that Congress assigned the USDA the task of ensuring beef exports met European standards. In 1891, the USDA started inspecting livestock slaughtered in the United States. Veterinarians were recruited to oversee the inspection process, with the goal of preventing diseased animals from entering the food supply.

During World War II, more women entered the workforce, and consumption of fast food increased. Ready-to-eat foods like processed hams, sausages, soups, hot dogs, frozen dinners, and pizza increased dramatically. The 1950s saw large growth in meat and poultry processing facilities. New ingredients, new technology, and specialization increased the complexity of the slaughter and processing industry. Slaughterhouses grew from small facilities handling hundreds of animals to large factories using high-speed processing techniques handling thousands. As a result, food technology, microbiology, and inspections became increasingly important tools to monitor safety.

The FSIS, the inspection arm of the USDA, monitors compliance with several federal statutes, including the Poultry Products Inspection Act, the Meat Inspection Act, and the Egg Products Inspection Act. The number of inspectors at FSIS grew to a high of more than 10,000 inspectors in 1981 (Government Accountability Office, 1994). As the meat and poultry industries grew, it became impossible for inspectors to evaluate each individual carcass. The 2016 FSIS workforce of about 9,400 inspectors is increasingly relying on risk-assessment techniques and other systematic approaches to manage these risks. The result of this is that a significant amount of meat and poultry processing facilities are not inspected regularly and food safety compliance is increasingly in the hands of manufacturers.

The FDA picks up programs specifically left out of the USDA's mandates. These include all domestic and imported foods, with the exception of meat and poultry products. FDA inspectors are responsible for a wide range of programs under its authorizing legislation, including drugs, medical devices, and foods (including dietary supplements). When a field inspector sees something at a facility that might be out of compliance with regulations, he or she records observations on a specific form. These forms are compiled on an annual basis into observational summaries; typically, observations related to food comprise the majority of concerns noted by inspectors (FDA, 2016b). The most common observations from field inspectors are those involving managing pests, monitoring sanitation, and implementing Hazard Analysis and Critical Control Points (HACCP) plans.

Other federal entities with responsibility for food safety include the Centers for Disease Control and Prevention (CDC), which is not a regulatory agency; rather, it focuses on preventing the spread of disease, educating the public, and assisting in outbreak investigations. Like the FDA, the CDC is housed in the Department of Health and Human Services. On the other hand, the U.S. Environmental Protection Agency (EPA) is an independent agency not located in the President's Cabinet. The EPA manages toxics, including pesticides and other chemicals such as heavy metals. The Department of Homeland Security (DHS) is newest to the Cabinet, formed in response to September 11, 2001. The DHS is responsible for the safety of many imported foods and to assessing vulnerabilities of the food supply to terrorism.

While federal statutes, regulations, and agencies are important components of the food safety regulatory system, it is the state and local health officials that are the essential frontline for consumers. These officials are authorized by state laws and local ordinances to conduct inspections at a variety of facilities. In most states, it is the local city or county health department that houses the workforce to inspect retail establishments, farmer's markets, groceries, and other facilities that sell directly to the consumer. There is no uniform set of food regulations, although many localities rely on the Federal Food Code in devising local laws and ordinances.

The food safety regulatory system is complex, involving key actors at all levels of government. These actors and agencies are responsible for specific foods or food processes in the context of an ever-expanding food industry. The regulatory system is not only fragmented; it is stretched thin, especially considering the critical role of local health agencies in protecting consumers. The hope is that the weaknesses in the food regulatory system can be at least partially addressed by non-regulatory approaches, including food safety management systems and strategies focusing on prevention rather than regulation.

Risk-Based Inspections

Inspections have been the foundation of the food safety management system in the United States for decades. Risk-based inspections target facilities handling foods that are the greatest public health risk or serve populations most susceptible to illness. For example, because of the potential for harm, preschools and hospitals should be inspected more often and more comprehensively than a convenience store. A processing facility that smokes or cures meat would be considered a greater risk than a facility that reheats prepared foods, and inspection protocols would address the risk differential. This approach prioritizes activities of food safety regulators so that limited resources can address the most significant risks first.

Annex 5 of the Federal Food Code and the National Voluntary Retail Food Regulatory Program Standards provide specific guidance on risk-based inspections. These inspections should focus on those factors that are likely to contribute the most to unsafe food. The factors are divided into five broad categories that FDA refers to as "foodborne illness risk factors":

1. Food from unsafe sources

2. Inadequate cooking

3. Improper holding temperatures

4. Contaminated equipment

5. Poor personal hygiene

In addition, the Annex provides an example of how to categorize facilities based on risk, with those establishments serving highly susceptible populations considered the greatest risks. During the inspection, the inspector must focus on observing behaviors and practices that could have the most significant impact on food safety. Most importantly, inspectors assess the effectiveness of "active managerial control" over the foodborne risk factors. This means that risk-based inspections could take more time than "routine" inspections because of the need for dialogue between the inspector and the operator. The inspection includes focusing on the issues that are most likely to lead to unsafe food, including knowledge of management and other personnel, temperature control of foods, and personal hygiene. Inspectors will review previous inspection reports, review menus and food items, complete a walk-through, determine how food flows through the establishment from receiving to serving, identify any foodborne illness risk factors, and evaluate managerial control of the risk factors. Active managerial control includes knowledge about proper temperatures for all food preparation techniques and personal hygiene protocols, among other items.

Until the FSMA of 2011, risk-based inspections were described in the Food Code as guidance to food regulators. The Code suggests four different categories of facilities with corresponding inspection logistics. As such, regulatory agencies could choose to develop their own system of risk-based inspections. With the FSMA, risk-based inspections are now mandatory, and all facilities that are considered high risk because of their product, processing, or population served must be inspected immediately and regularly. This mandate has led to the need to enhance the capacity of the food safety workforce and has created a new niche for trainers and educators to address this need. It has also created concerns among local health departments about their capacity to meet the requirements for risk-based inspections while not compromising overall food safety regulatory activities.

Non-Regulatory Food Safety Management

Ensuring food safety requires a systematic approach with capacity to evaluate all facets of the food supply, investigate outbreaks, conduct inspections, and educate consumers. All components of a highly effective system focus on preventing hazards and safeguarding public health. Many of the most important elements of food safety are non-regulatory because they offer guidance or are voluntary in nature. For example, the Federal Food Code is the framework for building food safety programs; it is not a set of regulations that the industry must comply with or health officials must implement. Risk analysis is a tool for assessing the safety of ingredients and processes. HACCP is a comprehensive strategy to ensure safe food processing. The National Voluntary Retail Food Regulatory Program Standards are available for regulatory agencies to use in assessing their effectiveness. Outbreak investigation techniques provide critical information on preventing the spread of illness and identifying dangerous food sources.

The Federal Food Code

The Federal Food Code is a guidance document grounded in science and research which serves as a model to state and local governments. It is not a law, regulation, or even requirement; it is a comprehensive document that offers advice from food scientists to protect the public from unsafe food. The first Food

Code was published in 1993, and until 2001 it was revised every two years. Starting in 2001, the code is revised every four years so that the most recent code is from 2013 (FDA, 2013a). The Code is written by scientists and experts in the FDA, CDC, and the FSIS and is intended to serve as a model and reference for local health agencies. Local health agencies are not required to adopt the Food Code, but the FDA encourages them to do so citing numerous benefits, including creating uniform standards that will aid manufacturers, operators, and others in creating safe food.

The 768-page Food Code includes a wealth of information related to management and personnel, equipment, plumbing, physical facilities, and compliance and enforcement, among many others. Science-based advice on proper temperatures for cooking, cooling, and reheating is contained in the Code, and the temperature "danger zone" is noted. The danger zone is a temperature range that is most conducive to pathogen growth, and the 2013 Food Code identifies this range as 41 to 135 degrees Fahrenheit. Perhaps the most useful components of the Code are the annexes offering specific guidance and examples for HACCP and risk-based inspections, as well as examples of forms and specific tools to use by state and local health officials.

The Food Code is likely the most important, non-regulatory component of food safety because of its specificity and wealth of information about a wide range of foods, food processing, and handling food in retail establishments. All 50 states have adopted some version of the Federal Food Code as their regulatory framework, although not all states use the most current version (Association of Food and Drug Officials, 2016).

Risk Analysis

Risk analysis is the process of evaluating food safety risks and determining whether ingredients can safely be consumed in the amounts likely to be present in a given food. The FDA uses the *Working Principles for Risk Analysis for Food Safety for Application by Governments* from Codex Alimentarius (2007).

Codex is an international organization that sets standards and guidelines for food safety. The Codex principles for risk analysis include three components: (1) risk assessment, (2) risk communication, and (3) risk management.

Risk assessment is a four-step scientific process: hazard identification, exposure assessment, dose-response assessment, and risk characterization. The purpose of risk assessment is to identify the probability of harm from a specific food, substance in food, or food-processing activity. For example, in 2014 FDA conducted a risk assessment of arsenic in rice and rice products. In assessing hazards from arsenic, scientists evaluated existing information related to its toxicity and the potential cancer and non-cancer health effects under various dose-response and exposure scenarios. The risk assessment report characterized the evidence and uncertainties related to the health effects from exposure to arsenic in rice products (FDA, 2016a).

After a public comment period and once the risk assessment was finalized, FDA policy makers determined approaches to manage the risks identified. In the case of arsenic in rice, FDA set an action level for the amount that is acceptable to be protective of infants. Risk communication specialists are involved throughout risk analysis in translating both the science and the decisions to the public. After the arsenic risks were characterized, FDA offered advice to parents, which includes varying diets for infants and pregnant women so there is less reliance on rice and rice products.

Hazard Analysis and Critical Control Points (HACCP)

HACCP, which was developed by Pillsbury for NASA in the late 1950s, is a systematic approach to identifying likely food hazards and establishing procedures at critical points to ensure safety. Since HACCP is tailored to specific foods, it can be applied at any point in food production. The steps include analyzing the potential problem areas, examining inputs to the system, determining prevention and control measures, taking action when controls and criteria are not met, and establishing and maintaining record-keeping procedures.

Guidance on implementing HACCP in the United States comes from the National Advisory Committee on Microbiological Criteria for Foods (NACMCF). The NACMCF consists of representatives from multiple federal agencies, including the FSIS, FDA, CDC, and the Departments of Commerce and Defense. The committee was formed by legislation in 1988 to provide guidance to the Secretaries of Agriculture and Health and Human Services related to controlling microbiological pathogens in foods. Since that time, the NACMCF has played an important role in developing and refining the HACCP system (NACMCF, 1997).

In order for HACCP to effectively address food safety, facilities must have additional policies and programs in place; these are referred to as "prerequisite" programs. Vendor Certification Programs and Sanitation Standard Operating Procedures are examples of prerequisite programs that are largely related to product quality. With prerequisite programs in place, HACCP can be implemented to focus on controlling hazards specifically from microbial contamination of food. HACCP is still voluntary in food retail establishments such as restaurants, cafeterias, and groceries. However, some states encourage the implementation of HACCP in these places by reducing the regulatory burden.

Until 2011, HACCP was mandatory only for meat, juice, and seafood-processing facilities in the United States. The 2011 FSMA mandates a preventive approach to ensuring food safety, which includes a HACCP-like system. Under FSMA, all food-processing facilities are required to have written prevention control plans that are similar to the HACCP approach. These plans must include the potential hazards and how these hazards will be monitored and controlled. In addition, the plans must address how the facility will respond if control protocols are breached and detail how records will be kept.

Voluntary National Retail Food Regulatory Program Standards

An additional approach to ensuring effective food safety protection is found in the Voluntary National Retail Food Regulatory Program Standards, or the "Retail Program Standards." These standards arose from discussions among federal agencies in 1996 to improve the safety of food retail establishments. These discussions led to two principles that serve as the basis for the Retail Program Standards (FDA, 2015):

1. Promote active managerial control of the risk factors most commonly associated with foodborne illness in food establishments, and

2. Establish a recommended framework for retail food regulatory programs with which active managerial control of the risk factors can be best realized.

As with the Food Code, local food regulatory agencies can choose to enroll in the Retail Standards Program. Once enrolled, these agencies complete self-assessments and audits of how their regulatory protocols adhere to the tenets of the Food Code. There are nine standards with specific requirements for regulatory agencies. For example, the standard for uniform inspection requires that "program management [establish] a quality assurance program to ensure uniformity among regulatory staff in the interpretation of laws, regulations, policies, and procedures." An agency enrolled in the program would conduct an assessment and submit documentation to the FDA that identifies their compliance with this standard.

Outbreak Investigations

Even with systems in place to analyze risks and hazards, conduct risk-based inspections, and manage and evaluate regulatory effectiveness, millions of people still get sick from eating contaminated food every year. A foodborne outbreak is defined as "an incident in which two or more persons experience a similar illness after ingestion of a common food, and epidemiologic analysis implicates the food as the source of the illness" (CDC, 2011). Investigating outbreaks involves several components with the goal of minimizing the public health impact of unsafe food. These components form an integrated approach that includes disease surveillance, epidemiology, laboratory analysis, environmental assessment, and trace-back/trace-forward practices. This holistic system works best when it involves a team comprised of regulators at all levels of government, scientists, farmers and food processors, and consumers.

Disease Surveillance

Monitoring disease is a critical element of outbreak investigations, and there are several tools in use to alert public health officials when an outbreak might be occurring. The National Outbreak Reporting System (NORS) is a web-based system that went live in 2009 and is available to state and local health officials to report potential outbreaks of enteric diseases. The benefit of NORS is that it allows the CDC to monitor information across the country to identify the possibility of a multistate outbreak. Figure 1.1 shows the flow of outbreak information in NORS.

NORS is a relatively new system, and it is only available to public health officials for reporting active outbreaks. Members of the public can access information in the CDC's Foodborne Outbreak Online Database (FOOD), which includes searchable data since 1998. In order for NORS and FOOD to be accurate, health officials rely on consumers to report illness either to their health provider or directly to the health department. Because most people are not likely to go to a doctor with diarrhea, vomiting, or other enteric symptoms, foodborne disease outbreaks are likely significantly underreported.

Prior to NORS, and since 1995, the CDC has collaborated with 10 state health departments to keep track of foodborne disease using the Foodborne Diseases Active Surveillance Network

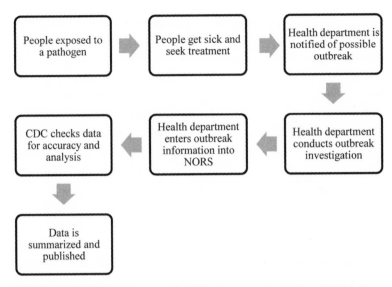

Figure 1.1   Flow of Information in the National Outbreak Reporting System (CDC, 2016c).

(FoodNet). FoodNet uses active surveillance in the 10 states, surveys, and epidemiological studies to monitor incidence and trends of illness caused by seven bacteria and two parasites. The annual report from FoodNet summarizes trends in illness associated with the nine microbes in the participating states. The CDC uses the FoodNet data to make estimates about the population impacts of foodborne disease in the United States, and current estimates are that 48 million Americans get sick every year.

Epidemiology

Much of what is known about foodborne illnesses started with epidemiology, the study of disease in populations. John Snow, a London anesthesiologist, used deductive reasoning, research, and interviews in the 1880s to determine the cause of a cholera epidemic that killed more than 500 people in one week. Snow's main tool to describe the prevalence of disease was a hand-drawn map locating cases and seeking a common exposure source, which was identified as a pump used for drinking water. Scientists used Snow's techniques to investigate infectious disease until the 1920s, when the field broadened to include clusters of all factors that apply to the incidence of disease among people.

Epidemiological techniques have improved over the years; it is now a science that uses both observation and statistics to understand disease. In the 1970s, Dr. Paul Blake developed the case-control method, which compares sick people with closely matched individuals who are well. By looking for differences between ill and well people, the source of infection can often be revealed. In the case of foodborne illness, an ill person is questioned about where and what he or she ate and matched as closely as possible in age, health status, and eating patterns to someone who stayed well in an effort to pinpoint differences.

In the United States, the CDC works to help treat and prevent disease at the national level and has increased its scope to lend epidemiological assistance worldwide because of the overlap between the developed and less developed countries. Most states have epidemiologists who coordinate outbreak investigations with assistance from local health officials. The Council of State and Territorial Epidemiologists is a membership-based nongovernmental organization that serves as a professional society for practicing epidemiologists.

Laboratory Analysis

After an outbreak is confirmed through surveillance and epidemiology, identifying the pathogenic culprit is a critical step to understanding and curtailing the spread of illness. In most cases, microorganisms, usually bacteria or viruses, are the cause of foodborne illness. However, because symptoms of many illnesses are often very similar, laboratory analysis is essential to linking specific foods to suspected cases. Since 1996, the CDC has used the National Molecular Subtyping Network for Foodborne Disease Surveillance (PulseNet), which is a web-based platform for communicating the results of bacterial analyses from public health laboratories across the country.

PulseNet includes information from three methods used in DNA fingerprinting bacteria. Pulsed-field gel electrophoresis (PFGE) is the most common method for distinguishing bacteria samples. PFGE allows the lab to create a DNA fingerprint, which is analyzed and then loaded into PulseNet so that labs and epidemiologists can be aware of possible connections between pathogens. In its 20 years of existence, estimates are that PulseNet has prevented at least 270,000 illnesses from *Salmonella, E. coli,* and *Listeria.*

In addition to bacteria, noroviruses are a major cause of foodborne outbreaks every year. The National Electronic Norovirus Outbreak Network (CaliciNet) allows for rapid communication among public health agencies to identify specific strains of the virus causing illness. Public health laboratories send information to CaliciNet about the genetic makeup of the noroviruses that are under investigation. The genetic sequencing can be compared with strains already extant in the database, or new strains can be identified. CaliciNet is linked to NORS, making it a powerful tool in managing foodborne illness outbreaks.

Traceback

Sometimes, the best approach to identifying the source of the pathogen, especially in the absence of laboratory samples, is to trace the food back to the source or forward from the source. Tracebacks can augment the outbreak investigation when disease surveillance, epidemiology, and laboratory analysis has implicated a specific food at a specific facility. The rationale for traceback investigations is that identifying what caused the illness, who is sick, and where people were exposed will not curtail an outbreak, especially when suspect foods were distributed in many states. So, tracing products, such as green onions, spinach, or ground beef, implicated in multistate outbreaks is a critical step in outbreak investigations.

Traceback relies on good inventory management by retail establishments so that investigators can identify specific shipments of product most likely involved in the outbreak. These investigations are also most successful when there is epidemiological data with exposure dates and places and inspection information from the facility implicated in the outbreak. Tracebacks are labor and time intensive and therefore not a common component of most outbreak investigations.

The Council to Improve Foodborne Outbreak Response offers guidance for when product tracing is appropriate, including the following: (1) there is laboratory analysis confirming a common pathogenic strain; (2) cases cover multiple states or localities; (3) there does not appear to be an exposure that is related to the local facility or point of sale, indicating that the source is likely a distributed product; and (4) epidemiology, laboratory analysis, and environmental assessments do not identify how the food became contaminated (Smith et al., 2015).

Environmental Investigation

Throughout the outbreak investigation, public health officials are seeking the environmental source of the pathogen. This could be any number of scenarios, including unsanitary growing conditions, inadequate food-processing protocols, unsafe water, or poor personal hygiene. As the CDC explains, epidemiological investigations answer the "where, when, and who" questions. Laboratory analysis answers the "what" question. Environmental assessments focus on "how" and "why" people got sick. Environmental assessments are also known as "root cause analysis" because they seek to understand the circumstances that caused the contamination, specifically the sanitation conditions related to its spread; it is part of a system of outbreak investigation (Selman and Guzewich, 2014).

Environmental assessment involves collecting samples, interviewing personnel, and observing food handling practices. Comprehensive environmental assessments will examine so-called contributing factors along the farm-to-fork continuum. This means an assessment must include conditions at the farm, in processing facilities, throughout the distribution chain, and into the point of sale. An example of environmental assessments can be found in the multistate outbreak of salmonellosis associated with cantaloupes (FDA, 2013b).

The cantaloupe multistate outbreak involved 261 reported cases of illness in 24 states, with the first cases documented in early July 2012. In this instance, trace-back analysis identified that one farm in Indiana was the likely source of the contaminated fruit. In addition, PFGE identified two strains of *Salmonella* that were causing the illnesses. Regulatory officials from the FDA and the state health department inspected the farm in August 2012 and determined that an environmental assessment was needed to identify how the cantaloupe became contaminated. The environmental assessment was conducted in September 2012 and included sampling growing equipment, water wells used for irrigation, the packinghouse, and processing equipment. The results of the environmental assessment suggested that the melons were likely contaminated while growing in the field and mishandled throughout the processing and distribution components leading to bacterial proliferation.

Public health agencies involved in environmental assessments are encouraged to join the National Environmental Assessment Reporting System (NEARS, 2015). NEARS is coordinated by the CDC and is an online platform to record information related to environmental assessments. This information is only available to registered users who are agencies involved in outbreak investigations. NEARS offers a source of information that these agencies can use to inform strategies for managing and preventing outbreaks in the future.

Food Recalls

Although manufacturers, processors, and restaurants all want to produce food cheaply and efficiently, they also have strong economic reasons for making safe products. If a product gets recalled, losses go far beyond just the revenue from the unsold product. Consumer confidence in the product must be reestablished before sales will resume to their normal level.

Until the FSMA of 2011, the federal government did not have the authority to mandate that food processors recall foods even if they were implicated in an outbreak. So, recalls were voluntary only and responsible parties could choose to keep their products on the market. The FSMA strengthened FDA's recall authority by allowing it to require a recall if the processor or responsible party does not stop distribution voluntarily. The FDA must give notice and allow for voluntary recall before a mandated recall, which could be more damaging to the processor than voluntarily removing product.

Table 1.1 summarizes some major food recalls and indicates that recalls do occur even without documented cases of

Table 1.1   **Summary of Recent Major Recalls**

Company/Product	Pathogen/Reason	Documented Illnesses	Scope of Recall
California Bagged Spinach	*E. coli* O157:H7	205	All bagged spinach from Natural Selection Food
Kraft Chicken Strips	*Listeria monocytogenes*	None	909,491 pounds
Menu Foods Pet Food	*Melamine*	At least 14 animals died	150 brands
Hallmark Beef	Sick cattle slaughtered	None	143,383,823 pounds
Peanut Corporation of America	*Salmonella* Typhimurium	714	Multiple lot numbers thousands of products
Nestle Toll House Cookie Dough	*E. coli* O157:H7	76	2,649,630 cases
SpaghettiOs with meatballs (Campbell Soup Company)	Food-processing error; no specific pathogen	None documented	3,771,102 pounds
Cargill Ground Turkey	*Salmonella* Heidelberg	None	2,029,374 pounds

human illness. Sometimes, recalls are issued when an inspection or sample at a processing facility identifies a problem with the product. Other times, as in the case of Peanut Corporation of America (PCA), hundreds of illnesses and deaths are linked to products. The PCA outbreak was a major event that ultimately led to criminal charges against the company. In September 2015, the former head of PCA was sentenced to 28 years of prison for knowingly providing unsafe food. This is the strictest sentence for foodborne illness in U.S. history.

Restaurant Ratings

One food safety tool that is being increasingly used by local health departments is a restaurant rating system. These systems correspond with inspections conducted by local sanitarians. Localities in almost every state have some sort of rating system, and many of these are available to the public (Food Safety News, n.d.). In some cities, such as Columbus, Ohio, placards alert consumers to the inspection result as they enter. Consumers can also go online to a searchable database to check restaurants before leaving the house. In addition, the inspection results are published by local news sources and often mentioned in a nightly news cast.

The idea behind a publicly available sanitation rating or grading system is that retail food service establishments would take steps to ensure safe food handling in order to obtain and maintain the highest scores possible. Consumers would be more inclined to patronize restaurants with higher ratings, so cleaner stores would benefit from achieving high scores. This was documented in an analysis of New York City's sanitation grading system as scores improved throughout the city after the grading system went into effect in 2010 (Wong et al., 2015). In addition, customers overwhelmingly supported the grading system and indicated that they made decisions based on how a restaurant was scored by the health department.

International Food Safety

Every industrialized country has agencies similar to the FDA and USDA, many with stricter regulations than those of the United States. In the European Union, for example, food irradiation and genetically modified foods are looked upon with suspicion, antibiotics in animal feed have been banned since 2006, and regulations regarding animal feeds and viral contamination are much more stringent than those in the United States. Since 2002, the European Food Safety Authority has been the pivotal organization involved in assessing risks from food. It is comprised of scientists who offer guidance to member states on a range of food safety topics, including animal health, pesticide uses, and nutrition claims on labels.

On a global level, the World Health Organization (WHO), an agency of the United Nations, is engaged with food safety worldwide. WHO works closely with the Food and Agriculture Organization (FAO) of the United Nations. Food safety is a priority to WHO because of estimates that 600 million (1 in 10) people get sick every year from foodborne pathogens, and as many as 420,000 people might die as a direct consequence.

The WHO has many safety-related programs to promote awareness, prevention, and control of food safety risks associated with biological and chemical contamination of foods. It also participates in the Codex Alimentarius Commission established in 1962 jointly with FAO. The purpose of the commission is to establish international standards for food to both ensure food safety and facilitate trade. In June 2016, Codex adopted new international standards and guidelines known as the new Codex Trust Fund (CTF2) (Codex Alimentarius, 2015). CTF2 offers assistance to countries to participate in the Codex Alimentarius Commission and apply international standards to reduce the burden of foodborne disease.

Microbes and Foodborne Illness

The CDC estimates that 1 in 6 Americans, 48 million people, suffer from foodborne illness every year. Of those who get sick, as many as 128,000 are hospitalized and 3,000 die from something they ate. Most of the illnesses are caused by what the CDC calls "unspecified" agents, meaning that the food could be contaminated with something that is not tested for or the cause is simply unknown (CDC, 2014a). According to the CDC, of the hundreds of pathogens known to cause illness, the most common causes are noroviruses, *Salmonella* spp., *Campylobacter* spp., *Clostridium perfringens*, and *Staphylococcus aureus*. These four bacteria and one virus account for an estimated 91 percent of all foodborne illnesses (CDC, 2014a).

Preventing the spread of microbes in food requires a basic understanding of microbiology. Bacterial pathogens are sensitive to temperature, moisture, pH, and in a few cases oxygen (e.g., *Clostridium botulinum* is most successful in environments without oxygen, such as canned foods). This means preventive approaches focus on minimizing temperature abuse of food products so that bacteria do not have optimal conditions to reproduce. Some bacteria do not grow well in cold temperatures, while others flourish. Some bacterial strains are extremely virulent, causing infection with as little as two bacteria. Other bacteria must be present in large numbers to cause any problems. In some instances people who become ill from bacteria in food can be treated with antibiotics; however, antibiotic resistance of some pathogens, specifically some strains of *Salmonella*, is increasing.

Viruses, on the other hand, are not generally sensitive to the same characteristics that promote bacterial growth. These organisms need a living host to survive and replicate. Even so, viruses can be spread from person to person, through food handled by infected individuals, or in the environment. Unlike single-celled bacteria, viruses are made up of a protein coat and either RNA or DNA; the RNA viruses are of most concern from the public health perspective.

The most common way microbes are transmitted is the fecal-oral route, where fecal matter from an animal or person contaminates foodstuffs. This contamination could result from inadequate hand washing, fecal matter from animals being transferred to meat during slaughter or processing steps, or even unsterilized manure being used to fertilize crops. Harmful bacteria can also be carried in animals and, even without fecal contamination, can be present in meat or eggs.

The summary in the next section offers an overview of the top five pathogens that cause foodborne illness in the United States. In addition, some important pathogens that have been implicated in recent outbreaks are summarized. For additional information about foodborne pathogens, the FDA publishes the "Bad Bug Book," which is available online and contains detailed information about numerous bacteria, viruses, parasites, and natural toxins (FDA, 2012). The Bad Bug Book contains both technical and nontechnical information about each pathogen, making it useful for food safety professionals and consumers alike.

Major Microbial Pathogens

Noroviruses

In 1968, there was an outbreak of gastrointestinal illness in Norwalk, Ohio, which is located near Cleveland in the northeastern part of the state. It was prominent because an unusual number of students in an elementary school were absent over the course of a few days, all with similar symptoms. Public health practitioners descended on Norwalk to investigate the outbreak, and they discovered a virus, initially naming it the "Norwalk virus." Since that time, multiple strains of this type of virus have been uncovered and the "Norwalk-like viruses" were renamed "norovirus" to signify all related viruses.

The symptoms of norovirus include a mild, self-limiting gastroenteritis with symptoms of nausea, vomiting, diarrhea, and abdominal pain. It is often referred to by patients and physicians alike as the "stomach virus" because it is so common and not linked to bacteria. It has been widely reported on cruise ships, where it is often spread by person-to-person contact or from infected food handlers. It is also associated with shellfish and salad ingredients including raw or inadequately steamed oysters and clams.

The CDC explains that noroviruses are the number one reason why children go to the doctor and that most years they are the leading cause of foodborne disease, making about 20 million people sick each year (CDC, 2016a). Furthermore, the CDC also estimates that 70 percent of all norovirus cases are caused by food workers who are infected with the virus and do not practice adequate personal hygiene. It only takes a few virus particles to make someone sick, and the virus is generally stable on surfaces and in the air for extended periods of time, contributing to the virulence of this group of pathogens. Noroviruses are monitored through CaliciNet, which specifically focuses on noroviruses.

Even though the CDC estimates that noroviruses cause about half of the foodborne outbreaks every year, most of these are in health care settings such as nursing homes and hospitals. Norovirus outbreaks linked to restaurants only account for about 22 percent of the illness. Recent outbreaks of foodborne norovirus include a multistate outbreak associated with Chipotle restaurants in 2015. Two stores were implicated in outbreaks, which made almost 400 customers sick. Chipotle concluded that an employee at each of these restaurants was the likely source of the virus, and they embarked on a major media campaign to address the issue. This included closing some stores for widespread employee training and modifying food handling guidelines across the franchise.

Campylobacter

Campylobacter is a bacterial pathogen derived from the Greek word "campyl," which means "curved." *Campylobacter jejuni* is the main species that is a leading cause of foodborne illness, but most people have never heard of it. This bacterium was first identified in fetal tissue of aborted sheep in 1913 but was not isolated from stool samples of patients with diarrhea until 1972. The most common food for transmission is raw or undercooked poultry; however, the prevalence of *Campylobacter* in retail chicken has been declining. *Campylobacter* was found in 38 percent of retail chicken samples in 2013, which is a decrease from 2003, when 52 percent of samples were contaminated (FDA, 2016c).

As the prevalence of *Campylobacter* in chicken declines, a new risk is emerging with raw milk consumption. *Campylobacter* is commonly associated with outbreaks involving raw milk, which are increasing in number. Of the known outbreaks related to raw milk, 81 percent are caused by *Campylobacter* (Mungai et al., 2015).

Most cases of campylobacteriosis are relatively minor, causing loose or sticky stools. More severe cases result in diarrhea, fever, and abdominal cramping. People who are immunocompromised are especially susceptible to getting sick. *Campylobacter* can cause bacteremia (bacteria gets into the bloodstream), hepatitis, pancreatitis, septic arthritis (bacteria gets into the joints and causes stiffening), and Guillain-Barré syndrome (GBS). GBS starts with fever, malaise, nausea, and muscular weakness. It affects the peripheral nervous system, especially the roots of the spinal cord that face the front of the body. The paralysis that follows may be mild or may require the patient to be placed on a ventilator to avoid respiratory failure.

There is no treatment for the disease besides providing supportive care. Most people recover within a few weeks or months. Preventing foodborne outbreaks caused by *Campylobacter* requires combining regulatory vigilance with public education. Because these bacteria are so prevalent in the environment, it is generally up to consumers to take steps to minimize exposure. This includes following guidelines on cooking temperatures for poultry and not consuming raw milk or products made with raw milk. Of the 404 outbreaks of *Campylobacter* that CDC documented from 1998 to 2014 in the FOOD Tool, 126 (31%) were linked to milk. The good news about *Campylobacter* is that it is not often implicated in large multistate foodborne outbreaks; rather, when an outbreak occurs, it is more localized.

Salmonella

On an annual basis, *Salmonella* is always one of the top five reasons why people get sick from food. It generally causes sudden headache, diarrhea, nausea, and vomiting, and the illness can persist for several days. Symptoms may be minor or severe, causing dehydration or even death. The CDC estimates there are one million cases each year, resulting in 19,000 hospitalizations and 380 deaths (CDC, 2016b).

Theobald Smith, who worked at Cornell as a laboratory assistant in the late 1800s, was the first to isolate the *Salmonella* bacterium. However, the bacterium was named after his boss, Daniel Salmon, who was the founder of the USDA Bureau of Animal Husbandry (later the Agricultural Research Service). Now, there are more than 2,500 strains, or serotypes, of *Salmonella* recognized as disease-causing organisms, and new ones are being discovered on a regular basis. The nomenclature of *Salmonella* is extensive and constantly under revision; however, most *Salmonella* strains are broken into two groups: those that cause typhoid and those that do not (non-typhoidal). The non-typhoidal strains cause foodborne illness in humans.

It used to be that *Salmonella* was most often associated with raw eggs and undercooked poultry. Poultry and eggs are still a significant source of this pathogen, but some of the largest multistate outbreaks in recent years have come from other foods such as alfalfa sprouts, cucumbers, and peanut products. One of the major concerns with *Salmonella* is that some strains are becoming resistant to antibiotics. Studies show that this both increases the rate of infection from *Salmonella* and increases the likelihood that treatment for the disease will be ineffective.

Data from the National Antibiotic Resistance System shows that the percentage of *Salmonella* resistant to commonly used antibiotics had increased between 1966 and 2014. Antibiotic resistance of *Salmonella* seems to be location specific, and some states have higher rates; for example, one out of six (16.7%) samples tested from Montana in 2014 showed antibiotic resistance to nalidixic acid.

Salmonellosis is generally a mild to moderate illness, and physicians are being cautioned not to prescribe antibiotics unless the victim is compromised by age or illness. As antibiotics become less effective at treating disease but *Salmonella* remains an important foodborne pathogen, some are hoping for a vaccine to prevent the illness. Scientists have been experimenting with vaccines for common strains of *Salmonella* with positive results, raising hopes of prevention (Kong et al., 2012).

Staphylococcus

Foods requiring extensive preparation and are kept at slightly elevated temperatures prior to consumption, including prepared egg, tuna, macaroni, potato, chicken salads, and bakery products like cream-filled pastries, are frequently carriers of *S. aureus*. This bacterium can also appear in meats, poultry, and dairy products and has been the source of at least one outbreak from cheese made from raw milk overseas (Johler et al., 2015).

S. aureus is nearly always present on the skin, and about one-half of healthy adults and nearly all children have these bacteria in their nasal passages. The rate is even higher among hospital workers. *S. aureus* can survive in air, dust, sewage, water, milk, and on food equipment and environmental surfaces. Because it is ubiquitous, it is difficult to prevent the transmission of this pathogen even with careful handling practices. Usually, symptoms of the disease occur very soon after consumption and include a very rapid onset of nausea, vomiting, and abdominal cramping. Symptoms generally last about two days. The CDC estimates that about 240,000 people suffer from foodborne illness caused by *S. aureus* annually.

Clostridium perfringens

C. perfringens is an anaerobic bacterium present in the environment and in the intestines of both humans and domestic and feral animals. Unlike *Salmonella* and *Campylobacter*, *C. perfringens* is similar to *S. aureus* in that it is a gram-positive bacterium. However, *C. perfringens* is also a spore-former. This bacterium is pervasive in the environment, and any food can become contaminated with it, especially meat and meat products. The small amounts of *C. perfringens* in foods do not cause problems unless the food is not cooled down quickly enough or stored properly. Outbreaks occur most commonly in institutional settings like hospitals, school cafeterias, prisons, and nursing homes, where food is prepared several hours before serving, giving this pathogen the nickname "cafeteria bug."

There are two types of illness associated with *C. perfringens*: diarrheal and emetic. Diarrheal symptoms can start 6 to 24 hours after consumption and generally consist of intense abdominal cramps and diarrhea that usually lasts about 24 hours. Occasionally, the diarrhea lasts up to two weeks. The emetic version, which manifests as vomiting and nausea, can happen much quicker, sometimes less than one hour after consuming the pathogen. This form is often linked to rice and pasta products that have not been handled correctly for temperature.

Other Microbes of Importance

Listeria

Listeria monocytogenes was discovered in the 1920s; however, it was not identified as a foodborne pathogen until the 1980s. It is a particularly pernicious bacterium found in soil and water that can survive refrigerator temperatures and even freezing in some cases. It can be found on some vegetables as well as on meat and dairy products. Heat kills *Listeria*, so foods that are consumed right after cooking are not at risk. If processed or ready-to-eat foods become contaminated after they are prepared but before they reach the consumer, they can develop sufficient levels of bacteria to sicken consumers.

Since 2011, there have been at least a dozen multistate outbreaks caused by *Listeria*. The foods implicated in these outbreaks are usually produce (e.g., cantaloupes) or dairy products (including soft cheeses and raw milk). Even though *Listeria* outbreaks in the United States are not as common as some of the other bacterial pathogens, illness can be catastrophic, especially to pregnant women. *Listeria* can cause stillbirth or miscarriage; as such pregnant women are often advised by doctors to refrain from eating hot dogs, deli meats, or soft cheeses because of the risk of exposure.

Listeria can also cause septicemia, meningitis, and encephalitis. The symptoms of listeriosis are usually influenza-like, including chills and fever. It may also cause gastrointestinal symptoms such as nausea, vomiting, and diarrhea. One of the challenges of tracing sources of the bacteria is its relatively long incubation period. Many cases take weeks to manifest, increasing the range of possible tainted foods.

The public health consequences of *Listeria* are so significant that the CDC and other agencies have focused a great deal of effort on improving surveillance, including a whole genome sequencing project and "The *Listeria* Initiative." Both of these endeavors have enhanced understanding of *Listeria*, preventing the spread of the pathogen.

E. coli

E. coli are a type of bacteria that thrives in our intestines and helps digest food. It was named for Theodor Escherich, who was a pediatrician in Germany in the late 1880s and discovered the bacteria was making children ill with diarrhea. He called it the "common colon bacteria," but this was eventually changed to *E. coli*. *E. coli* are identified by serotypes and labeled according to O and H antigen combinations in the bacteria. There are least 174 known O antigens and 53 H antigens. Most strains are beneficial, but a few release harmful toxins that can cause great discomfort and even death.

There are four classes of *E. coli* that cause illness in humans: enteroinvasive, enteropathogenic, enterotoxigenic, and the most toxic, enterohemorrhagic, caused by Shiga toxin-producing *E. coli* (STEC), one strain of which is O157:H7. All four types start with watery diarrhea, but include other symptoms as well, such as cramps or abdominal pain. STEC is the most frightening because of its potential to harm all vital organs and cause death. The CDC estimates that there are about 265,000 STEC infections every year in the United States, and almost 40 percent of these are caused by O157:H7.

E. coli O157:H7 is the most common STEC and was first isolated in 1982, when 47 people in Michigan and Oregon became violently ill. The bacterium contained a few strands of genetic material that caused it to produce a *Shigella*-type toxin. Scientists believe the toxin first destroys blood vessels in the intestines, causing bloody diarrhea. Bloody diarrhea is the most telling symptom of this type of *E. coli* infection, and most people recover, but about 5 to 10 percent develop hemolytic uremic syndrome. HUS is a disease of the blood and kidneys that is now the leading cause of kidney failure in U.S. and Canadian children. HUS develops when the toxin penetrates the intestinal wall and passes into the bloodstream. Once in the bloodstream, the toxin damages vessels throughout the body (Jay et al., 2005).

E. coli O157:H7 is most commonly associated with cattle and is generally harmless to the animals. Bacteria can get in the food supply during slaughter if fecal matter from the intestines contaminates the meat. When beef is ground to make hamburger, bacteria can be integrated into the meat, and hamburger from pooled animals can contaminate large batches of meat. *E. coli* bacteria will be destroyed in the cooking process, as long as the hamburger reaches an internal temperature of 160 degrees Fahrenheit.

The most publicized *E. coli* O157:H7 outbreak occurred in 1993 when more than 500 people got sick from eating improperly cooked hamburgers from a Jack-in-the Box restaurant in Washington State. Several children died, and this led to parent activism and litigation. Even though hamburger is most often thought to be the source of most *E. coli* outbreaks, several outbreaks have involved produce such as sprouts, ready-to-eat salads, spinach, and unpasteurized apple cider. In addition, other STEC strains are responsible for multistate outbreaks. For example, in 2016, *E. coli* O121 has been identified as the strain that is involved in an outbreak linked to flour. As of July 11, 2016, 42 people were sick and 21 states involved in the outbreak. General Mills recalled several lots of Gold Medal flour because some tested positive for the pathogen. This outbreak is especially compelling because people are sick from eating raw flour in uncooked products such as cookie dough or cake batter.

Vaccines for cattle have been available since 2009 and show great promise in reducing the prevalence of *E. coli* O157:H7 bacteria (Varela et al., 2013). However, beef producers have been slow to accept and use the vaccine, likely for economic reasons (Tonsor and Schroeder, 2015). Vaccination is only one approach to controlling the spread; sound farm management and slaughtering practices are critical elements.

Hepatitis A

Hepatitis A is a relatively mild hepatitis that causes sudden onset of fever, malaise, nausea, abdominal discomfort, and loss of appetite, followed by several days of jaundice since the liver is involved. The incubation period of 10 to 50 days is so long that it can be difficult to locate the source of infection. It is also communicable between individuals, making it hard to know whether the transmission was person-to-person contact or foodborne. Hepatitis A does not cause chronic health issues like the other strains of the virus, and most people who are infected might be asymptomatic. A vaccine is available for Hepatitis A, and people traveling to countries with substandard water sanitation are advised to be vaccinated. In addition, first responders, health care workers, and others who might be involved in disaster management are expected to be vaccinated.

The virus is excreted in the feces of infected people, and food can become contaminated when food handlers are not rigorous about personal hygiene. Additionally, inadequately treated water can contaminate foods during washing, making the virus a significant problem with imported produce and shellfish. Ready-to-eat foods such as cold cuts, sandwiches, fruit, vegetables, salads, shellfish, and iced drinks have often been implicated in outbreaks. Although outbreaks are rare, a high-profile outbreak occurred in Pennsylvania in 2003, when more than 600 people became ill and 4 people died after eating green onions from Mexico at a Chi Chi's restaurant. This was the largest Hepatitis A outbreak ever in the United States. Chi Chi's, which was already in financial trouble before the outbreak, never recovered, and all of its U.S. restaurants closed in 2004. A more recent outbreak in 2013 also involved imported produce, and 162 cases in the United States were linked to pomegranate seeds from Turkey (CDC, 2013b).

Parasites

Parasites, small microscopic animals that need a host to survive, are other pathogens transmitted through the fecal-oral route. They live in the intestines of humans and other animal hosts. They are excreted in the feces and enter a new host through feces-contaminated drinking water, contaminated water on produce, manure used as fertilizer, carcasses that become contaminated during the slaughter process, and poor personal hygiene of food handlers. Unlike bacteria, which often take large numbers to cause infection, a single parasite can cause illness.

Perhaps the best-known parasite in the United States is *Trichinella*, a small roundworm found in raw meat that causes trichinosis. The life cycle of *Trichinella* is similar to that of many other parasitic infections. When a person eats meat contaminated with the parasite, the coating is digested freeing the larvae to invade the lining of the small intestine. Sometimes, the adult worm deposits larvae in the lymphatic system, where they enter the bloodstream and can spread throughout the body. Very few infected people have sufficient symptoms to recognize the disease. Early symptoms include diarrhea, vomiting, and nausea. These can be followed by pain, stiffness, swelling of muscles, and swelling in the face. Cases and outbreaks of trichinellosis have declined in the United States, especially those linked to pork products. When an outbreak does occur, it is likely to be associated with wild game, including bear meat (Wilson et al., 2015).

Although *Trichinella* has been well understood for years, it does not cause as much foodborne illness as three other parasites: *Giardia*, *Cryptosporidium*, and *Cyclospora*. These waterborne parasites can be transferred to food from infected food handlers or from contaminated water used to irrigate or wash fruits or vegetables. Of these three parasites, *Cyclospora* is most often linked to foodborne outbreaks. From 2000 through 2014, there were 31 reported foodborne outbreaks of cyclosporiasis, affecting more than 1,500 people. The food documented in every outbreak was produce such as raspberries and basil and is often imported produce (CDC, 2015). In 2015, an outbreak involving more than 500 cases in multiple states was linked to cilantro from Mexico. The parasite causes watery diarrhea and intestinal cramps that can last for weeks. Washing produce can help but usually does not completely eliminate the problem. Some delicate fruits, such as raspberries, have many crevices enabling parasitic abundance. Blast freezing is one of the techniques that kill parasites.

Prions

Bovine spongiform encephalopathy (BSE) is a disease that strikes cows, causing them to suffer neurological damage. When the disease was first noticed in the United Kingdom in 1986, some cows were found staggering around in circles, hence the name "mad cow disease." In addition to the toll on cattle, humans began developing a related disease, variant Creutzfeldt-Jakob disease, at earlier ages than normal and in increasing numbers and severity.

The most widely accepted theory is that BSE is caused by a prion. A prion is a protein molecule that, instead of forming a spiral like a telephone cord, forms a straight fiber. This deformed protein molecule then attaches to a healthy protein molecule, and it becomes a straight fiber also. The two molecules then split apart and go on to attack other healthy protein molecules. Because these straight fibers cannot be organized correctly by the cell, the cell eventually dies. Some people may be more susceptible to the infection than others. Scientists think that there may be a genetic variation in the coding for a particular amino acid (proteins are made up of amino acid chains) at the DNA level. If this variation is present, then the person is more likely to be affected by a prion if he or she is exposed (Pennington, 2003). The prion is resistant to common sterilization methods, including bleach, boiling, alcohol, exposure to chemical agents, and irradiation. Even after burning infected tissue, the prion can still be detected in the ashes.

Prion diseases are also known as transmissible spongiform encephalopathies. Creutzfeldt-Jakob disease (CJD) was first described in the 1920s by Hans Gerhard Creutzfeldt and Alfons Jakob. Symptoms can include loss of coordination, personality changes, mania, and dementia. People usually die within a year or two of diagnosis. It generally affects about one in one million people age 50 or older through spontaneous means or as an inherited condition. In 1995, scientists in the United Kingdom identified a new type of CJD called variant CJD (vCJD). This new type strikes mostly younger people, and the brain tissue of its victims looks exactly like the brain tissue of cows that die of BSE.

As epidemiologists studied vCJD, they began to suspect a species-to-species transfer was taking place. People who had consumed brain or spinal tissue from cows were getting the disease. Although the incubation period can be as long as 20 to

25 years, it appears the risk is greatest to those who contract it before the age of 15. As of late 2016, 220 people have been diagnosed with vCJD. Most of these (177) were from the United Kingdom (CDC, 2014b). In 2014, one case was confirmed in Texas in an individual who was not born in the United States, making it the fourth confirmed case in the country.

In 2008, the FDA published interim regulations to prohibit cattle materials in animal feed, including those that are from animals who have BSE and brain and spinal cord from animals over 30 months old. In 2016, FDA issued a final rule related to BSE that included the 2008 interim rule and two other rules as well (2004 and 2005). The final rule clearly defines prohibited feed materials and food that is not considered dangerous for BSE. It also identifies restrictions on importing meat and meat products based on the country of origin.

Food Safety at the Consumer Level

Although outbreaks of foodborne illness on cruise ships or at restaurants receive a lot of media attention, most foodborne illness occurs because of improper food handling at home. Yet, with an understanding of the causes of foodborne illness, and adherence to a few simple rules, the hazards can largely be prevented. Since microbes cause most illnesses, understanding how to control their growth and spread is critical to minimizing risk. When it comes to bacteria, temperature control of food products is the most critical step. Since bacteria will generally reproduce best at room temperature (about 70 degrees Fahrenheit), keeping hot foods hot and cold foods cold is one way to curtail their growth. The food safety danger zone is 41 to 135 degrees Fahrenheit, so minimizing the time food is held in the danger zone will go a long way to stopping bacterial growth.

On the other hand, viruses are best controlled through good sanitation. This includes equipment and kitchen sanitation as well as personal hygiene. Adequate hand washing with soap and warm water is the best way to manage viruses.

The Partnership for Food Safety Education launched the FightBac! consumer food safety campaign in 1997 to simplify the food safety message into four steps: clean, separate, cook, and chill to keep food safe from harmful bacteria. Although these steps are targeted to reduce bacterial growth, following them will help eliminate viruses as well. The first step, clean, includes hand washing, surface cleaning, and washing produce. Hand washing is a critical part of safe food handling. Hands should be washed before handling food. During preparation, hands should be washed after handling animal proteins and before handling something that will not be cooked before serving, after handling garbage, and after taking a break from kitchen activities. It should also be done after completing food preparations.

Besides washing hands, surfaces need to be cleaned to stop contamination. So if raw meat comes in contact with a kitchen surface, it needs to be cleaned thoroughly with hot soapy water afterward. Produce should be washed under cold running water. Even foods in modified atmospheric packaging (prewashed bags of lettuce, for example) should be washed.

One of the major ways bacteria can spread in a kitchen is through cross-contamination. If uncooked eggs or meat come in contact with something that is going to be consumed without further cooking, such as salad, the normal cooking step that would adequately kill the bacteria is eliminated. So anything that could transfer bacteria from meat to foods that are ready-to-eat, such as salad or bread, needs to be thoroughly cleaned before it is reused (e.g., hands, cutting boards, knives, and kitchen counters).

The third FightBac! step is cook. Meat should be tested for doneness with a meat thermometer inserted into the thickest part of the meat to check that it has reached an internal temperature of 145 degrees Fahrenheit for a beef roast and fish and 160 degrees Fahrenheit for ground meats and poultry. It is particularly important for ground meats to be thoroughly cooked inside since bacteria get mixed throughout ground meats, and

Table 1.2.   Minimum Safe Cooking Temperatures for Select Foods

Food	Minimum Temperature (°F)	Minimum Holding Time at Specified Temperature
Raw eggs prepared for immediate service	145	15 seconds
Commercially raised game	145	15 seconds
Fish, pork, and meat	145	15 seconds
Raw eggs not prepared for immediate service	158	<1 second
	155	15 seconds
Mechanically tenderized	150	1 minute
meat	145	3 minutes
Poultry	165	15 seconds
Stuffed fish, meat, pasta, poultry		
Wild game		
Food cooked in a microwave	165	Hold for 2 minutes after removing from microwave

Source: FDA (2013a).

cooking on the outside is insufficient to kill bacteria that are inside the burger or loaf. Table 1.2 offers guidance from the 2013 Food Code on safe cooking temperatures.

Inadequate chilling, the subject of the fourth FightBac! step, causes many foodborne illnesses, and the CDC considers it the leading cause of foodborne illness in restaurant settings. Keeping foods chilled, ensuring that refrigerators are set below 41 degrees Fahrenheit, and promptly chilling leftovers prevent bacteria from being in the danger zone for too long. Soups and other large containers of cooked foods need to be chilled in shallow containers to ensure that the food cools quickly enough.

Eating Out Safely

In addition to being careful at home, you can eat more safely in restaurants by taking a few precautions: (1) wash your hands or use an alcohol-based hand sanitizer before consuming restaurant meals; (2) observe the restaurant environment before choosing to eat there; if local health department ratings are unavailable, note whether the employees are well groomed and whether the bathrooms are clean and well maintained; and (3) ensure all leftovers are refrigerated within two hours or throw them away.

References

Association of Food and Drug Officials. 2016. Real Progress in Food Code Adoption. http://www.fda.gov/downloads/Food/GuidanceRegulation/RetailFoodProtection/Food Code/UCM476819.pdf

CDC. 2011. Foodborne Disease Outbreak 2011 Case Definition. https://wwwn.cdc.gov/nndss/conditions/food borne-disease-outbreak/case-definition/2011/

CDC. 2013a. Ten Great Public Health Achievements in the 20th Century. http://www.cdc.gov/about/history/tengpha.htm

CDC. 2013b. Multistate Outbreak of Hepatitis A Virus Infections Linked to Pomegranate Seeds from Turkey (Final Update). http://www.cdc.gov/hepatitis/outbreaks/2013/a1b-03-31/index.html

CDC. 2014a. CDC 2011 Estimates: Findings. http://www.cdc.gov/foodborneburden/2011-foodborne-estimates.html

CDC. 2014b. Variant Creitzfeldt-Jakob Disease (vCJD). http://www.cdc.gov/prions/vcjd/news.html

CDC. 2015a. U.S. Foodborne Outbreaks of Cyclosporiasis—2000–2014. http://www.cdc.gov/parasites/cyclosporiasis/outbreaks/foodborneoutbreaks.html

CDC. 2015b. National Environmental Assessment Reporting System (NEARS). https://www.cdc.gov/nceh/ehs/nears/index.htm

CDC. 2016a. Norovirus. http://www.cdc.gov/norovirus/index.html

CDC. 2016b. Salmonella. https://www.cdc.gov/salmonella/

CDC. 2016c. National Outbreak Reporting System. https://www.cdc.gov/nors/about.html

Codex Alimentarius Commission. 2007. Working Principles for Risk Analysis for Food Safety for Application by Governments In *Codex Alimentarius Commission: Procedural Manual, 17th ed.* Rome: Food and Agriculture Organization of the United Nations. ftp://ftp.fao.org/docrep/fao/010/a1472e/a1472e.pdf

Codex Alimentarius Commission. 2015. Codex Trust Fund-2. http://www.who.int/foodsafety/areas_work/food-standard/codextrustfund/en/

FDA. 2012. *Bad Bug Book*, 2nd ed. http://www.fda.gov/Food/FoodborneIllnessContaminants/CausesOfIllnessBadBugBook/

FDA. 2013a. Food Code 2013. http://www.fda.gov/downloads/Food/GuidanceRegulation/RetailFoodProtection/FoodCode/UCM374510.pdf

FDA. 2013b. Environmental Assessment: Factors Potentially Contributing to the Contamination of Fresh Whole Canteloupe Implicated in a Multi-State Outbreak of Salmonellosis. http://www.fda.gov/Food/RecallsOutbreaksEmergencies/Outbreaks/ucm341476.htm

FDA. 2015. Voluntary National Retail Food Regulatory Program Standards—September 2015. http://www.fda.gov/Food/GuidanceRegulation/RetailFoodProtection/ProgramStandards/ucm245409.htm

FDA. 2016a. Arsenic in Rice and Rice Products Risk Assessment Report. Center for Food Safety and Applied Nutrition. http://www.fda.gov/Food/FoodScienceResearch/RiskSafetyAssessment/ucm485278.htm

FDA. 2016b. Inspection Observations. http://www.fda.gov/ICECI/Inspections/ucm250720.htm

FDA. 2016c. The 2012–2013 Integrated NARMS Report. http://www.fda.gov/AnimalVeterinary/SafetyHealth/ AntimicrobialResistance/NationalAntimicrobial ResistanceMonitoringSystem/ucm059103 .htm

Food Safety News. n.d. Restaurant Inspections in Your Area. http://www.rwjf.org/en/library/funding-opportunities/2015/evidence-for-action-investigator-initiated-research-to-build-a-culture-of-health.html

Government Accountability Office. 1994. Risk-Based Inspections and Microbial Monitoring Needed for Meat and Poultry (GAO Publication No. GAO/RCED-94-110). http://www.gao.gov/assets/220/219682.pdf

Government Accountability Office. 2011. Federal Food Safety Oversight: Food Safety Working Group Is a Positive First Step but Government Planning Is Needed to Address Fragmentation (GAO Publication No. GAO-11-289). Retrieved from http://www.gao.gov/assets/320/316742.pdf

Government Accountability Office. 2014. Federal Food Safety Oversight: Additional Actions Needed to Improve Planning and Collaboration (GAO Publication No. GAO-15-180). http://www.gao.gov/assets/670/667656.pdf

Jay, James M., Martin J. Loessner, and David A. Golden. 2005. *Modern Food Microbiology*. 7th ed. New York: Springer Science.

Johler, Sophia, Delphine Weder, Claude Bridy, Marie-Claude Huguenin, Luce Robert, Jörg Hummerjohann, and Roger Stephan. 2015. Outbreak of Staphylococcal Food Poisoning among Children and Staff at a Swiss Boarding School Due to Soft Cheese Made from Raw Milk. *Journal of Dairy Science* 98(5): 2944–2948.

Johnson, Renée. 2014. *The Federal Food Safety System: A Primer* (Congressional Research Service Publication No. RS22600). https://www.fas.org/sgp/crs/misc/RS22600.pdf

Kong, Wei, Matthew Brovold, Brian A. Koeneman, Josephine Clark-Curtiss, and Roy Curtiss III. 2012. Turning Self-Destructing Salmonella into a Universal DNA Vaccine Delivery Platform. *Proceedings of The National Academy of Sciences of the United States of America* 109(47): 19414–19419.

Law, Mark T. 2003. The Origins of State Pure Food Regulation. *Journal of Economic History* 63(4): 1103–1130.

Mungai, Elisabeth A., Casey Barton Behravesh, and L. Hannah Gould. 2015. Increased Outbreaks Associated with Nonpasteurized Milk, United States, 2007–2012. *Emerging Infectious Diseases* 21 (1). DOI: 10.3201/eid2101.140447

National Advisory Committee on Microbiological Contamination in Foods (NACMCF). 1997. HACCP Principles & Application Guidelines. http://www.fda.gov/Food/GuidanceRegulation/HACCP/ucm2006801.htm

Pennington, T. Hugh. 2003. *When Food Kills: BSE, E. Coli, and Disaster Science.* New York: Oxford University Press.

Selman, C.A., and J.J. Guzewich. 2014. Public Health Measures: Environmental Assessment in Outbreak Investigations. *Encyclopedia of Food Safety* 4: 98–106. https://www.cdc.gov/nceh/ehs/nears/docs/ea-encyclopedia-foodsafety.pdf

Smith, Kirk, Ben Miller, Katie Vierk, Ian Williams, and Craig Hedberg. 2015. Product Tracing in Epidemiologic Investigations of Outbreaks Due to Commercially Distributed Food Items—Utility, Application, and Considerations. http://www.cifor.us/clearinghouse/tooldetail.cfm?id=290

Tai, Stephanie. 2015. Whole Foods: The FSMA and the Challenges of Defragmenting Food Safety Regulation. *American Journal of Law & Medicine* 41(2–3): 447–458.

Tonsor, Glynn T., and Ted C. Schroeder. 2015. Market Impacts of *E. coli* Vaccination in U.S. Feedlot Cattle. *Agricultural Food Economics* 3. http://agrifoodecon .springeropen.com/articles/10.1186/s40100-014-0021-2

U.S. Department of Agriculture. 2015. FSIS History. http:// www.fsis.usda.gov/wps/portal/informational/aboutfsis/ history/history

Varela, N.P., P. Dick, and J. Wilson. 2013. Assessing the Existing Information on the Efficacy of Bovine Vaccination against *Escherichia coli* O157:H7—A Systematic Review and Meta-analysis. *Zoonoses and Public Health* 60: 253–268.

Wilson, Nana O., Rebecca L. Hall, Susan P. Montgomery, and Jeffrey L. Jones. 2015. Trichinellosis Surveillance— United States, 2008–2012. *Morbidity and Mortality Weekly Report* 64(SS01): 1–8. http://www.cdc.gov/mmwr/preview/ mmwrhtml/ss6401a1.htm

Wong, Melissa R., Wendy McKelvey, Ito Kazuhiko, Corinne Schiff, J. Bryan Jacobson, and Daniel Kass. 2015. Impact of a Letter-Grade Program on Restaurant Sanitary Conditions and Diner Behavior in New York City. *American Journal of Public Health* 105(3): e81–e87.

2   Problems, Controversies, and Solutions

While microbiological contamination of food with bacteria, viruses, and parasites is the main concern of many public health professionals, there are other food safety issues which are often more concerning to consumers. These include food additives, pesticides, hormones in milk and cattle, antibiotics in farm animals, genetically modified organisms, and chemicals. In addition, exotic and unusual issues such as bird flu, pink slime, raw milk, and melamine are examples of food-related controversies that raise public alarm about the overall safety of the food supply.

Food Additives and Contaminants

A food additive is

> a substance not normally consumed as a food by itself and not normally used as a typical ingredient of the food, whether or not it has nutritive value, the intentional addition of which to food for a technological (including organoleptic) purpose in the manufacture, processing, preparation,

---

The beef product known as "pink slime" or lean finely textured beef (LFTB) is seen in a tray on a table in front of (from left to right): Kansas governor Sam Brownback, Texas governor Rick Perry, Iowa governor Terry Branstad, and South Dakota lieutenant governor Matt Michels, during a tour of Beef Product Inc.'s plant in South Sioux City, Nebraska, on March 29, 2012. LFTB is made from high fat beef scraps and is added to ground beef as a cost-saving measure. Several manufacturers curtailed the production of LFTB in 2012 as the demand for the product plummeted as a result of public concern. (AP Photo/Nati Harnik)

49

treatment, packing, packaging, transport or holding of such food results, or may be reasonably expected to result, (directly or indirectly) in it or its by-products becoming a component of or otherwise affecting the characteristics of such foods. The term does not include "contaminants" or substances added to food for maintaining or improving nutritional qualities. (Codex Alimentarius, 2013)

A food contaminant is

any substance not intentionally added to food, which is present in such food as a result of the production (including operations carried out in crop husbandry, animal husbandry and veterinary medicine), manufacture, processing, preparation, treatment, packing, packaging, transport or holding of such food or as a result of environmental contamination. The term does not include insect fragments, rodent hairs and other extraneous matter. (Codex Alimentarius, 2013)

In other words, additives become part of the food supply intentionally, usually in order to improve food quality, aesthetics, or shelf life. Olestra and aspartame (marketed as Equal or NutraSweet) are examples of additives causing debate in recent years. However, many more additives are used, some of which are inert, but some of which are considered unhealthy even if they are not unsafe. For example, arsenic is an additive to animal feed at low levels; as such it is regulated in the human supply as a residue in meat. On the other hand, contaminants are found in foods because of processing or other means. Some contaminants can be dangerous compounds which form during cooking or storage, such as acrylamide and benzene; other contaminants migrate into foods, like mercury and polychlorinated biphenyls (PCBs) into fish and bisphenol A (BPA), which contaminates foods from certain plastic containers. Both additives and contaminants have the potential to impact

Table 2.1   Select Food Additives and Contaminants

Substance	Additive[1]	Contaminant
Acrylamide	X	X
Antibiotics	X	
Arsenic	X	X
Aspartame	X	
Benzene	X	X
Carbon monoxide[2]		X
Growth hormones	X	
Melamine		X
Mercury		X
Olestra	X	
Polychlorinated biphenyls		X

[1] See FDA Food Additives Status List: http://www.fda.gov/Food/Ingredients PackagingLabeling/FoodAdditivesIngredients/ucm091048.htm.

[2] Generally recognized as safe (GRAS) at levels of 0.4%.

food safety, and both raise concerns from consumers who are increasingly vocal about unnatural substances in their foods. Table 2.1 provides an overview of the additives and contaminants discussed in this section.

Acrylamide

In 2002, scientists in Sweden first raised concerns about the presence of an industrial pollutant, known carcinogen, and human neurotoxin known as acrylamide in foods (Tareke et al., 2002). Using different cooking techniques under laboratory conditions, they measured levels of acrylamide in various food products and determined potatoes cooked with high heat or fried showed the highest level of this contaminant. Since that time, acrylamide has become a major concern among food safety advocates because they are chemicals used in adhesives and grouts and should not be in foods. Under California Proposition 65, companies are required to warn consumers if their products contain carcinogens. As such, the California attorney general has successfully settled lawsuits with many major companies, including McDonalds, Frito-Lay, and Heinz, because they did not comply with the law since some of their products contain acrylamide.

In March 2010, the EPA published the *Toxicological Review of Acrylamide* and characterized acrylamide as "likely to be carcinogenic to humans" (EPA, 2010a). The EPA bases its evaluation on studies conducted with laboratory animals in addition to limited epidemiological studies. The agency does not determine regulatory levels for contaminants in foods but has set the maximum contaminant level goal of acrylamide in drinking water at 0 parts per billion (ppb). The EPA report found the median level of acrylamide in french fries and potato chips is 318.0 ppb, with some studies finding more than 2,700 ppb. Levels of acrylamide measured in ground coffee have been as high as 539 ppb, thus raising additional concerns from consumers.

In March 2016, the FDA issued *Guidance for Industry: Acrylamide in Foods* for public comment (FDA, 2016a). This guidance document lays out suggestions for reducing acrylamide in food from farm to table but does not identify a specific regulatory limit for the amount allowed in food. For example, in order to reduce acrylamide content in fried potatoes, the guidance recommends using potatoes with lower sugar content and cutting french fries in a way to reduce the surface area.

Antibiotics

Antibiotics are the most effective tool ever developed for fighting infection. These drugs act directly on bacteria (but not viruses), destroying them or inhibiting their growth. However, bacteria are continually evolving, making some drugs ineffective as bacteria become resistant to them. Overuse of antibiotics in people and animals has contributed to resistant strains of bacteria. The CDC estimates that more than two million people in the United States are infected with antibiotic-resistant strains of bacteria and at least 23,000 die as a result of these infections (CDC, 2013).

Tuberculosis (TB) offers a well-documented illustration of how drug-resistant strains can affect severity, treatment, and costs. Drug-resistant strains of TB began to emerge when TB patients failed to complete the three- to six-month courses of antibiotic therapy or they were prescribed the ineffective drugs. Multidrug-resistant TB strains emerged in the 1980s, and now there is a "virtually untreatable" strain that is resistant to five classes of antibiotic drugs. There are three other classes of antibiotics that can still be used, but they are more toxic, less effective, and more expensive. It can take as long as two years to treat multidrug-resistant TB, and surgery to remove diseased portions of the lung may be required. Mortality is also greater with multidrug-resistant TB.

In 1949, Dr. Thomas Jukes, then director of Nutrition and Physiology Research at Lederle Pharmaceutical Company, discovered that animals, especially pigs, fed small doses of antibiotics gained weight faster and did not suffer from diarrhea as much as those who did not receive doses (Jukes, 1972). In the early 1950s, farmers began to incorporate antibiotics into livestock feed to promote growth, cut production costs, and treat subclinical diseases—diseases that do not cause obvious symptoms but nevertheless are taxing to the animal. It did not take long for scientists to question the consequences of so-called subtherapeutic use of antibiotics. In 1969, the Swann Committee in England recommended that antibiotics only be used to treat animals when prescribed by a veterinarian. Further, the report stated that penicillin and tetracycline should not be used at subtherapeutic doses for growth promotion. In the early 1970s, most western European countries banned the two drugs for livestock use, but the United States did not. Following the Swann report, many other researchers raised similar concerns about antibiotic use in livestock, specifically related to potential effects on human health (Landers et al., 2012). Figure 2.1 shows how antibiotic resistance emerges in humans and animals.

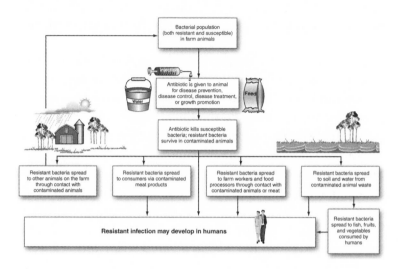

Figure 2.1   Antibiotic Resistance (Government Accountability Office, 2011)

Salmonella, Campylobacter, and *Shigella,* three leading causes of foodborne illness, are among the pathogens monitored by the National Antimicrobial Resistance Monitoring System (NARMS). As these pathogens become increasingly drug resistant, patients face more and longer illnesses and increased illness severity. Because *Salmonella* and *Campylobacter* are such common bacteria, it is relatively easy for them to become resistant. For example, antibiotic use in both humans and animals affects the intestinal tract, making it more susceptible to infection from certain bacterial strains because antibiotics kill not only disease-causing bacteria but also bacteria aiding in healthy digestion. If a person takes a drug for a sinus infection, for example, the presence of antibiotic-resistant bacteria in the gut from eating food containing a resistant strain can cause an infection. In addition, if a person ill with *Salmonella* is treated with antibiotics and does not complete the prescription, the most virulent bacteria will survive. This survival of the fittest has contributed to evolving strains of many pathogens resistant to common antibiotics.

Tracking antibiotic resistance in the United States involves multiple agencies and is not keeping pace with the evolution of antibiotic resistant pathogens (Government Accountability Office, 2011). The CDC tracks humans, the FDA tracks retail meats, and the U.S. Department of Agriculture (USDA) tracks food animals. In addition, states are involved in surveillance and providing samples for laboratory analysis. *Salmonella* is of special concern because of the evidence of multidrug resistance. The fact that there are more than 2,700 strains of *Salmonella* contributes to the magnitude of the problem in that antibiotic resistance varies by strain. In some cases, the prevalence of antibiotic-resistant strains is stabilizing; in others it is increasing (NARMS, 2013). In the case of *Salmonella* Typhimurium, it is becoming more resistant to some common antibiotics but less resistant to others (NARMS, 2016). In the United States, it is estimated that there are 100,000 infections with drug-resistant *Salmonella* every year, resulting in more than $365 million in medical costs (CDC, 2013).

While the situation with *Salmonella* is alarming, *Campylobacter* is even more so. As many as 310,000 people are infected with drug-resistant strains of *Campylobacter* every year in the United States, 13,000 are hospitalized, and 120 die as a result. These numbers, along with the emerging human health research, contributed to public concern about antibiotic levels in food—to the point that now the USDA or "federal government" considers antimicrobial resistance "one of the most serious health threats to both animals and humans" and has created a plan to address the issue (USDA, 2014).

Despite the USDA and FDA's efforts to curtail antibiotic use in animals, including new legislation since 2006, antimicrobials sold for use in food animals grew during 2013–14 (FDA, 2015a). An FDA report compiles data required under the Animal Drug User Fee Amendments of 2008 (ADUFA). ADUFA reports sales of antimicrobials intended for use in food animals; however, it does not identify if the drugs are actually used. The food industry is responding to consumer concerns over the presence of antibiotics in food. Many of the largest meat producers in the United States, restaurant chains, and retailers are eliminating products that contain antibiotics. As a result, consumer spending on chicken raised without antibiotics has seen a tremendous increase since 2009 (Kesmodel, 2014).

Arsenic

Arsenic is a naturally occurring heavy metal that is released into the environment from volcanoes and from minerals. There are also anthropogenic sources of arsenic, such as burning fossil fuels and as a component of pesticides and wood preservatives. The biochemistry of arsenic is complex, but arsenic can be categorized as either inorganic or organic. The inorganic forms of arsenic are of greatest concern from the public health perspective. There are areas in the United States that have documented high levels of arsenic in the drinking water. In addition, several foods are known to have high levels of arsenic, including seafood, mushrooms, and rice.

In 2012, concerns over arsenic as a contaminant in apple and grape juice were raised, and *Consumer Reports* analyzed grocery store juices (*Consumer Reports*, 2012a). After testing 88 samples and evaluating data from the National Health and Nutrition Examination Survey (NHANES), they concluded that apple and grape juices were sources of arsenic. This finding alarmed some health professionals and frightened parents who believed their children were being exposed to a carcinogen on a daily basis. Following the outcry about the potential health risks from arsenic, the FDA conducted a risk assessment of inorganic arsenic in apple juice (Carrington et al., 2013) and set an action level for arsenic at 10 micrograms/kilogram (or parts per billion). In their support documentation for this decision, the FDA notes that the source of arsenic in apple juice is somewhat uncertain but it could be the consequence of the metal's persistence in the environment.

In late 2012, *Consumer Reports* continued its investigation of arsenic in foods with a study finding high levels of arsenic in rice and rice products (*Consumer Reports*, 2012b). After testing more than 200 samples of rice products, they found arsenic in almost every one. Once again, the impact on children is high-lighted as a concern because of common baby foods, such as rice cereals.

Aspartame

Aspartame, sold under the brands NutraSweet and Equal, was discovered accidentally by a scientist at G.D. Searle Laboratories in 1965 who was testing new drugs for gastric ulcers and licked his fingers before picking up a piece of paper (Bilger, 2006). Aspartame turned out to be a failure as an ulcer drug, but it has become a well-received sweetener that has found its way into more than 6,000 processed foods, including sodas, desserts, candy, and yogurt.

The safety of aspartame has been questioned as some people have reported dizziness, hallucinations, and headaches after drinking diet sodas made with aspartame. Limited research suggests that consuming high levels of aspartame is linked to neurobehavioral effects, including changes in mood and memory loss (Lindseth et al., 2014). Phenylalanine and aspartic acid are metabolites of aspartame, and both are known to be involved in regulating behavior.

The potential for aspartame to cause cancer has added to the controversy surrounding its widespread use. A review and commentary of aspartame carcinogenicity studies since it was introduced in the 1960s argues that some of these studies are inadequate to determine whether there is a cancer risk (Soffritti et al., 2014). Even so, the lack of valid scientific research and adequate data to prove that there is no cancer risk has led to calls to warn pregnant women and children to avoid aspartame completely. On the other hand, the American Cancer Society agrees with the FDA, the National Cancer Institute, and many other scientists that aspartame is safe to consume and does not increase the risk of cancer.

The debate about aspartame is compelling because it has been studied extensively in governmental research facilities (National Toxicology Program, 2005) as well as by numerous independent researchers. Nevertheless, there are calls for banning it as an approved food additive, fueled by public fears over cancer. Responding to consumer concerns, Pepsi decided to replace aspartame in its diet sodas with sucralose in 2015; they were vilified by many Pepsi lovers over the end product.

Benzene

Benzene is an organic chemical found in gasoline and cigarette smoke and emitted from coal-burning power plants. Benzene is one of only a few chemicals identified as a *cause* of cancer rather than just being *associated* with it. It occurs naturally in some foods like meat, eggs, and bananas. In the early 1990s, scientists discovered that benzene can form in soft drinks that contain both ascorbic acid (vitamin C) and sodium benzoate (a preservative) if the soft drink is exposed to high heat.

In response to test results in 2005, the FDA's Center for Food Safety and Applied Nutrition (CFSAN) analyzed soft drinks specifically for benzene. CFSAN found negligible levels of benzene in the vast majority of samples tested. The CFSAN study, however, identified elevated benzene levels in several products, including Safeway Select Diet Orange Soda, AquaCal Strawberry Flavored H2O Beverage, Crystal Light Sunrise Classic Orange, Giant Light Cranberry Juice Cocktail, and BellyWashers Black Cherry Blast (FDA, 2015b). According to the FDA, all products that tested high for levels of benzene have been reformulated by the manufacturers. In some cases, this involved removing vitamin C from their beverages. The FDA worked with manufacturers at that time to reformulate their beverages so that the drinks would not pose a safety risk (FDA, 2006).

The EPA set a maximum contaminant limit (MCL) of 5 ppb of benzene for drinking water, and this standard is serving as a benchmark for FDA. The FDA conducts a Total Diet Study to determine levels of contaminants and nutrients in a wide variety of foods. The analytical procedures are designed to detect multiple pesticide residues, industrial chemicals, and levels of both toxins and nutrients found in foods. Benzene levels are calculated as part of these tests. When the FDA evaluated its data from the 1995 to 2001 diet study, it found some beverage levels that were substantially above the EPA level of 5 ppb. There is currently no regulatory limit for benzene in soft drinks or other beverages.

Carbon Monoxide

Modified atmospheric packaging (MAP) has been used to package meats since 1980 because it helps to maintain the appearance of meat while in grocers' meat cases. Packages are injected with carbon dioxide, nitrogen, and very small (0.4%) amounts of carbon monoxide. The carbon monoxide binds with the muscle tissue and gives it a rosy appearance. Without this treatment, the iron in the meat reacts with oxygen and creates a brown color on the surface of the meat. Although carbon monoxide is toxic to humans in large quantities, the small amounts used in packaging are considered harmless by the FDA.

Consumer groups complain that this practice takes away one of consumers' tools for determining freshness: appearance. This leads to a misrepresentation of the freshness of meat and hiding the presence of bacteria that cause spoilage. Grocers would like consumers to rely more on expiration dates on packages since meat can still be safe to eat even after it has browned due to oxidation. Meat that is still wholesome, and has not exceeded its expiration date, often must be sold at a discount or discarded because it has developed a brown color.

The FDA and USDA's FSIS have a Memorandum of Understanding regarding ingredients added to meat and poultry products. Under this Memorandum of Understanding, the FDA is responsible for determining the safety of additives, and the FSIS is responsible for determining if the additive is safe as used in meat and poultry products. Carbon monoxide is classified as GRAS (generally recognized as safe) for use in MAP under the Food Additives Act. This classification is science based even though FDA relies on studies by others, including the food industry, to make this determination. The FSIS agrees with the classification and allows carbon monoxide at low levels to preserve the freshness of some meats and fish.

Research related to consumer perceptions indicates a preference for ground beef that is red in color and has an extended shelf life. However, when consumers are informed about the MAP-CO technology used to enhance color and extend shelf life, their acceptance declines (Grebitus et al., 2013). This research contributes to debates over labeling products in which carbon monoxide is used. On one side of the debate are consumer advocates arguing that meat should be labeled as if carbon monoxide were an additive, while the meat industry expresses concerns about the impact of such labels on the marketability.

In 2007, the U.S. House of Representatives considered a bill, H.R. 3115—the Carbon Monoxide Treated Meat, Poultry, and Seafood Safe Handling, Labeling, and Consumer Protection Act. The intent of the bill was to require labeling of foods treated with carbon monoxide. On July 19, 2007, the bill was introduced to the House Committee on Energy and Commerce and then referred to the Subcommittee on Health, where it was never discussed. In September of 2007, an additional bill, the Food and Drug Import Safety Act of 2007, was introduced in the House, and it included a revision to the definition of "color additive" that would identify carbon monoxide as such. This bill was also referred to the Subcommittee on Health, and hearings were held; however, the bill never left the subcommittee.

Growth Hormones

Since the 1950s, hormones have been used to increase meat and milk production. Three naturally occurring hormones—estridiol, progesterone, and testosterone—and their synthetic equivalents—zeranol, melengestrol acetate, and trenbolone—are injected into calves' ears as time-release pellets. This implant under the skin causes the steers to gain an extra 2 to 3 pounds per week and saves money in production costs, because the steers gain more weight with the same amount of feed. In the United States, estimates are that about two-thirds of all cattle and almost all cattle in large commercial feedlots are treated with hormones. The European Union banned the practice in 1981, and in 1989 it banned imported beef unless it is certified hormone free, setting off a dispute between the United States and the European Union that has been "long-standing and acrimonious" (Johnson, 2015).

While the FDA and the FSIS were endorsing the safety of hormones in food, the European Commission's Scientific Committee for Veterinary Measures Relating to Public Health concluded that adverse effects from hormones include developmental, neurobiological, genotoxic, and carcinogenic effects. They further concluded that existing studies do not point to any clear tolerance level and thus banned the hormones outright (European Commission, 1999). The U.S. beef industry claims that natural hormone levels in the aging bulls and dairy cows used for beef in Europe can be many times higher than those from steers treated with hormones.

Similar controversy surrounds recombinant bovine growth hormone (rBGH), also called recombinant bovine somatotropin (rBST), which is administered to dairy cattle to help them produce more milk. Developed by the Monsanto Corporation and marketed under the name Posilac, it has generated a lot of debate since it was approved by the FDA in 1993. The United States is the only major industrialized nation to approve rBGH. Health Canada, the food and drug regulatory arm of the Canadian government, rejected rBGH in early 1999 and stirred up more controversy in the process. They rejected the drug after careful review of the same data that was submitted to the FDA, finding that it did not meet standards for veterinary health and might pose food safety issues for humans.

In 2014 The Joint Expert Committee on Food Additives issued a report summarizing veterinary drug residues in foods and included an assessment of rBGH (World Health Organization [WHO], 2014). After reviewing existing and new data, they concluded that rBGH poses a "negligible" harm to human health. The report specifically discusses FAO/WHO concerns about the increase in antibiotic use related to higher levels of mastitis that are associated with rBGH use in cows. Concerns have been raised that the mechanism by which rBGH works may also create dangerous hormones for people consuming the dairy products from treated cows. As a by-product, rBGH causes cows to produce more insulin growth factor 1 (IGF-1). IGF-1 is present in milk at higher levels in cows that take rBGH. IGF-1 causes cells to divide but the FAO/WHO Committee found no basis for a connection between cancer and rBGH.

The USDA estimated that approximately 22 percent of the dairy cows in the United States were treated with rBGH in 2002 and that number declined to about 14 percent in 2014 (USDA, 2016a). Since rBGH was approved in 1993, milk production per cow has grown significantly and so have large farms, which are more likely to use rBGH than smaller farms. The USDA also analyzed more than 40,000 samples of pasteurized fluid milk in 2012 and found that none of them contained any antibiotic residues.

Consumer advocacy groups remain concerned about the levels of rBGH in milk and have demanded that milk be labeled so that people can be aware if it contains these growth hormones. FDA rules do not permit a dairy to declare its milk rBGH free. However, individual states can allow or restrict labeling of milk products if they are proven to be from cows that have not been given rBGH. In 2010, Ohio tried to ban the labels with this claim, but their ban was ruled unconstitutional by the Sixth Circuit Court of Appeals (Bottemiller, 2010).

Melamine

Melamine was the cause of a massive pet food recall in 2007. More than 180 different brands were part of the recall, including Hills, Del Monte, Nestle, and Iams. Concerns about pet food began after several animals died during laboratory taste testing and the manufacturer, Menu Foods, contacted the

FDA. Ultimately, many more pets likely died as a result of consuming foods contaminated with melamine (FDA, 2009). In 2008, Menu Foods settled a class action lawsuit involving more than 250 pet owners which would compensate most for veterinary fees in addition to a small cash payment (Schmit, 2008).

In late 2008, the FDA issued a public health alert related to consuming dairy-based products that originated in China (FDA, 2008). Specific concerns were raised about imported infant formula in the wake of hundreds of thousands of Chinese children suffering severe illness, and six children died. The children suffered kidney stones and in some cases complete renal failure. Melamine-contaminated products from China were found in 47 countries, including the United States. It was determined that this was a case of deliberate contamination as melamine was added to make milk more profitable by diluting it (Gossner et al., 2009).

Melamine is an organic chemical that is used in plastics and adhesives, among other things. It is combined with formaldehyde to make a range of plastic products, including tableware and other food service containers. Recently, concerns have been raised about the ability of melamine to migrate from plastic containers and contaminate food. This is a valid concern, and the FDA cautions consumers not to use containers made with melamine in the microwave. Under normal use, melamine tableware does not pose a health risk.

Mercury

Mercury is a heavy metal that is both naturally occurring and anthropogenic. Mercury is emitted by some natural processes, but major sources in the atmosphere are mining and smelting of mineral ores, burning fossil fuels (especially coal), and incinerating wastes. Mercury in the environment can be in elemental form or as the organic chemical methylmercury; either form of mercury can end up in food products.

Mercury causes both neurological and heart problems. In the 1800s, hat makers used mercury in the shaping process and developed neurological symptoms, including trembling and twitching. These symptoms, which people associated with madness, led to the term "mad as a hatter." A disaster in the 1950s made people think about the dangers of mercury in fish. In the Japanese fishing village of Minimata, local cats began to stumble around, and some went into the bay and drowned. Later, dozens of people died, and women gave birth to babies with severe disabilities and neurological problems. The cause of the tragedy was traced to a nearby chemical plant that had dumped tons of mercury into the bay. The fish became contaminated by the mercury, as did the cats and humans who ate the fish. A similar case occurred in Iraq in the 1970s, in which more than 50,000 people were exposed to methylmercury in a pesticide and several hundred people died as a result.

Ultimately, the health effects from mercury poisoning became known as "Minimata disease." In 2013, the United States signed a global treaty, the *Minimata Convention on Mercury*, to protect human health and the environment from mercury. In August 2015, the EPA and the Japanese Ministry of the Environment agreed to formally collaborate to reduce sources of environmental mercury (EPA, 2015).

Mercury bioaccumulates, so older fish and those fish higher on the food chain have higher concentrations of mercury in their systems. The dangers of exposure to high levels of mercury are well documented; however, the dangers from low levels of contamination were not well understood until the 1960s. The FDA set guidelines for permissible levels of mercury in 1969; this action level of 1 ppm of edible fish is still in place in 2016.

In 2004, the EPA and FDA issued a joint warning statement about fish because of high levels of mercury (FDA, 2004). Children, pregnant women, and women of childbearing age were advised to avoid shark, swordfish, king mackerel, and tilefish and to eat no more than 12 ounces of fish per week total. Further, the agencies recommended that this group of consumers eat only low-mercury fish such as shrimp, canned light tuna, pollock, and catfish. Albacore tuna is higher in mercury and should be avoided by this group. Complicating the safety issues are the known benefits of fish consumption, including better cardiovascular health and fewer heart attacks and strokes, due to the consumption of omega-3 fatty acids. One large 2011 study determined that mercury in fish was not related to adverse cardiovascular effects (Harvard School of Public Health, 2011). Regardless of mercury-related research and action levels enforced by the FDA, the messages about mercury consumption can be confusing to the public. Pregnant women are not advised to eliminate fish from their diets entirely because it is possible they will not pass on the cognitive benefits to their unborn children.

In 2014, the agencies revised the 2004 advisory and focused on the benefits of eating 8 to 12 ounces of fish each week but still cautioned pregnant women and young children to choose fish known to be lower in mercury (FDA, 2014a). The EPA provides numerous tools for consumers to use in self-regulating their mercury intake. For example, fish consumption advisories by states are available online. Some states have issued their own safety warnings to further protect their citizens, specifically including other fish species on the "do not eat" list. There are multiple sources of information and tools available to help consumers understand how to manage mercury in their diets, including the following:

- Fish Advisories Where You Live from EPA: https://fishadvi soryonline.epa.gov/General.aspx. Identifies local and state-level advisories on the amounts and species of fish suitable for distinct population groups.

- The Environmental Working Group's Seafood Calculator: http://www.ewg.org/research/ewg-s-consumer-guide-sea food/seafood-calculator. After you enter your age, weight, gender, and heart disease status, this tool provides a list of fish, including their mercury content, by how often you should eat them.

- Mercury Calculator from the Turtle Island Restoration Network: https://seaturtles.org/programs/mercury/. In this tool, you enter your weight and the type and amount of fish you plan to eat in the week and the result is an estimated dose of mercury.

Olestra

Olestra, the fat substitute, was first synthesized at Procter & Gamble in 1968 by researchers looking for a way to increase fat intake in premature babies. Chemically, olestra is a table sugar (sucrose) molecule to which as many as eight fatty acid residues are attached. The molecule is so large and fatty that it cannot be broken down by the intestinal enzymes and absorbed by the body, so it did not work as a product to help babies gain weight. An alternative use was suggested as an indigestible fat substitute to make low-calorie food. Researchers discovered quickly that eating even small amounts, such as the quantity in one ounce of potato chips, could cause digestive problems like diarrhea, abdominal cramping, gas, and fecal incontinence.

Because olestra is such a bulky fat molecule, fat-soluble vitamins such as vitamins A, D, E, and K and some plant nutrients (phytochemicals) called carotenoids (like beta-carotene found in many vegetables, including carrots, and lycopene found in tomatoes) are attracted to it in the intestine and are excreted with the olestra instead of being absorbed by the body. These carotenoids are one of the benefits of eating fruits and vegetables and appear to prevent cancers and other degenerative diseases. So even if a person did not experience intestinal distress from eating olestra, there would be negative nutrition consequences from having vitamin absorption reduced.

Originally, Procter & Gamble envisioned many applications for olestra, and branded it Olean. They sought approval for savory snack foods first. In 1996, the FDA approved olestra for snacks such as potato chips, crackers, and tortilla chips, but because of the adverse effects, the products had to carry a label: "This product contains olestra. Olestra may cause abdominal cramping and loose stools. Olestra inhibits the absorption of some vitamins and nutrients. Vitamins A, D, E, and K have been added." Procter & Gamble test marketed fat-free Pringles; Nabisco test-marketed Wheat Thins and Ritz Crackers; and Frito-Lay started the Wow line of chips. Consumer complaints began to roll in to the FDA. The FDA had received almost 20,000 complaints about olestra by 2002, more than all other consumer complaints about other food additives combined.

In 2003, Procter & Gamble lobbied the FDA to remove the warning label for foods containing olestra. The FDA granted the request despite lobbying by consumer groups that wanted the labels to stay. Frito-Lay changed the name of its Wow chips to Light in 2004 and removed the warning label. Olestra is still listed in the ingredient list, and a small Olean logo is located on the front of the package.

The Center for Science in the Public Interest (CSPI) is supporting a consumer lawsuit filed in 2006 against Frito-Lay to restore the warnings, even though the FDA has ruled that the warnings do not need to be there. The CSPI claims that Frito-Lay engaged in deceptive marketing practices when it renamed the Wow line, but Frito-Lay says it renamed the brand to be more descriptive of the contents (Mohl, 2006). In order to avoid the lawsuit, Frito-Lay agreed to include a warning to consumers on the labels of foods containing olestra and to donate money to the Harvard Medical School. By 2002, olestra had essentially disappeared from the radar; in 2010, *Time Magazine* identified olestra as one of the 50 Worst Inventions of all time (Gentilviso, 2010).

Even if olestra has serious problems as a fat substitute, one interesting potential use for the substance has been found. Olestra seems to bind to PCBs, dioxins, and other dangerous chemicals in the body, causing these toxins to be excreted (Jandacek et al., 2010; Potera, 2005).

Polychlorinated Biphenyls

For many years, salmon has been the second most popular fish food in the United States; shrimp is the most popular (NFI, 2016). The amount of farm-raised salmon consumed has increased steadily since 2004, and today it is the dominant source of salmon in the food supply (Marine Harvest, 2015). Specifically, farm-raised Atlantic salmon is the most common species of salmonoid by quantity, and aquaculture is the only way to keep up with consumer demand for salmon.

PCBs are organic chemicals that were mostly used in electrical equipment, such as transformers, because they were effective insulators. Their chemical characteristics contribute to their persistence in the environment, so even though they were banned in the United States in 1979, they are still creating problems. In 2003, the Environmental Working Group tested farm-raised salmon for PCBs; they found levels in farmed salmon more than 16 times higher than wild salmon (Environmental Working Group, 2003). The Environmental Working Group study was controversial because of its methods, but it still contributed to public concerns about eating farm-raised salmon.

In follow-up studies, including a large study funded by the Pew Charitable Trust's Environment Program, scientists found large differences in contaminant levels between farmed and wild salmon. The Pew study sampled about 700 salmon from around the world and analyzed them for more than 50 contaminants, including PCBs and two other persistent pesticides, dieldrin and toxaphene. All three of these contaminants have been associated with increased liver and other cancer risk. The research was published in *Science* in 2004, a top-tier, peer-reviewed journal, and called for clear labeling as to whether salmon is farmed or wild (Hites et al., 2004).

Farmed salmon are fed a diet of fish meal, made from ground-up small fish. This meal is high in fish oil, to help the fish increase the weight of salmon. In fact, farmed salmon is higher in omega-3 fatty acids than wild salmon because wild salmon eat a variety of fish, many of which are low in fat. PCBs bioaccumulate in fat, and the more fat the fish consumes, the greater the concentration of PCBs in the fish. Fish farms have been working to develop new feeds that are low in contaminants and are experimenting with using transgenic canola oil, which is a precursor to omega-3s (Stokstad, 2004).

The American Heart Association recommends eating at least two servings, or 7 ounces, of fish per week, especially fish high in omega-3 fatty acids. However, they follow guidance from the FDA and EPA in issuing warnings to pregnant women and parents about the types of fish that are least likely to be contaminated with pollutants. Some consumer groups caution people to avoid farmed salmon; however, there has been little new research since 2004 examining this issue.

Controversies

Avian and Swine Influenza

Influenza viruses are typed into three categories: A, B, and C. All three can affect humans, but C viruses do not lead to widespread epidemics. The influenza A viruses are named by the combination of antigens hemagglutinin (H) and neuraminidase (N), which are proteins comprising the virus particle. Viruses are spheres that have a central core containing genetic material. This core is covered by another layer, called the capsid, and a third layer known as the envelope. Both the capsid and the envelope are made up of antigens. When a virus infects a cell, it turns its host into a biological factory, making more copies of the virus and eventually causing the cell to burst, spilling virus into surrounding tissue. New viruses are always emerging, creating a need for vigilant surveillance and new vaccines with each flu season.

If a healthy person is infected with a virus his or her body does not recognize, it can take two to three weeks before the immune system responds with specific antibodies to kill the virus. While the body is learning the virus, the virus is invading healthy cells and causing them to make more viruses. When the cells die, they spill their contents, stimulating pain and inflammation and encouraging white blood cell production to increase. Current influenza viruses that cause human disease have antigen combinations H1N1 and H3N2.

Avian influenza (also known as the "bird flu") and swine flu are animal diseases that can affect human health. Both influenzas are exacerbated by highly concentrated farming practices prevalent in the United States. Bird flu is caused by influenza A viruses, typically H5 or H7 strains. Avian influenzas are categorized as those with low pathogenicity (LPAI) and those that are highly pathogenic (HPAI). Specific strains of avian influenza can become more or less pathogenic over time. This was the case in 2016, when a new strain of H7N8 virus was found in turkeys in Indiana. The USDA's Animal and Plant Health Inspection Service worked with local authorities to identify the strain and take steps to stop the virus from spreading (USDA, 2016b).

Although the viruses affecting poultry and birds rarely infect humans, there have been enough human cases that it concerns public health authorities in the United States and abroad. Almost every human case has been the result of extended contact with infected animals. The most common avian influenza found in humans is the H5N1 strain; the WHO confirmed 450 human cases between 2003 and 2016 (WHO, 2016). The few human-to-human cases that have occurred are usually members of the same family who are in proximity to animals.

One emergent concern, with bird flu especially, is related to the local foods movement. In many places in the United States, people are growing their own poultry in so-called backyard flocks. In March 2016, the USDA issued procedures for monitoring backyard flocks that are near places with confirmed infections (USDA, 2016c). While these backyard flocks have the potential to contribute to more sustainable agriculture, they also have the potential to put more people in contact with circulating avian influenzas.

Swine flu is more of a public health concern because of its ability to infect people, even though this is still a rare occurrence.

The most common swine flu strains in the United States are H1N1, H3N2, and H1N2, and in most cases these strains are only found in swine. However, a new variant of H1N1 emerged in 2009, creating the first global pandemic in more than 40 years; it was eventually linked to swine flu (CDC, 2010).

Since viruses are constantly mutating, vaccines with specific antibodies cannot be made until the exact nature of the virus is known. Before each flu season, scientists must determine which strains are the most prevalent and choose which strains to target in vaccines. Then the time-consuming process of individually inoculating chicken eggs begins. Developed in the 1940s, this process produces vaccine in several months. Research is being conducted to improve and increase vaccine production. Scientists are attempting to find ways to make vaccine without using chicken eggs because production times could be shortened and the process could be independent of the chicken egg supply.

Bioterrorism

After the terrorist attacks of September 11, 2001, all sectors of the United States examined vulnerability to terrorism, and the food industry is no exception. Food processing and agricultural facilities provide potential avenues for terrorist attacks, although the likelihood of this is unknown. The only documented case of food-related bioterrorism with political aims occurred in The Dalles, Oregon, in 1984. At the time, The Dalles was a small farming community of about 11,000 residents, located near the Columbia River. In 1981, followers of Bhagwan Shree Rajneesh purchased a ranch in the county where The Dalles is located, with the intent of building an international headquarters for the guru. The group incorporated as a town called Rajneeshpuram in order to circumvent local zoning ordinances and thus build their facilities as they wished. Their incorporation was challenged in court, and the sect was prevented from building as they planned. The group believed that the outcome of the November 6, 1984, elections for the county commissioners would affect their ability to get their zoning petitions approved. Their strategy was to sicken a significant portion of the local population to limit the turnout in the election.

Members of the group purchased stocks of *Salmonella* Typhimurium from a biological supply house. In two episodes, from September 9 to September 18, 1984, and September 19 to October 10, 1984, group members visited local restaurants and were able to successfully inoculate various salads, blue cheese dressing, and some creamers with bacteria. At least 751 people contracted *Salmonella* Typhimurium and 45 people had to be hospitalized. It appears that the two episodes were trial runs for contaminating the water supply nearer the time of the election.

Although intentional contamination was considered early in the investigation, it was rejected because there was no apparent motive. There was concern in The Dalles about potential election fraud, but since the outbreak occurred too early to affect the election, the incident was not linked in the investigators' minds to the election. No one claimed responsibility for the attacks; law enforcement officers questioned a few restaurant employees, but there was no recognizable pattern of unusual behavior. By considering the epidemic exposure curves, it appeared that the salad bars were contaminated multiple times during a several-week period. This indicated that a sustained source of *S.* Typhimurium was necessary, a situation more likely to occur from a sick employee than from multiple sabotage attempts.

When the Rajneesh commune collapsed in 1985, the Federal Bureau of Investigation and the Oregon Public Health Laboratory investigated the clinic and lab facilities at Rajneeshpuram. A sample seized at the facility's medical center lab on October 2, 1985, matched the outbreak strain. A confession by one of the members of the group provided further clues about the plot. On March 19, 1986, two commune members were indicted for conspiring to tamper with consumer products by poisoning food in violation of the federal anti-tampering laws; they pled guilty in April 1986. They were subsequently sentenced to four-and-a-half years in prison (Torok et al., 1997).

Another case of intentional contamination occurred in 1996, when 12 laboratory workers at a large Texas medical center contracted *Shigella dysenteriae* type 2 after eating muffins and doughnuts left in their break room. On October 29, 1996, an unsigned e-mail from a supervisor's computer appeared on lab computer screens inviting coworkers to eat pastries in the lab break room. Twelve workers ate the pastries, and all 12 developed diarrhea; 4 workers had to be hospitalized, with an average stay of four days, and 5 others were treated in emergency rooms, some with intravenous fluids.

Investigation of the lab storage freezer suggested that the reference culture of *Shigella dysenteriae* type 2 had been disturbed. An uneaten muffin was contaminated with the same strain of *S. dysenteriae* as the reference culture—a strain that is uncommon in the United States. The researchers investigated other possible sources of contamination, including a lab accident or contamination during commercial handling but concluded that the most likely occurrence was intentional tampering by someone with access to the freezer, the lab skills to culture the organism and inoculate the pastries, and access to the locked break room. The dosage on each pastry was not determined, but *S. dysenteriae* causes illness with as little as 10 to 100 organisms. A lab technician was found guilty of contaminating the food and sentenced to 20 years in prison. This case was not politically motivated but appeared to be the result of an unstable employee with a history of attempting to poison her boyfriend.

These two incidents illustrate the potential for intentional biological contamination of food. In each of these cases, the food products were tainted right before serving. This time frame results in the most concentrated effect; however, the risk of detection for the perpetrator is high, and the number of people that can be affected is low. Each of these incidents used agents that were meant solely to induce illness and not death. This method also reduced the risk to the perpetrators since accidental self-contamination would not be lethal.

If an outbreak is detected, it may not be immediately apparent whether it is intentional or unintentional. Intentional adulteration of food is not the first thing that comes to mind when an outbreak occurs; however, there are some clues that should alert investigators to consider it (Dembek et al., 2007). For example, in the case of the Texas pastry poisoning, the pathogen was uncommon, the episode occurred over a narrow window of time, and there was direct evidence. The best defense against intentional food poisoning is an effective and efficient surveillance system that uses multiple tools, as described in the Outbreak Investigations section of Chapter 1.

The Food Safety Modernization Act (FSMA) required the FDA to develop rules to mitigate the likelihood and consequences of bioterrorism. The *Final Rule for Mitigation Strategies to Protect Food against Intentional Adulteration* was published in May 27, 2016 (FDA, 2016b). Under this rule, certain facilities are required to have a written food defense plan that includes (1) vulnerability assessment; (2) mitigation strategies; (3) food defense monitoring procedures; (4) food defense corrective actions; and (5) food verification procedures. In addition, there are specific requirements for training all personnel and for keeping records pertaining to food defense.

Bisphenol A

There are chemicals that, when ingested, mimic hormones even at low doses; these are referred to as endocrine disruptors. Some research suggests that certain chemicals used in food containers may have endocrine-disrupting effects. Bisphenol A (BPA) is used in making hard, clear polycarbonate plastics formed into baby bottles, water bottles, and other food and beverage containers. If the containers are heated, cleaned with harsh detergents, or exposed to high-acid food or drinks, BPA can leach from the container into the food.

In the 2003–04 National Health and Nutrition Examination Survey (NHANES), BPA was detected in nearly every person tested in the United States. As people became more aware of BPA and more concerned about possible health effects, researchers began to evaluate the safety of these chemicals. At the same time, the government was conducting its own research in attempts to set regulatory limits on the amount of BPA allowable in food and noted some health concerns from exposure (National Toxicology Program, 2008). In many cases the results from the studies were not in agreement, leading to a challenging regulatory environment in which the uncertainties heightened consumer concerns. The food industry responded by labeling products as BPA-free in order to reassure the public.

Because the health effects can be subtle, the chemicals are ubiquitous in the environment, and there is not enough information about health effects from low doses, the EPA has not regulated BPA. Instead, the agency created a Bisphenol A Action Plan in 2010 that expresses the EPA's intentions to "consider initiating rulemaking" under the Toxic Substances Control Act (TSCA) (EPA, 2010b). In the Action Plan, the EPA explicitly states that it is not regulating BPA under TSCA because human exposure to the chemical is mainly from food, which is the FDA's jurisdiction.

The FDA convened a BPA Joint Emerging Science Working Group to review the research related to the human health effects of BPA, including their own risk assessment that had been released in 2008. In 2014, the Working Group issued their findings and concluded that BPA is safe at current levels in food contact products (FDA, 2014b). In 2012 and 2013, the FDA amended regulations pertaining to food additives, because BPA is no longer used in baby bottles, sippy cups, or packaging for infant formula.

As a result of the myriad challenges with the scientific understanding of the health effects from BPA and in the context of public outrage about involuntary exposure to this chemical, the National Institute of Environmental Health Science

(NIEHS) and the National Toxicology Program assembled a consortium of researchers focused solely on this chemical. In 2016, the Consortium Linking Academic and Regulatory Insights on BPA Toxicity (CLARITY-BPA) is an ongoing endeavor that involves clinical, occupational, and laboratory studies to assess levels of BPA in humans (Heindel et al., 2015).

Factory Farming

When people imagine farming, some may consider images of pastoral acreage dotted with cows or perhaps memories of a grandparent or neighbor who kept chickens or pigs. Today's reality is much different from those images of the past. As world population and incomes grow, farming methods producing greater yields are needed. Farming is influenced by business thinkers who advocate economies of scale, and, as in many businesses, sometimes large-scale production is more cost effective than small-scale production. As such, small, independent farms have merged and/or were bought by large corporations resulting in the so-called factory farms of today. Other factors, such as increased demand for meat and certain agricultural policies, spurred changes in agricultural methods (United Nations Environment Program, 2012).

Scientific advances in manipulating nitrogen led to the ability to synthesize ammonia, a potent fertilizer. Eventually, so much ammonia was produced that chemical fertilizers enhanced with nitrogen were commonplace, creating what was called the "Green Revolution" in the 1960s, when crop yields increased substantially worldwide. The greater yields and the ability to farm land that was previously thought not to be arable enabled the earth to support a much greater population but also enabled wealthier countries to put more meat in their diets as there were more crops available to use as animal feed.

As scientists were creating ways to enhance plant growth, several historical events contributed to the current situation in which we rely on intensive agriculture to meet today's food supply demands. First, a shipping mistake in the 1920s transformed poultry farming in the Delmarva Peninsula, which is named for portions of Delaware, Maryland, and Virginia. Mrs. Cecile Steele ordered 50 chicks to supplement her flock of laying hens but received 500 chicks instead; she decided to keep the hens and build a small shed to raise them indoors. Instead of raising them to lay eggs, she sold the chickens for meat and earned more than what she would have earned had she kept them as part of her egg business.

The second event occurred in 1936, when John Tyson, a truck driver from Arkansas, picked up a load of chickens and drove to Chicago instead of taking them to the local slaughterhouse, effectively breaking the connection between local farmers and local slaughterhouses. Tyson went on to buy feed plants, start hatcheries, contract with producers, and build processing plants.

Third, U.S. farm policy encouraged large-scale farming because farm subsidies designed to compensate farmers during times of economic downturn created crop surpluses. These surpluses resulted from growing more than could be sold since farmers were paid per bushel. At times, the U.S. government has warehoused large surpluses under this policy. Thus, simple economics has the effect of promoting farming methods to maximize production rather than maintain and improve the land.

Today, much of the world's meat supply is grown on large-scale feeding operations where thousands of animals are housed in relatively small areas. These farms, called animal feeding operations (AFOs), are defined by the EPA as

a lot or facility (other than an aquatic animal production facility) where the following conditions are met:

- animals have been, are, or will be stabled or confined and fed or maintained for a total of 45 days or more in any 12-month period, and
- crops, vegetation, forage growth, or post-harvest residues are not sustained in the normal growing season over any portion of the lot or facility.

A Concentrated Animal Feeding Operation (CAFO) is an AFO that houses quantities of animals as specified in regulations and summarized in Table 2.2.

CAFOs create a range of environmental, health, nutrition, and food safety problems, not only in the meat they produce but also for the food raised nearby. The main issue that underscores all environmental problems related to CAFOs is manure and the fact that these facilities generate more manure than the local environment can handle. The EPA (2004) noted in their risk assessment of CAFOs that the manure includes pathogens, nutrients, and chemicals such as antibiotics that can contaminate local water supplies. Food safety is further compromised by CAFOs because of the challenges created in adhering to inspection protocols required in federal law (Follmer and Termini, 2009).

Table 2.2   Regulatory Definitions of CAFOs

Animal	Number of Animals		
	Large	Medium	Small
Cattle or cow/calf pairs	1,000 or more	300–999	Less than 300
Mature dairy cattle	700 or more	200–699	Less than 200
Veal calves	1,000 or more	300–999	Less than 300
Swine (over 55 pounds)	2,500 or more	750–2,499	Less than 750
Swine (less than 55 pounds)	10,000 or more	3,000–9,999	Less than 3,000
Sheep or lambs	10,000 or more	3,000–9,999	Less than 3,000
Turkeys	55,000 or more	16,500–54,999	Less than 16,500
Laying hens or broilers with liquid manure handling systems	30,000 or more	9,000–29,999	Less than 9,000
Chickens other than laying hens other non-liquid manure handling system	125,000	37,500–124,999	Less than 37,500
Laying hens with other non-liquid manure system	82,000 or more	25,000–81,999	Less than 25,000

Source: EPA (2004).

Economics and cheap corn affected livestock farming. In the United States, meat formerly raised in pastures is now raised in feedlots or large indoor complexes and are fed corn instead of grass or hay. In the case of cattle, in less than 50 years, farmers reduced the time it takes to bring animals to the market from years to months. Unfortunately, this adaptation causes nutritional and food safety problems for humans (such as fattier cattle with fewer omega-3 fatty acids and more likelihood of harboring and transmitting *Escherichia coli* O157:H7) and health problems for the cattle.

On most CAFOs, cattle are regularly fed antibiotics to mitigate infections that result from a combination of an unnatural diet and unsanitary living conditions. The combination of animals living in close quarters, heavy use of antibiotics, and large quantities of waste is providing a hospitable environment for creating new diseases and may be making certain diseases foodborne that were previously acquired in other ways.

Genetically Modified Organisms

Perhaps no other food safety issue has been more controversial than genetically modified organisms (GMOs). GMOs have inflamed numerous consumer groups, exasperated scientists, created trade disagreements between countries, and rallied some components of the food industry to use the controversy to improve their image. The core of the controversy is answering questions about the impacts of transferring DNA from one species to another in order to improve yields or make crops more resistant to pests and pesticides. For example, Monsanto, the agriculture bioengineering giant, and maker of the herbicide Roundup, markets "Roundup Ready Soybeans." These seeds are resistant to Roundup, so the herbicide can be sprayed on the crops, killing the weeds and leaving the soybeans intact. The hope is that fewer herbicides can be used to control weeds, which would make the crops cheaper to grow and put fewer chemicals into the soil and groundwater. This reduction in herbicide use could also mean fewer chemical residues on food. Specific concerns have been raised about the long-term food safety and environmental health issues from using genetic engineering in agriculture.

Since ancient times, farmers have looked for ways to increase yields. Three-inch-long corncobs grown by Native Americans in Arizona have been replaced by the 10- and 12-inch ears we see today. People saved seeds from successful plants, created hybrids, and enriched soil, among other methods of enhancing yields. Within the last 50 years or so, the efficiency of agriculture has improved to the point that global acreage in crops is no longer increasing even though the population is. According to the United Nations, the world population will be 8.5 billion people in 2030, an increase of more than 1 billion from 2015. Currently, the United Nations estimates almost 800 million people in the world are undernourished, about one in every nine people. World hunger will increase with growing population, urbanization, and climate change. At the same time, agricultural acreage is likely to decrease with increasing population and climate conditions that reduce arable land. In the midst of this somewhat dire future, increased activity in genetically engineering crops has arisen as one solution to the problem.

Some genetically engineered corn seeds have a gene from the bacterium *Bacillus thuringiensis*, or Bt. This gene makes the corn plant produce a toxin in all its tissues, including the edible grain, thus killing insects harmful to the corn, including the European corn borer that eats its way into the stalk and weakens the plant. Fields planted with the altered corn produce 6 to 8 percent greater yields on average. However, this toxin may harm more than the insects it is designed to repel. In 1999 and 2000, several studies suggested that pollen from genetically engineered Bt corn can kill Monarch butterflies who feed on milkweed near cornfields (Jesse and Obrycki, 2000; Losey et al., 1999). These conclusions further enraged people, and even though additional research suggested no impact on Monarch butterflies (Sears et al., 2001), it is still an argument made by opponents of GMOs.

Additionally, opponents of genetic engineering fear that these techniques will have only short-term benefits and that "superweeds" will develop requiring the use of more toxic and greater quantities of herbicides. If superweeds develop, they could crowd out indigenous plants and thus impair biodiversity. Genetically modified crops are also difficult to contain to one area because cross-pollination occurs with neighboring fields planted with the same crop. So one variety of corn planted next to a different variety will be cross-pollinated, causing the resultant crop in the two fields to be a mixture of the two varieties. For organic farmers or farmers exporting to Europe or Japan, this type of cross-pollination poses real problems. They cannot get their crops certified as free of GMOs.

Cross-pollination also poses problems for people who find themselves allergic to genetically modified crops. It is impossible to know whether a new strain will cause allergies because new proteins are being created. When a crop that produces a known allergen, such as nuts or wheat, mixes with a crop that does not produce an allergen, the new crop could be problematic. Aside from the dangers of allergies, the quality of genetically engineered produce has been questioned. The FlavrSavr tomato, which was one of the earliest and most publicized genetically engineered products, was not a resounding commercial success and caused some to raise the issue of "faux freshness." If the tomato is engineered to have a long shelf life, will a consumer actually be purchasing an old tomato that looks fresh but has long since lost its nutritional value?

In the United States, genetically engineered crops have grown from below 25 percent of all acreage in 1996 to 94 percent of acreage in 2016 for some crops such as herbicide-resistant soybeans. Bt corn was about 8 percent of all acreage planted in the United States in 1997 and now comprises 79 percent of the crop (USDA-ERS, 2016). There are no specific or distinct regulations pertaining to GMOs in food, but the FDA does encourage manufacturers of genetically engineered plants to voluntarily consult with them prior to marketing their seed.

The FDA maintains a database of consultations that includes letters sent to the manufacturers summarizing the FDA's assessment of the product.

Foods can be voluntarily labeled to indicate their status with regards to GMO, and the FDA recommends using language such as "not bioengineered" or "not genetically engineered." The FDA does not recommend the use of labels such as "GMO free" because it would be difficult for the manufacturer to prove that there are no genetically modified organisms in their product. According to USDA regulations for organic labeling, organic foods cannot be produced with genetic engineering, so a food cannot be labeled "organic" if it has been bioengineered.

In Europe, genetically engineered foods have met with great resistance. In 2002, the European Union created the European Food Safety Authority (EFSA) to provide scientific support on a variety of food safety topics including GMO products. However, the EFSA is not the regulatory authority when it comes to genetically modified products—the European Commission is. In 2015, the Commission authorized member countries to make their own determination as to whether to allow GMOs. The result of this policy change is that 17 countries, including France, Germany, and Greece, banned all genetically modified crops, a move that could cripple biotechnology in Europe. The bans could also result in additional trade disputes with countries, such as the United States, that allow genetically modified crops.

So far, scientific studies have not shown significant environmental or human health problems with genetically engineered foods. Even though we have been selectively breeding crops since the birth of agriculture, the technology surged in the mid-1990s, creating some fears that there may be long-term, unforeseen consequences as a result of the widespread use of genetic engineering. In many other areas, changes in the ways food is grown and processed have created niches for harmful bacteria and viruses. Genetic engineering has much to offer in increasing the amount of food available to the world's expanding population, but some argue that the process should be carefully and continuously evaluated to avoid creating new food risks and environmental catastrophes (Freedman, 2013).

Irradiation

Just as science has brought us new food production techniques, it has also brought new food safety strategies, such as irradiation. Irradiation is the process of treating food to electron beams or gamma rays to kill bacteria. The radiation damages bacteria so that it cannot reproduce, making the food safer from microbes and delaying spoilage. The amount of radiation is not enough to make the food radioactive; it is just enough only to kill bacteria. Currently, irradiation is used to sterilize medical supplies and cosmetics and a limited number of foods.

Irradiation is the only way to kill *E. coli* O157:H7 in food besides cooking to proper temperatures. After the deaths of four children from *E. coli* O157:H7 were traced to Jack in the Box restaurants in 1993, enthusiasm for irradiation grew, and the USDA approved irradiation of beef in 1999. Under congressional mandate, the USDA announced in 2003 that it would allow school districts to purchase irradiated beef for school cafeterias. There was not much interest in the irradiated meat, though, because of the increased cost and because parent groups were not in favor of irradiated food. In addition, sanitarians at school districts believed that their procedures were sufficient to safely handle beef without irradiation.

Meat producers have been cautious about introducing irradiated beef because of the added cost and because it can darken meat and change the flavor enough to be noticeable. Irradiated food must be marked with the Radura symbol, or it must say "irradiated" on the food label. The marketing departments of the grocery and meat trade organizations have found that considerable education of consumers is needed before they will accept irradiated food. The FDA expanded the definition of pasteurization in 2004 to be "any process, treatment, or combination thereof that is applied to food to reduce the most resistant microorganism(s) of public health significance to a level that is not likely to present a public health risk under normal conditions of distribution and storage" (Sugarman, 2004). The FDA considers irradiation to be "cold pasteurization" and has approved several foods for irradiation, including beef and pork, some shellfish, fresh fruits and vegetables, lettuce and spinach, poultry, seeds for sprouting, shell eggs, and spices and seasonings.

Besides increased cost and potential reduction of food taste, there are several drawbacks to irradiation. However, after decades of research, there have been no documented health effects from consuming irradiated food. On the other hand, it is possible that more widespread use and acceptance of irradiation might have minimized some major outbreaks, including the 2006 spinach outbreak involving *E. coli* O157:H7. The CDC, the WHO, and the FDA all endorse the safety of irradiation. However, there are still arguments against radiating foods; the most compelling is that if better farming practices were employed, then there would be no need to decontaminate meats, produce, and spices.

Local Foods Movement

The local foods movement is a contemporary food issue that has the potential to impact food safety in multiple ways. Although there is no consensus on what is required for food to be considered "local," in most cases local foods are those that are grown close to the market, directly sold to the consumers, or grown by consumers themselves. There are several components of this movement that create food safety challenges, including farmers' markets and homegrown meats and produce.

Farmers' markets are one method of direct to consumer (DTC) food sales that has seen a rapid rise in popularity. The number of farmers' markets in the United States grew 180 percent between 2006 and 2014, and there are more than 8,000 markets listed in the USDA's database. In addition, farm to school programs have seen a 430 percent increase since 2006 (Low et al., 2015). DTC activities create food safety challenges for local sanitarians, especially when a significant percentage of items for sale at some markets are from the "cottage industry"— that is, they are made in an unlicensed or uninspected home kitchen. In addition, some farm products, such as eggs and meats, are subject to strict temperature controls that are sometimes not available at farmers' markets. States are creating and revising their food safety regulations in order ensure that products purchased at farmers' markets are safe.

Another local foods movement–related situation comes in the form of "backyard flocks," in which homeowners raise their own hens for egg and meat production, creating small-scale manure problems. There are documented outbreaks of foodborne illness pathogens associated with backyard flocks. In 2016, there was a series of outbreaks of *Salmonella* linked to backyard flocks that sickened more than 600 people. Simple sanitation methods such as adequate hand washing could minimize the spread of pathogens circulating in these flocks, but a combination of a lack of education and a lack of attention to personal hygiene is creating concerns about these illnesses affecting the community.

The 2011 FSMA exempts some small farmers from complying with some regulations. For example, under the Produce Safety Rule, farmers who have food sales averaging less than $500,000 per year during the previous three years are exempt. Farms that sell most of their product less than 275 miles from their farm are also exempt. These exemptions have stirred debate because they were not originally in the rule, prompting local and small farmers to argue that they could not afford to comply with all of the requirements of the rule. Once the FDA made the exemptions, larger farms and some food safety professionals argued that they would make food from local farmers less safe.

Manure

Historically, animal waste was considered to be relatively benign. In fact, manure is generally considered a "soil builder" because it contributes so much to soil quality. Manure reduces nitrate leaching, reduces soil erosion and runoff, increases soil carbon and reduces atmospheric carbon levels (potentially reducing global warming), reduces energy demands for natural gas–intensive nitrogen fertilizers, reduces demand for commercial nitrogen and phosphorous fertilizers, and improves productivity of cropping systems. Table 2.3 provides estimates of the amounts of manure produced by some common livestock.

Referring back to the regulatory definition of CAFO, a large poultry CAFO could house 30,000 or more chickens. Using a formula provided by Penn State Extension (2016), this could result in more than 223 tons of manure per year for an average farm. Federal regulations allow for manure to be used as a fertilizer with certain restrictions in timing and amount; however, CAFOs are subject to more stringent requirements than non-CAFOs. States establish and enforce regulations pertaining to manure as fertilizer in terms of amounts allowable per acre. Even with permission to spread manure on fields, the large feedlots generate too much waste for land application methods.

Table 2.3   Estimates of Average Daily Production of Total Manure, Nitrogen, and Phosphorus

Livestock	Total Manure (pounds/ animal/day)[1]	Nitrogen (pounds/ton)[2]	Phosphorus (pounds/ton)[2]
Heifer (dairy)	60	10	3
Lactating cows (dairy)	111	10	4
Cow and calf (beef)	90	11	7
Swine—farrow to wean	11	18	18
Swine—grow to finish	7	31	24
Poultry (layer)	26	37	55
Poultry (broiler)	20	66	63
Turkey (tom)	13	52	76

[1] Varies depending on weight of animal.

[2] Swine estimates are based on pounds/1,000 gallons of waste rather than pounds/ton.

Source: Penn State Extension (2016).

Animal manure contains more than 150 pathogens associated with risks to humans, including the 6 human pathogens that account for a significant percentage of foodborne and waterborne diseases: *Salmonella, E. coli, Giardia, Campylobacter, Cryptosporidium parvum,* and *Listeria monocytogenes* (Hribar, 2010). If these pathogens come in contact with a drinking-water supply or are used for irrigation of fruits and vegetables, human health can be affected. In addition to microbial pathogens, heavy metals, nutrients including nitrogen, and synthetic chemicals such as antibiotics are found in manure.

Foodborne illness attributable to fruits and vegetables has increased dramatically, and some of the increase can be attributed to higher rates of consumption, self-service salad bars (since there are opportunities for greater contamination from patrons and cross-contamination), improved surveillance, global and centralized production facilities, and more vulnerable populations (such as children, the elderly, and immune-compromised individuals). Manure that contains potential foodborne pathogens can directly contaminate produce, which is a special concern for produce that is intended to be consumed raw. Once a pathogen makes contact with the soil, its survival depends on environmental factors. Some microorganisms thrive in cold temperatures, some prefer heat, some like moisture, while some favor dry conditions. Pathogens like *L. monocytogenes, Bacillus cereus,* and *Clostridium botulinum* flourish in soil; it is one of their natural habitats, and they can survive there indefinitely. Some bacteria, such as *E. coli* O157:H7, survive longer if they are in proximity to the root area of plants, called the rhizosphere, but this affinity only occurs with certain types of plants. Soil characteristics can either enhance or interfere with pathogen growth.

The 2011 FSMA addresses concerns with "biological soil amendments of animal origin" (i.e., manure) contaminating produce by proposing regulations restricting the timing of when manure can be spread on fields. Specifically, the proposed 2013 Produce Safety Rule stated that at least nine months had to pass between applying raw manure and harvesting produce. The FDA was immediately confronted with arguments from both the organic and conventional food industries because the proposed regulations were more stringent than those required by the USDA, specifically in terms of organic food production. In response to comments from a variety of perspectives, the FDA decided to conduct a risk assessment of foodborne illness that could be related to using untreated manure as a fertilizer. The FDA was accepting information from stakeholders until mid-July 2016, so the risk assessment is likely several years from completion.

Manure can contaminate irrigation water, which is a significant source of contamination in fruit and vegetable production. Irrigation water can also be contaminated by sewage spills, runoff from feedlots, storm-related contamination (as when manure lagoons overflow during storms), illicit discharge of waste, and uncontrolled animals that get into irrigation water. In the final Produce Safety Rule, irrigation water that is applied directly to crops must meet minimum standards for levels of *E. coli*. If the water does not comply with the standards, the farmer must take corrective action within one year of when the water was tested.

In the meantime, some farmers are addressing the manure problem with economic strategies. In some states, "Manure Share" programs are emerging that connect farms with excess manure to other farms and individuals who want manure. For example, the University of Illinois Extension coordinates a Manure Share program that provides a listing and online forms for sharing manure among farms.

Pesticides

The U.S. Federal Insecticide, Fungicide, and Rodenticide Act defines pesticides as "any substance or mixture of substances intended for preventing, repelling, or mitigating any insects, rodents, nematodes, or fungi, or any other forms of life declared to be pests." This definition includes substances or mixtures intended for use as plant regulators, defoliants, or desiccants. Pesticides are an integral part of U.S. agricultural practice, and the USDA estimates that close to 100 percent of all corn grown in the United States has been treated with herbicides (USDA-ERS, 2014).

Pesticides are comprised of active and inert ingredients. Active ingredients are chemicals that affect the target pest, whether it is a plant or insect. Inert ingredients generally improve the efficacy of the active ingredients or make the product more marketable. There are hundreds of active ingredients registered in pesticides in the United States. Pesticides can be naturally occurring substances such as nicotine, pyrethrum (found in chrysanthemums), hellebore, rotenone, and camphor, or synthetically produced substances such as metals, metallic salts, organophosphates, carbamates, and hydrocarbons. The four most common active ingredients in pesticides applied to crops are glyphosate, atrazine, acetochlor, and metolachlor, all of which are herbicides and target weeds that compete with the cash crop.

Glyphosate is the most common herbicide used in the United States; it is the active ingredient in Roundup and has been used to control weeds since the 1970s. There are more than 750 products that contain glyphosate on the market in the United States, and almost 300 million pounds are applied to farms in the United States annually. Glyphosate is related to genetic engineering because of the drive to make crops that are "Roundup-Ready," meaning that they can tolerate glyphosate. On the other hand, using glyphosate without other herbicides and not rotating crops is creating glyphosate-resistant weeds as well.

The Government Accountability Office (2014) recommended that the FDA and the USDA take steps to improve monitoring pesticide residues in foods and improve transparency about the data they gather. The FDA is responsible for testing food to ensure that the amount of pesticide residues comply with levels set by the EPA. The FDA compiles a report that summarizes their annual testing of specific foods for residues, but the methods were called into question by the Government Accountability Office. In addition, there is a considerable lag from the time of monitoring to the time the report is published; the 2013 report was posted to FDA's website in 2016.

Before a company can market a pesticide in the United States, it must demonstrate that it is safe. Pesticides are regulated by three agencies at the federal level; all three work under the 1996 Food Quality Protection Act, which specifically addressed pesticide safety. The EPA registers the pesticide and sets maximum levels (tolerances) allowed in food. The FDA monitors pesticide residues in domestic and imported foods, except for meat, poultry, and some egg products. The Food Safety Inspection Service of the USDA has responsibility for ensuring tolerance levels in products not in the FDA's jurisdiction. The FDA also conducts the Total Diet Study program, which involves taking retail samples of food products and testing them for a wide range of elements, nutrients, pesticides, and radionuclides.

Although the FDA and the EPA regulate pesticides used in this country, some pesticides that have been banned from *use* in the United States continue to be *manufactured* in the United States and sold abroad. In many less-developed countries, the regulatory infrastructure does not exist to require testing, labeling, and product review of imported pesticides. Pesticide poisoning is common among foreign farmworkers, and some of the pesticides come back to the United States in the form of residues on imported produce.

Pink Slime

In 2012, a food controversy developed after the public was alerted to the use of lean finely textured beef (LFTB) in hamburgers used in fast food restaurants and school lunches. LFTB was used for many years as a way to address both wasted meat scraps and to enhance the economics of ground beef production. The controversy arose when LFTB was rebranded by the media, specifically Diane Sawyer of ABC News, as "pink slime" (Engber, 2012). Every night for more than a week in March 2012, ABC News covered the story of how pink slime is made and added to the food supply with the blessing of the USDA. The reaction from the public, especially parents of school-aged children, was swift, and within a few weeks, the two companies that manufactured the product closed several processing facilities and laid off hundreds of workers. Major grocery stores, including Kroger and Safeway, stopped selling ground beef that contain the product and McDonald's did so as well.

LFTB is made from high-fat beef scraps that are by-products in meat-processing facilities. The amount of fat in these scraps limits their potential for human consumption, although they have been used in pet food. Two companies, Beef Products Incorporated (BPI) and Cargill, used these scraps to create LFTB by heating them to soften the fat, spinning the heated material in centrifuges to separate the fat from the meat, and then treating the residual meat with either ammonia (BPI) or citric acid (Cargill) to kill pathogens. The BPI process using ammonia was especially concerning because of claims that the smell of ammonia made the meat unpalatable at least and unsafe at most.

The USDA did not require beef products made with LFTB to be labeled as such; this contributed to public outcry. Celebrity chef Jamie Oliver spoke out about pink slime and demonstrated how it is made on his show, to the disgusted looks of his audience. In the meantime, BPI made a weak attempt to assure the public that the product was safe and was not made of anything other than beef. The public relations approaches did not appease consumers and demand for ground beef made with the product plummeted in 2012. As a result, BPI filed a lawsuit against ABC News and other media outlets for defamation; this suit continues into 2016 with a court date sometime in early 2017.

The market for LFTB started to rebound in 2014 as the price of beef began to climb due to a variety of factors (Bunge and Gee, 2014). BPI and Cargill are reopening some of the facilities that manufacture this product as demand rises; however, it is unclear which retailers are creating the demand. Furthermore, the case of pink slime has been described as an example of the power of social media in influencing food safety perceptions (Runge, 2016). The Internet was used by consumers in this case for everything from seeking information to circulating a petition to remove the substance from school lunches.

Raw Milk

Raw, or unpasteurized, milk concerns and perplexes public health professionals. Concerns with raw milk come from estimates that it accounts for about 1 to 3 percent of all milk sales in the United States but 97 to 99 percent of all illnesses associated with dairy products. The reason why public health professionals are perplexed is due to the long history of pasteurization and the fact that milk sanitation is one of the cornerstones of environmental health. With more than 100 years of successfully managing the nation's milk supply by heat treating it, it is alarming to see cases of illness associated with raw milk consumption rising.

One reason for the increasing demand for raw milk is linked to beliefs that it is healthier than pasteurized milk. While most scientists and regulatory agencies dispute this, it hasn't stopped companies such as Organic Pastures in California from promoting health benefits of raw milk. According to raw milk retailer Organic Pastures and organizations such as the Weston A. Price Foundation, raw milk is healthier because it decreases conditions such as allergies and asthma. Weston A. Price takes the support for raw milk a step further in accusing the government of unfairly blaming raw milk for outbreaks of foodborne illness. In addition to unsubstantiated and anecdotal health claims in favor of raw milk, assertions are also made that pasteurization makes milk less healthy by killing nutrients along with pathogens.

On the other hand, there is evidence that raw milk causes debilitating illness. The CDC has not only compiled data in this regard—they feature people who have been affected by raw milk in short videos on their website, *Real Stories of the Dangers of Raw Milk* (http://www.cdc.gov/foodsafety/rawmilk/raw-milk-videos.html). One of these stories is from Mary McGonigle-Martin, whose 7-year-old son almost died after she gave him raw milk. She explains in the video that she believed the claims that raw milk was healthier than pasteurized product but now she is an outspoken critic of raw milk and has even testified to Congress against it.

While the federal government offers stern warnings, provides data, and encourages consumers to choose pasteurized dairy products, they do not regulate sales of these products. States are responsible for determining if it is legal to sell raw milk; as of 2015, retail sales of raw milk was legal in 11 states, on-farm sales was legal in 19 states, and it was illegal to sell raw milk for human consumption in 17 states (Farm-to-Consumer, 2016). Consumers in 10 states can buy raw milk as part of an agreement with farmers in a herd- or cow-sharing program. Under these programs, the consumer contributes to raising the animal so is considered part owner. As an owner, it is legal to consume raw milk.

The debate about raw milk is likely to continue, but it is more a debate about choice than about health. Much like parents who demand a choice in whether to vaccinate their children, they also want to choose whether to give their children raw milk. Both of these choices have significant public health consequences and are based on questionable science.

References

Bilger, Burkhard. 2006. The Search for Sweet. *The New Yorker*, May 22, 40–46.

Bottemiller, Helena. 2010. Ban on Milk Labeling Ruled Unconstitutional. *Food Safety News*, October 4. http://www.foodsafetynews.com/2010/10/court-rules-ohio-ban-on-hormone-labeling-unconstitutional/#.V40sDqJWJK4

Bunge, Jacob, and Gee, Kelsey. 2014. "Pink Slime" Makes a Comeback as Beef Prices Spike. *Wall Street Journal*. http://www.wsj.com/articles/SB10001424052702303749904579579991127674958

Carrington, Clark D., Clarence Murray, and Shirley Tao. 2013. *A Quantitative Assessment of Inorganic Arsenic in Apple Juice*. http://www.fda.gov/downloads/Food/FoodScienceResearch/RiskSafetyAssessment/UCM360016.pdf

CDC. 2010. 2009 H1N1 Flu. http://www.cdc.gov/h1n1flu/

CDC. 2013. Antibiotic Resistance Threats in the United States, 2013. http://www.cdc.gov/drugresistance/threat-report-2013/index.html

Codex Alimentarius Commission. 2013. *Procedure Manual*. 21st ed. Rome: Join FAO/WHO Food Standards Committee. http://www.fao.org/3/a-i3243e.pdf

Consumer Reports. 2012a. Arsenic in Your Juice. How Much Is Too Much? Federal Limits Don't Exist. http://www.consumerreports.org/cro/magazine/2012/01/arsenic-in-your-juice/index.htm

Consumer Reports. 2012b. Arsenic in Your Food. Our Findings Show a Real Need for Federal Standards for This Toxin. http://www.consumerreports.org/cro/magazine/2012/11/arsenic-in-your-food/index.htm

Dembek, Z.F., M.G. Kortepeter, and J.A. Pavlin. 2007. Discernment between Deliberate and Natural Infectious Disease Outbreaks. *Epidemiology and Infection* 135(3): 353–371. http://www.ncbi.nlm.nih.gov/pmc/articles/PMC2870591/

Engber, Daniel. 2012. The Sliming: How Processed Beef Trimming Got Rebranded, Again and Again and Again. *Slate.com*. http://www.slate.com/articles/news_and_politics/food/2012/10/history_of_pink_slime_how_partially_defatted_chopped_beef_got_rebranded.html

Environmental Working Group. 2003. PCBs in Farmed Salmon. http://www.ewg.org/research/pcbs-farmed-salmon

EPA. 2004. Risk Assessment Evaluation for Concentrated Animal Feeding Operations. https://www.epa.gov/npdes/animal-feeding-operations-afos

EPA. 2010a. Toxicological Review of Acrylamide. EPA/635/R-07/009F. https://cfpub.epa.gov/ncea/iris/iris_documents/documents/toxreviews/0286tr.pdf

EPA. 2010b. Bisphenol A Action Plan. https://www.epa.gov/sites/production/files/2015–09/documents/bpa_action_plan.pdf

EPA. 2015. Environmental Policy Dialogue between the U.S. Environmental Protection Agency and the Ministry of the Environment Japan. https://yosemite.epa.gov/opa/admpress.nsf/21b8983ffa5d0e4685257dd4006b85e2/9186ae6a6ce6f62685257eab004c5106!OpenDocument

European Commission. 1999. Opinion of the Scientific Committee on Veterinary Measures Relating to Public Health: Assessment of Potential Risks to Human Health from Hormone Residues in Bovine Meat and Meat Products. http://ec.europa.eu/food/safety/docs/cs_meat_hormone-out21_en.pdf

Farm-to-Consumer Legal Defense Fund. 2016. Raw Milk Nation—Interactive Map. http://www.farmtoconsumer.org/raw-milk-nation-interactive-map/

FDA. 2004. What You Need to Know about Mercury in Fish and Shellfish. http://www.fda.gov/Food/FoodborneIllnessContaminants/Metals/ucm351781.htm

FDA. 2006. FDA Statement: Benzene in Soft Drinks. http://www.fda.gov/NewsEvents/Newsroom/PressAnnouncements/2006/ucm108636.htm

FDA. 2008. "Dear Colleague": Letter to the United States Food Manufacturing Industry, Regarding Melamine.

http://www.fda.gov/Food/FoodborneIllnessContaminants/ChemicalContaminants/ucm164514.htm

FDA. 2009. Melamine Pet Food Recall—Frequently Asked Question. http://www.fda.gov/AnimalVeterinary/SafetyHealth/RecallsWithdrawals/ucm129932.htm

FDA. 2014a. Fish: What Pregnant Women and Parents Should Know. http://www.fda.gov/Food/FoodborneIllnessContaminants/Metals/ucm393070.htm

FDA. 2014b. 2014 Updated Safety Assessment of Bisphenol A (BPA) for Use in Food Contact Applications. http://www.fda.gov/downloads/NewsEvents/PublicHealthFocus/UCM424266.pdf

FDA. 2015a. 2014 Summary Report on Antimicrobials Sold or Distributed for Use in Food-Producing Animals. http://www.fda.gov/downloads/ForIndustry/UserFees/AnimalDrugUserFeeActADUFA/UCM476258.pdf

FDA. 2015b. Data on Benzene in Soft Drinks and Other Beverages. http://www.fda.gov/Food/FoodborneIllnessContaminants/ChemicalContaminants/ucm055815.htm

FDA. 2016a. Guidance of Industry: Acrylamide in Foods. http://www.fda.gov/Food/GuidanceRegulation/GuidanceDocumentsRegulatoryInformation/ucm374524.htm

FDA. 2016b. Final Rule for Mitigation Strategies to Protect Food against Intentional Adulteration. http://www.fda.gov/Food/GuidanceRegulation/FSMA/ucm378628.htm

Follmer, Julie, and Roseann B. Termini. 2009. Whatever Happened to Old Mac Donald's Farm . . . Concentrated Animal Feeding Operation, Factory Farming and the Safety of the Nation's Food Supply. *Journal of Food Law & Policy* 5(1): 45–67.

Freedman, David H. 2013. The Truth about Genetically Modified Food. *Scientific American* 309(3): 80–85.

Gentilviso, Chris. 2010. The 50 Worst Inventions: Olestra. *Time Magazine.* http://content.time.com/time/specials/packages/article/0,28804,1991915_1991909_1991785,00.html

Gossner, C.M., J. Schlundt, P. Ben Embarek, S. Hird, D. Lo-Fo-Wong, J.J. Beltran, K.N. Teoh, A. Tritscher. 2009. The Melamine Incident: Implications for International Food and Feed Safety. *Environmental Health Perspectives* 117: 1803–1808. http://dx.doi.org/10.1289/ehp.0900949

Government Accountability Office. 2011. Antibiotic Resistance: Agencies Have Made Limited Progress in Addressing Antibiotic Use in Animals. GAO-11-801. http://www.gao.gov/assets/330/323090.pdf

Government Accountability Office. 2014. FDA and USDA Should Strengthen Pesticide Residue Monitoring Programs and Further Disclose Monitoring Limitations. GAO-15-38. http://www.gao.gov/products/GAO-15-38

Grebitus, Carola, Helen H. Jensen, Jutta Roosen, and Joseph G. Sebranek. 2013. Fresh Meat Packaging: Consumer Acceptance of Modified Atmosphere Packaging Including Carbon Monoxide. *Journal of Food Protection* 76(1): 99–107.

Harvard School of Public Health. 2011. Study Finds No Association between Mercury Exposure and Risk of Cardiovascular Disease. https://www.hsph.harvard.edu/news/press-releases/mercury-exposure-cardiovascular-disease/

Heindel, Jerrold J., Retha R. Newbold, John R. Bucher, Luísa Camacho, K. Barry Delclos, Sherry M. Lewis, Jennifer Fostel, et al. 2015. NIEHS/FDA CLARITY-BPA Research Program Update. *Reproductive Toxicology* 58: 33–44. doi:10.1016/j.reprotox.2015.07.075

Hites, Ronald A., Jeffery A. Foran, David O. Carpenter, Coreen M. Hamilton, Barbara A. Knuth, and Steven J. Schwager. 2004. Global Assessment of Organic

Contaminants in Farmed Salmon. *Science* 303: 226–229. http://www.pewtrusts.org/~/media/legacy/uploadedfiles/wwwpewtrustsorg/reports/protecting_ocean_life/salmonstudy1pdf.pdf

Hribar, Carrie. 2010. *Understanding Concentrated Animal Feeding Operations and Their Impact on Communities.* Bowling Green, OH: National Association of Local Boards of Health. https://www.cdc.gov/nceh/ehs/docs/understanding_cafos_nalboh.pdf

Jandacek, R., T. Rider, E. Keller, and P. Tso. 2010. The Effect of Olestra on the Absorption, Excretion and Storage of 2,2',5,5' Tetrachlorobiphenyl; 3,3',4,4' Tetrachlorobiphenyl; and Perfluorooctanoic acid. *Environment International* 36: 880–883. doi:10.1016/j.envint.2009.06.010

Jesse, Laura C. Hansen, and John J. Obrycki. 2000. Field Deposition of Bt Transgenic Corn Pollen: Lethal Effects on the Monarch Butterfly. *Oecologia*, 125: 241–248.

Johnson, Rene. 2015. The U.S.-EU Beef Hormone Dispute. Congressional Research Service Report R40449. https://www.fas.org/sgp/crs/row/R40449.pdf

Jukes, T. 1972. Antibiotics in Animal Feeds and Animal Production. *BioScience* 22(9): 526–534.

Kesmodel, David. 2014. Meat Companies Go Antibiotics-Free as More Consumers Demand It. *Wall Street Journal*, November 3. Retrieved from http://www.wsj.com/articles/meat-companies-go-antibiotics-free-as-more-consumers-demand-it-1415071802

Landers, Timothy F., Bevin Cohen, Thomas E. Wittum, and Elaine L. Larson. 2012. A Review of Antibiotic Use in Food Animals: Perspective, Policy, and Potential. *Public Health Reports*. 127(1): 422.

Lindseth, G.N., S.E. Coolahan, T.V. Petros, and P.D. Lindseth. 2014. Neurobehavioral Effects of

Aspartame Consumption. *Research in Nursing & Health* 37(3): 185–193. doi:10.1002/nur.21595

Losey, John E., Linda S. Rayor, and Maureen E. Carter. 1999. Transgenic Pollen Harms Monarch Larvae. *Nature* 399(6733): 214.

Low, Sarah, Aaron Adalja, Elizabeth Beaulieu, et al. 2015. Trends in U.S. Local and Regional Food Systems: Report to Congress. AP-068. U.S. Department of Agriculture, Economic Research Service. http://www.ers.usda.gov/media/1763057/ap068.pdf

Marine Harvest. 2015. *Salmon Farming Industry Handbook 2015*. http://www.marineharvest.com/globalassets/investors/handbook/2015-salmon-industry-handbook.pdf

Mohl, Bruce. 2006. Nutrition Group Seeks Warning Labels for Olestra; But State Law May Help Frito-Lay If Lawsuit Is Filed. *Boston Globe*, January 5, E3.

NARMS. 2013. National Antimicrobial Resistance Monitoring System: Enteric Bacteria, 2013. Human Isolates Final Report. http://www.cdc.gov/narms/pdf/2013-annual-report-narms-508c.pdf

NARMS. 2016. NARMS Now: Human Data. Retrieved from http://wwwn.cdc.gov/narmsnow/

National Toxicology Program. 2005. NTP Report on the Toxicology Studies of Aspartame. NIH Publication No. 06-4459. https://ntp.niehs.nih.gov/ntp/htdocs/gmm_rpts/gmm1.pdf

National Toxicology Program. 2008. NTP-CEHR Monograph on the Potential Human Reproductive and Developmental Effects of Bisphenol A. http://ntp.niehs.nih.gov/ntp/ohat/bisphenol/bisphenol.pdf

NFI (National Fisheries Institute). 2016. U.S. Per-Capita Consumption by Species in Pounds. http://www.aboutseafood.com/wp-content/uploads/2016/05/Top-Ten-Seafood.pdf

Penn State Extension. 2016. Average Daily Production and Total Content of Manure. *Penn State Agronomy Guide, 2015–2016.* http://extension.psu.edu/agronomy-guide/cm/tables/avg-daily-production-and-total-content-of-manure

Potera, Carol. 2005. Olestra's Second Wind. *Environmental Health Perspectives* 8: A518.

Runge, Kristin. 2016. Pink Slimed: The Beef Industry Learns the Importance of Social Media Literacy. Wisconsin Public Radio. Retrieved from http://www.wpr.org/pink-slimed-beef-industry-learns-importance-social-media-literacy

Schmit, Julie. 2008. Tainted Pet Food Suit Settled for $24 Million. *USA Today.* http://usatoday30.usatoday.com/money/industries/2008-05-22-petfood-lawsuit-settled_n.htm

Sears, Mark K., Richard L. Hellmich, Diane E. Stanley-Horn, Karen S. Oberhauser, John M. Pleasants, Heather R. Mattila, Blair D. Siegfried, and Galen P. Dively. 2001. Impact of Bt Corn Pollen on Monarch Butterfly Populations: A Risk Assessment. *Proceedings of the National Academy of Sciences of the United States of America* 98 (21): 11937–11942.

Soffritti, M., M. Padovani, E. Tibaldi, L. Falcioni, F. Manservisi, and F. Belpoggi. 2014. The Carcinogenic Effects of Aspartame: The Urgent Need for Regulatory Re-Evaluation. *American Journal of Industrial Medicine* 574: 383–397. doi:10.1002/ajim.22296

Stokstad, Erik. 2004. Toxicology: Salmon Survey Stokes Debate about Farmed Fish. *Science*, January 9, 154–155.

Sugarman, Carole. 2004. Pasteurization Redefined by USDA Committee. *Food Chemical News* 30: 21–22.

Tareke, Eden, Per Rydberg, and Patrik Karlsson. 2002. Analysis of Acrylamide, a Carcinogen Formed in Heated

Foodstuffs. *Journal of Agricultural & Food Chemistry* 50(17): 4998–5006.

Torok, Thomas, Robert Tauxe, Robert Wise, John Livengood, Robert Sokolow, Steven Mauvais, Kristin Birkness, Michael Skeels, John Horan, and Laurence Foster. 1997. A Large Community Outbreak of Salmonellosis Caused by Intentional Contamination of Restaurant Salad Bars. *Journal of the American Medical Association* 5: 389–395.

United Nations Environment Program. 2012. Growing Greenhouse Gas Emissions Due to Meat Production. http://www.unep.org/pdf/unep-geas_oct_2012.pdf

USDA. 2014. Antimicrobial Resistance Action Plan. http://www.usda.gov/documents/usda-antimicrobial-resistance-action-plan.pdf

USDA. 2016a. Diary 2014: Dairy Cattle Management Practices in the United States, 2014. https://www.aphis.usda.gov/animal_health/nahms/dairy/downloads/dairy14/Dairy14_dr_PartI.pdf

USDA. 2016b. FY2016 HPAI Response: Surveillance of Backyard Flocks around Infected Premises. https://www.aphis.usda.gov/animal_health/emergency_management/downloads/hpai/survsampling_byflocks.pdf

USDA. 2016c. USDA Confirms Highly Pathogenic H7N8 Influenza in a Commercial Turkey Flock in Dubois County, Indiana. https://www.aphis.usda.gov/aphis/newsroom/news/sa_by_date/newsroom-2016/newsroom-january-2016/ct-hpai-indiana-turkeys

USDA-ERS. 2014. Pesticide Use in U.S. Agriculture: 21 Selected Crops, 1960–2008. http://www.ers.usda.gov/publications/eib-economic-information-bulletin/eib124.aspx

USDA-ERS. 2016. Adoption of Genetically Engineered Crops in the U.S. http://www.ers.usda.gov/data-products/

adoption-of-genetically-engineered-crops-in-the-us/recent-trends-in-ge-adoption.aspx

WHO. 2014. Evaluation of Certain Veterinary Drug Residues in Food. http://apps.who.int/iris/bitstream/10665/127845/1/9789241209885_eng.pdf?ua=1

WHO. 2016. Cumulative Number of Confirmed Human Cases of Avian Influenza A (H5N1) Reported to WHO. http://www.who.int/influenza/human_animal_interface/H5N1_cumulative_table_archives/en/

3   Perspectives

Food safety is multifaceted, including a range of scientific disciplines, multiple regulatory systems, numerous food manufacturing and processing interests, and millions of consumers. There are seemingly unlimited perspectives on how to make our food safe. Some of these perspectives are based on concerns about specific issues such as genetically modified organisms (GMOs); others are more broad and include our overall capacity to ensure that all foods are safe. This chapter offers perspectives from food safety professionals and scholars who have a wealth of diverse experiences in the field.

In crafting these essays, the author was asked to respond to questions about the most important issues relative to food safety today and into the future. The first two perspectives offer insights from two local health department environmental health practitioners. One is from a large city health department, and the other is from a smaller, more rural, county health department. These are the "boots on the ground" personnel who oversee inspections at retail establishments and are critical to keeping food safe. Even though the authors work in different

Protestors stand beside a giant "Frankenfish" sculpture installed by Avaaz at FDA Headquarters in Silver Spring, Maryland, on April 22, 2013. One million people signed an Avaaz petition urging the FDA to reject the approval of the world's first genetically engineered (GE) salmon for human consumption. The FDA ultimately approved GE salmon as safe for human consumption. (Paul Morigi/AP Images for Avaaz) conditions and with very different populations, they share similar concerns about the need to educate both the workforce and consumers to address the current and future challenges of food safety.

Three scholars offer perspectives about some of the emerging scientific and societal challenges related to food safety. First, a professor in nutrition with expertise in food security makes the connection between safety and security. Second, a PhD candidate in communication studies writes about the communication challenges and opportunities regarding genetically engineered salmon. The final scholar is a researcher at a major land grant university whose essay envisions a future with smart technology in every home helping to keep food safe.

Two representatives from the food industry contribute to this section; one is a food safety consultant and the other works for a major food and beverage retail trade organization. Both of these professionals talk about the role that new technologies will have in making food safer in the future. Both also talk about the challenges the food industry is facing with these rapidly emerging technologies.

Even though these perspectives come from people with different backgrounds and experiences, the common themes of educating consumers and professionals and the role of technology in food safety emerge as the overall message from these essays.

Evolution of Local Environmental Health and Food Safety: From Observing Deficiencies to Reducing Risks
Luke Jacobs

Local public health agencies typically take the lead in ensuring food is prepared, served, and sold in a manner that will help prevent foodborne illness and injury. As scientific understanding has evolved over the past 40 years, and so has the focus of inspection practices. We have moved away from emphasizing physical structures and cleanliness to assessing how food is processed and evaluating critical control points. This new approach has changed the landscape of how inspections are conducted. In addition, the use of environmental health informatics allows for new and improved ways for investigating foodborne illness, including clear collaboration with nurses and epidemiologists. Even with all of these advances, local public health officials still face challenges in the fight to prevent foodborne illness in our communities.

It is vital for environmental health professionals to move away from performing "inspections" because it implies making observations. Observations are critical, but an inspection-only approach does not speak to the critical work of ensuring that risk is reduced based on what observations are made. *The work of environmental health must involve and focus on evaluating and determining risk related to the observations made during inspections.* This work is more challenging and often times more rewarding than the act of performing an inspection.

Risk assessment and intervention requires environmental health professionals to understand how to modify behavior. Almost every practice in a food service establishment can be boiled down to learned behavior. This applies to not only the staff preparing and serving food, but those managing and supervising employees as well. The most common example of this is hand-washing practices and habits. Lack of proper hand washing is a major risk factor in transmitting pathogenic organisms, particularly viruses and bacteria. Therefore, increasing effective hand washing, which requires behavior change, must be a priority in food safety. Educational institutions and public health agencies have to focus coursework and training on behavior, including strategies for modifying unsafe behaviors in addition to enhancing techniques for observation if the evolution of this profession is to continue to move in a forward direction.

Risk communication is another practice environmental public health professionals need to be well versed with in order to successfully protect the public from threats. Good communication of findings and solutions to operators is vital to the success of a collaborative food safety system. Cultivating relationships with food service operators is important in getting them to "buy" what we are selling. That is correct: what we do is essentially sales. We are selling people on the concepts of food safety; we are selling people solutions for their deficiencies. Without this, the likelihood of making an idea stick becomes much more difficult. The art of communicating our messages becomes as important as the science helping drive this work. Taking the time to understand an operator's values, interests, and expectations can go a long way to tailor communication that more soundly resonates. Culturally sensitive visual aids, such as brochures, handbooks, and posters, can assist operators in understanding the concepts of food safety principles.

Social and political matters continue to affect environmental public health. Workplace sick leave policies can literally be the difference between life and death. When food service employees are not mandated by law to stay home while exhibiting symptoms of a foodborne illness (i.e., diarrhea, vomiting, etc.), and paid sick leave is not an option, it creates a recipe for disaster. A sole provider for a family missing an 8- to 12-hour shift because of diarrhea is, unfortunately, unlikely. You only have to put yourself in the shoes of an individual who may be in this situation to see the struggle of making a decision whether or not to go to work. No risk assessment or intervention that public health professionals can do will stop this situation from taking place. Public policy must be developed, providing some form of paid sick time to food workers. Employers in this industry would be wise to develop internal policies that support this concept as well. Ultimately, the cost of a foodborne outbreak of norovirus from a sick worker is exponentially more than paying a sick worker for an eight-hour shift.

If you ever want to get a sense of how important food safety is, all you have to do is read testimony provided by a parent whose child died from a foodborne infection. A simple

Google search can provide this. As a parent, there is nothing more gut wrenching than to read about a child going from a perfectly healthy child to deceased in a matter of days: how they go from playing in their backyard, to a coffin. The worst part about these stories is how preventable almost all of these cases are—if only someone would have been able to stay home instead of come to work sick; if only someone would have washed his or her hands appropriately; if only someone would have cooked the meat to the proper temperature. All of us working in this food safety system do everything we can to ensure that not one more parent has to lose his or her child to foodborne disease.

While environmental health has come a long way in the past decades to use science to dictate food safety principles, more work is needed. Rest assured, the news is not all bad for this profession. Industry leaders are collaborating with local public health agencies to develop more efficient food safety systems. As pathogens emerge with resistance to antibiotics, ensuring that the tail end of the "farm to table" food system is safe is more important now than it ever has been. Local public health officials have the responsibility to protect public health, but it is a job that we cannot do alone. To continue the evolution, partnerships across the food industry must continue to strengthen their bond to assure the public has confidence in the food industry and are protected from environmental health hazards.

Luke Jacobs, MPH, RSs graduated from Eastern Kentucky University in 2002 with a Bachelor's of Science in Environmental Health. Luke went on to complete a Master's of Public Health program at Eastern Kentucky University in 2005. He has been working in the public health sector for various county and city governments for 14 years and is currently the Assistant Environmental Health Administrator at Columbus (Ohio) Public Health. Luke serves as Adjunct Professor at Ohio University and teaches introductory environmental health. He has also served as President of the Ohio Environmental Health Association.

Education and Actions for Ensuring the Future of Safe Food
Chad Brown

As a local public health Environmental Health Director and Sanitarian for nearly 20 years, I've seen many changes related to how food safety is viewed and implemented at the local level. Early in my career, there was an emphasis on just completing as many inspections as possible to comply with state mandates. This emphasis was a result of a lack of funding and mostly a lack of understanding that it was our job at the local level to prevent foodborne illness, not just write violations at facilities with missing light bulbs or stained ceiling tiles. It would be easy to state that funding local health department food safety programs is the most important food safety issue moving forward, but over the years, I've learned it's not always best to do what's easy, especially, in the field of environmental health.

In my opinion, the most important food safety issue over the next 50 years will be effectively implementing food safety education programs aimed at preventing foodborne illnesses and outbreaks. There are a variety of factors that will impact this issue; however, the most important factor is the constantly evolving food environment in which we live. When I was a young sanitarian, our department licensed a total of four food trucks. Today, there are thousands of mobile food operations in our area, offering everything from hamburgers to southern barbeque to sushi. These operations are transient, and they often are not properly inspected as a result. While conducting food safety inspections is a pivotal role of local public health departments, it is much more important to properly train and educate operators during inspections. This allows them to implement techniques and procedures to prevent customers from suffering illness because of their lack of knowledge. No operator intentionally makes his or her customers ill; however, a poorly trained operator can easily make numerous people sick.

While the expansion of food trucks is taxing local health departments to prevent foodborne illness, one of the most important obstacles to overcoming outbreaks continues to be educating consumers regarding how to properly grow, prepare, serve, store, and reheat food. We are constantly receiving information regarding a wide variety of topics from our phones, computers, TVs, kids, coworkers, family members, and many other sources. Often conversations start with "Well, I read online that . . ." As technology continues to evolve, the amount of information available will only increase. This will make it extremely difficult for food safety professionals to provide accurate information regarding food safety to the general consumer.

We often hear about foodborne outbreaks associated with national restaurant chains, such as Chipotle, but there are a significant number of outbreaks resulting from food prepared at church potlucks, family reunions, graduation parties, weddings, and other private functions. More often than not, people will immediately blame the last restaurant they ate at when they get sick. However, it is more likely their illness was caused by the improperly cooled and stored leftovers they did not reheat properly two days before they became ill. People do not make themselves sick on purpose; they just are not properly educated on about ensuring their food is safe.

Another growing trend that will impact the ability to educate vendors selling food is the increasing popularity of farmers' markets. As a public health professional, I understand the many benefits these markets offer. However, many of the food products sold at these venues are either grown or prepared in private homes without any type of regulation or inspections. While these individuals have the best of intentions, I'm always wary of consuming a product that is labeled as being a homemade product. This is because I have no idea of the cleanliness of their home, but I do know that a food safety professional has not inspected the home to ensure that it is not only clean, but to determine if other critical food safety practices are being implemented as well. As the number of farmers' markets increases, so does the number of these types of vendors. Reaching a completely unregulated population of operators with accurate food safety education will be an enormous challenge. Again, I'm not against these types of vendors, and I'm not advocating for increased regulations, but I do believe they pose a risk to food safety. This risk will be difficult to mitigate through education by food safety professionals simply due to the sheer number of these vendors.

Food safety programs are by far the biggest and most impactful programs operated by local health departments. Everyone has to eat, whether they eat at a licensed restaurant or buy food from a licensed grocery store; every one of our constituents is eating food from a facility we regulate. However, most facilities are only inspected once or twice a year. This means properly educating operators regarding food safety principles is imperative to their implementing these principles during the 364 days a year a food safety professional is not in their operation. Additionally, we need to educate consumers to properly prepare and serve food to their families. This will be a challenge, but environmental Health professionals have dealt with many challenges in the past, and we will do so again to ensure consumers can be as protected as possible from contracting a foodborne illness.

It is nearly impossible to accurately correlate how many foodborne illnesses are prevented through food safety education. However, food safety professionals must continue to provide accurate information to operators and the general public. This will be increasingly difficult over the next 50 years, but that should not deter us from reaching out to and educating operators as well as our friends and family to prevent them from becoming ill or possibly even dying as a result of improperly prepared food.

Chad Brown, RS, REHS, MPH, is the Director of Environmental Health and Deputy Health Commissioner at the Licking County Health Department located in Newark, Ohio. Mr. Brown obtained a Bachelor of Science degree in Environmental Health from Ohio University and a Master's degree in Public Health from Walden University. Mr. Brown has worked in public health for over 17 years and has worked for several local health departments in Ohio and the Ohio Department of Health. He also led the effort that resulted in the Licking County Health Department becoming one of the first 22 health departments in the country to be accredited by the Public Health Accreditation Board.

The Dynamic Duo—Food Security and Food Safety
David H. Holben

Setting the Stage

There is no food in the cupboards. My children and I are hungry. I do not have money to buy food. What do I do? Where do I turn? How can I feed my family?

This situation is all too familiar to millions of individuals and families living in the United States, in spite of living in *The Land of the Free and Home of the Brave*. In America, however, the buzz around food often relates to eating locally produced, organically grown, and non-genetically modified foods. Apart from the aforementioned (what some may consider) "elitist" food worries, what about *food safety*, especially for those who have limited access to food? In my view, for those most vulnerable to eating unsafe foods and experiencing the negative consequences of eating those foods, *food safety* may be the last thing on a household provider's mind when resources to buy food are scarce. This *perspective* focuses on the intersection of food security and food safety.

Food Security? I'm Confused . . .

To clarify upfront, the security of our food supply, from intentional contamination and biosecurity standpoints, is of utmost importance, especially since September 11, 2001. Ensuring safe food is the responsibility of numerous governmental bodies, including the U.S. Department of Agriculture (USDA), Food Safety and Inspection Service, Food and Drug Administration (FDA), Centers for Disease Control and Prevention, Environmental Protection Agency, U.S. Customs Service, and state and local agencies (United States Department of Agriculture & Food

Safety and Inspection Service, 2013). This section, however, focuses on securing food by individuals and households—being food secure, that is, having adequate resources (money, transportation, social capital) to access enough food for an active, healthy life—and the intersection of food security with food *safety*.

The intersection of food *security* and food *safety* has not been explored extensively. As summarized in Figure 3.1, however, food security relates to food availability, food access, and food

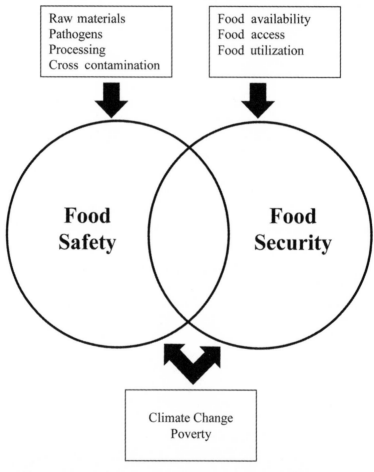

Figure 3.1   The Intersection of Food Safety and Food Security (Hanning et al., 2012)

utilization. Food safety, on the other hand, relates to pathogens, processing, cross-contamination, and others. Yet, Hanning and colleagues (Hanning et al., 2012) view both as being influenced by poverty and climate change.

Plain and Simple—Food Insecurity Is When the Cupboards Are Bare . . . or Getting There

The antithesis of food *security* is food *insecurity*. Food insecurity, lacking access to enough nutritionally adequate and *safe* food for an active, healthy life due to insufficient resources (Anderson, 1990), affects millions of individuals and households across the United States. Figure 3.2 summarizes U.S. household food insecurity trends over the period 1995–2013. According to the USDA, more than 17 million households, representing 48.1 million individuals, experienced food insecurity sometime during 2014 (Coleman-Jensen et al., 2015). Of all U.S. households, 8.4 percent (10.5 million households) suffered from low food security, and 5.6 percent (6.9 million households) were faced with very low food security. Those

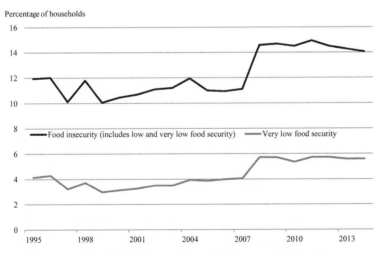

Percentage of households

Food insecurity (includes low and very low food security)   Very low food security

Figure 3.2   Food Insecurity Prevalence Trends in the United States (Calculated by USDA Economic Research Service)

households struggling with poverty experience food insecurity at greater rates than other households.

Essentially, living with food insecurity means not having enough resources to acquire food to meet nutritional needs. While food insecurity can be episodic, on average, a U.S. household lacking access to food experiences this phenomenon for seven months annually. As such, food may be more readily available at some points in the year leading to many different coping strategies to manage the lean times. Coping strategies include purchasing and eating low-cost, empty-calorie foods that are filling, participating in federal food and nutrition assistance programs, obtaining food from charitable organizations (food pantries, soup kitchens, and shelters), growing food (gardening) at home or in a community garden, receiving aid from family and friends, and borrowing, begging, or stealing food (Seligman et al., 2010; Weinfield et al., 2014). Some of these coping strategies and adaptive behaviors may compromise the *safety* of the food of those struggling with food insecurity.

The U.S. Food Supply Is Safe . . . for Most of Us

Cody and Stretch (2014) reviewed the topic of food and water safety and asserted that all people should have access to safe food and water. Chan (2014) further underscored that food safety must be aligned with food security efforts through agricultural, trade, health, education, and social protection policies to ensure that everyone has access to a safe and healthy diet. However, what happens in the face of food insecurity?

The behaviors observed among individuals and families experiencing food insecurity may increase their risk of eating unsafe foods. Those struggling with food insecurity often make difficult tradeoffs, that is, choosing between buying food and other things, such as medical treatments/medications, rent/mortgage, or utilities (Biros et al., 2005; Cook et al., 2006; Frank et al., 2006; Nord & Kantor, 2006; Sullivan et al., 2010; Weinfield et al., 2014). Eating *unsafe* food may be the only choice.

Research shows that food insecurity has consequences, including physical impairments related to insufficient foods (e.g., illness, fatigue), psychological issues related to a lack of food access (e.g., feelings of constraint against held norms and values, stress at home), and socio-familial disturbances (e.g., modification of eating patterns and related ritual, disruption of household dynamics, distortion of the means of food acquisition and management) (Rose, 1999). Anater and colleagues (Anater et al., 2011) found that not only did those experiencing food insecurity acquire foods in a manner that posed illegal or regulatory risks such as begging for or stealing food, but they also legally acquired foods posing food safety risks. For example, some bought foods in dented or damaged packaging, ate expired foodstuffs, ate others' leftovers, ate perishable foods not properly stored, removed mold from grain-based foods before eating, and even ate road kill. Thus, when household food is scant, eating leftovers accidentally left on the counter all night, cooking meat that doesn't quite look right, or digging in a dumpster for food may be primary coping mechanisms for securing the next meal.

While the benefits of charitable food organizations cannot be minimized, Chaifetz and Chapman (2015) provided a glimpse into how some food pantries operate, from a food safety perspective. Their study revealed that pantries would benefit from food safety training to improve food safety knowledge and practice, but more evaluation of the emergency food supply chain and food acquisition practices of those suffering from food insecurity is needed. Some charitable food and other community organizations are turning to gardening as a means to improving food access. As such, there is need to further study urban, school, and community gardening practices to ensure production of *safe* foods, especially when empty lots, urban or otherwise, are the gardening sites. For example, Kaiser et al. (2015) found that soil contaminants (e.g., lead, zinc, cadmium, copper) may be present in urban gardening sites; there is also potential for foodborne pathogens to be lurking.

Finally, while the safety of genetically engineered crops and food will undoubtedly be revisited and continue to be explored, the National Academies of Sciences has weighed in on the issue. The consensus report (National Academy of Sciences, 2016) objectively examines the economic, agronomic, health, *safety*, and other effects of genetically engineered crops and food. The authors recommended *safety* testing for products, rather than specific processes (e.g., conventional breeding versus genetic engineering), using a tiered approach that includes testing for potential hazards and exposure. The National Academies of Sciences found no substantiated evidence to support differences in risks to human health or environmental problems between genetically engineered and conventionally bred crops. This type of evidence-based research has not stopped food retailers from taking steps to alert consumers that their products are "GMO-free" in order to appease public perceptions about the risks.

Wrapping It Up

Ensuring that all people have access to enough wholesome and *safe* food for an active, healthy life is vital. Being cognizant of the intersection of food *security* and food *safety* is vitally important. Food safety, health, nutrition, and other professionals and volunteers must be aware that those most vulnerable to having poor food availability, food access, and food utilization may employ coping strategies and adaptive behaviors compromising the *safety* of their food. Taking steps to eliminate food insecurity while minimizing food safety risk to those vulnerable to poor food access is warranted.

References

Anater, A.S., R. McWilliam, and C.A. Latkin. 2011. Food Acquisition Practices Used by Food-Insecure Individuals

When They Are Concerned about Having Sufficient Food for Themselves and Their Household." *Journal of Hunger and Environmental Nutrition* 6: 27–44.

Anderson, S.A. 1990. Core Indicators of Nutritional State for Difficult-to-Sample Populations. *The Journal of Nutrition* 120(s11): 1559–1600. http://search.ebscohost.com/login .aspx?direct=true&db=cmedm&AN=2243305&site= ehost-live&scope=site

Biros, M.H., P.L. Hoffman, and K. Resch. 2005. The Prevalence and Perceived Health Consequences of Hunger in Emergency Department Patient Populations. *Academic Emergency Medicine: Official Journal of the Society for Academic Emergency Medicine* 12(4): 310–317. http:// search.ebscohost.com/login.aspx?direct=true&db=cmedm& AN=15805321&site=ehost-live&scope=site

Chaifetz, A., and B. Chapman. 2015. Evaluating North Carolina Food Pantry Food Safety-Related Operating Procedures. *Journal of Food Protection* 78(11): 2033–2042.

Chan, Margaret. 2014. Food Safety Must Accompany Food and Nutrition Security. *Lancet* 384(9958): 1910–1911.

Cody, Mildred M., and Theresa Stretch. 2014. From the Academy: Position of the Academy of Nutrition and Dietetics: Food and Water Safety. *Journal of the Academy of Nutrition and Dietetics* 114: 1819–1829.

Coleman-Jensen, A., M.P. Rabbitt, C. Gregory, and A. Singh. 2015, September. Household Food Security in the United States in 2014. ERR-194. http://www.ers.usda.gov/ webdocs/publications/err194/53740_err194.pdf

Cook, John T., Deborah A. Frank, Suzette M. Levenson, Nicole B. Neault, Tim C. Heeren, Maurine M. Black, and Mariana Chilton, et al. 2006. Child Food Insecurity Increases Risks Posed by Household Food Insecurity to

Young Children's Health. *Journal of Nutrition* 136(4): 1073–1076.

Frank, D.A., N.B. Neault, A. Skalicky, J.T. Cook, J.D. Wilson, S. Levenson, C. Berkowitz, et al. 2006. Heat or Eat: The Low Income Home Energy Assistance Program and Nutritional and Health Risks among Children Less Than 3 Years of Age. *Pediatrics* 118(5): E1293–E1302.

Hanning, I.B., C.A. O'Bryan, P.G. Crandall, and S.C. Ricke. 2012. Food Safety and Food Security. *Nature Education Knowledge* 3(10): 9. http://www.nature.com/scitable/knowledge/library/food-safety-and-food-security-68168348 (accessed November 2016).

Kaiser, Michelle L., Michele L. Williams, Nicholas Basta, Michelle Hand, and Sarah Huber. 2015. When Vacant Lots Become Urban Gardens: Characterizing the Perceived and Actual Food Safety Concerns of Urban Agriculture in Ohio. *Journal of Food Protection* 78(11): 2070–2080.

National Academy of Sciences. 2016. *Genetically Engineered Crops: Experiences and Prospects.* https://nas-sites.org/ge-crops/

Nord, Mark, and Linda S. Kantor. 2006. Seasonal Variation in Food Insecurity Is Associated with Heating and Cooling Costs among Low-Income Elderly Americans. *The Journal of Nutrition* 11: 2939.

Rose, D. 1999. Economic Determinants and Dietary Consequences of Food Insecurity in the United States. *Journal of Nutrition* 129(2): 517S–520S.

Seligman, H.K., B.A. Laraia, and M.B. Kushel. 2010. Food Insecurity Is Associated with Chronic Disease among Low-Income NHANES Participants. *Journal of Nutrition* 140(2): 304–310. doi:10.3945/jn.109.112573.

Sullivan, A.F., S. Clark, D.J. Pallin, and C.A. Camargo, Jr. 2010. Food Security, Health, and Medication Expenditures of Emergency Department Patients. *Journal of Emergency*

Medicine (0736–4679) 38(4): 524–528. doi:10.1016/j.
jemermed.2008.11.027.

United States Department of Agriculture, & Food Safety and
Inspection Service. 2013. Food Safety and Security: What
Consumers Need to Know. http://www.fsis.usda.gov/wps/
wcm/connect/ebaabfa4-e6a0–4201–9f12–9fd65b46447e/
foodsec_cons.pdf?MOD=AJPERES

Weinfield, Nancy S., et al. 2014. Hunger in America
2014. National Report. http://help.feedingamerica.org/
HungerInAmerica/hunger-in-america-2014-full-report.pdf

*David H. Holben, PhD, RDN, LD, FAND, is a registered dieti-
tian, nutritionist, and former commissioned officer in the United
States Army Reserves Medical Specialist Corps. Dr. Holben completed his doctoral studies at The Ohio State University, Columbus,
Ohio. Building upon a clinical nutrition and basic science background, his research focuses on food insecurity and health outcomes
of individuals in North America. Exploring the relationship of
diabetes, obesity, and other conditions to food access across the lifes-
pan and optimizing solutions for food access and security to promote health and wellness are of particular interest to Dr. Holben.*

How Fishy Is It? Risk Communication and Perceptions of Genetically Engineered Salmon
Sarah M. Parsloe

Biotechnology, also referred to as bioengineering, genetic
engineering, and the development of GMOs, is a rapidly
expanding field, particularly in the United States. It involves
designing new varieties of plants and other organisms by manipulating DNA material. The debate regarding the relative
safety of GMOs that are in the food supply is a complex one.
Opponents have become increasingly strident in publiciz-
ing the technology's potentially negative consequences with
regard to crops, including the development of "superweeds," the

"corporate control of GMO seeds and patents, the potentially negative effects of genetic engineering on wildlife (such as the monarch butterfly) and ecosystems, and GMO contamination of organic crops" (Bain & Dandaci, 2014, p. 9464). Still, some evidence indicates GMOs have the potential to increase the productivity of farms and fisheries, alleviate the threat of food insecurity, remove allergens, and minimize the need for pesticides (Amin et al., 2014).

In November of 2015, the FDA took the historic step of approving the first genetically engineered animal developed for human consumption. The agency gave the green light to AquAdvantage's genetically engineered (GE) salmon, designed to grow to market size in half the time as conventional salmon (Pollack, 2015). The FDA (2015) issued a statement claiming that scientific data had shown that the "inserted genes remained stable over several generations of fish, that food from the GE salmon is safe to eat by humans and animals, that the genetic engineering is safe for the fish, and the salmon meets the sponsor's claim" that it grows rapidly (p. 1). Further, the FDA reassured the public that, because the fish would be sterilized and grown in land-based tanks, the potential for the fish to escape into the environment was minimal (FDA, 2015).

However, the future market success of GE salmon and other developing genetic engineering technologies depends on public acceptance of the idea that GMOs' benefits outweigh both the risks of their creation and consumption with the risks of allowing current food production systems to continue unaltered. Public risk perceptions are shaped in large part by media framings. When biotechnology was first being developed in the 1990s, media coverage was largely positive (Shanahan et al., 2001; Bain and Dandachi, 2014). However, with the advent of the new millennium, coverage shifted to focus on risks. Visual representations of GMOs in online media are overwhelmingly negative and inaccurate, most commonly emphasizing the creation of bizarre plants, animals, and humans and GMOs' danger to the environment (Rodriguez and Asoro, 2012). Already, the *New York Post* and CNN have begun referring to GE salmon as "Frankenfish" (Associated Press, 2015; Goldschmidt, 2015), while *NPR* and *The New York Times* have focused on human health threats and the possibility that an escaped fish might contaminate the environment (Pollack, 2015; Rack, 2015).

Negative media coverage stokes public fears and feeds the growing demand to mandate labeling of GMO products (Bain and Dandachi, 2014), a policy change that would allow the public to actively avoid purchasing GE foodstuffs. Labeling GMO products would give consumers a choice to avoid GE foods that are being vilified in the media. The importance of public perception leads companies like AquAdvantage, who have a vested interest, to conducting research to document GE salmon-specific risk perceptions. For instance, a 2014 survey study in Malaysia revealed that factors related to a willingness to consume GMOs depend on whether the food was a plant or animal that had been genetically modified. Whereas perceived benefits most strongly predicted support of GMO crops, perceptions of risk most directly predicted support of GE salmon (Amin et al., 2014). This research suggests that developing a risk communication strategy that focuses on minimizing the public's concerns about GE salmon risks (rather than on emphasizing its benefits) will be particularly important for ensuring its success in the marketplace.

GE salmon may well minimize some of the health and environmental concerns that initially informed the movement to demand GMO labeling. Because GE salmon are sterile and raised in isolated tanks, they pose only a limited threat to the wild salmon population and the surrounding ecosystem. In addition, the FDA can argue, as it has with GE crops, that the processes involved in genetic engineering are no riskier than the long-accepted technique of selective breeding. What remains, then, is the threat of corporate greed. As companies like AquAdvantage develop and patent food technologies, they gain control over the means of production. Increasingly, such technologies shift resources from the hands of the impoverished to the hands of those who own capital. Propelled by neoliberal discourses that emphasize growth and glorify technological solutions, such companies invade communities and displace the local population (Dutta, 2015). By unsettling indigenous fishing industries, companies creating and managing GMO fisheries participate in perpetuating poverty. In addition, technologies like GE salmon may not alleviate food insecurity when the product is extracted from disadvantaged regions and sold to wealthier areas. Thus, technologies like GE salmon may pose indirect risks to human health by threatening local economies.

In summary, GE salmon, like other GMOs, provides a potential pathway to addressing the risks of food insecurity, climate change, and unsustainable fishing practices. However, in order for technologies like this to take root in the marketplace, the industry and organizations like the FDA must develop strategic risk communication campaigns that address fears circulated in the popular press. In addition, if technologies like GE salmon are implemented in ways that displace and exploit local populations, the promise of genetic engineering technologies may be undercut by the risk corporate greed poses to economic and, ultimately, human health.

References

Associated Press. 2015. "Frankenfish" Won't Be Labeled: FDA. *New York Post*, November 20. http://nypost.com/2015/11/20/frankenfish-salmon-coming-soon-to-a-super market-near-you/

Amin, Latifah, Md., Abul Kalam Azad, Mohd Hanafy Gausmian, and Faizah Zulkifli. 2014. Determinants of Public Attitudes to Genetically Modified Salmon. *Plos ONE* 9(1): 1–14.

Bain, C., and T Dandachi. 2014. Governing GMOs: The (Counter) Movement for Mandatory and Voluntary Non-GMO Labels. *Sustainability* 6(12): 9456–9476.

Dutta, Mohan J. 2015. *Neoliberal Health Organizing: Communication, Meaning, and Politics.* n.p. Walnut Creek, CA: Left Coast Press.

FDA. 2015. FDA Has Determined That the AquAdvantage Salmon Is as Safe to Eat as Non-GE Salmon. http://www.fda.gov/ForConsumers/ConsumerUpdates/ucm472487.htm

Goldschmidt, D. 2015. Genetically Engineered "Frankenfish" Salmon Wins FDA Approval. *CNN.* http://www.cnn.com/2015/11/19/health/genetically-engineered-salmon/

Pollack, A. 2015. Genetically Engineered Salmon Approved for Consumption. *New York Times*, November 19. http://www.nytimes.com/2015/11/20/business/genetically-engineered-salmon-approved-for-consumption.html?_r=0

Rack, J. 2015. Genetically Modified Salmon: Coming to a River Near You? *National Public Radio*, June 24. http://www.npr.org/sections/thesalt/2015/06/24/413755699/genetically-modified-salmon-coming-to-a-river-near-you

Rodriguez, Lulu, and Ruby Lynn Asoro. 2012. Visual Representations of Genetic Engineering and Genetically Modified Organisms in the Online Media. *Visual Communication Quarterly* 19(4): 232–245. doi:10.1080/15551393.2012.735585.

Shanahan, James, Dietram Scheufele, and Eunjung Lee. 2001. Trends: Attitudes about Agricultural Biotechnology and Genetically Modified Organisms. *The Public Opinion Quarterly* 65(2): 267.

Sarah Parsloe earned her MA in communication studies from San Diego State University in 2013. She is currently a doctoral candidate studying health communication at Ohio University. Her

research focuses on how individuals communicatively construct empowering health/(dis)ability identities in the face of stigma, uncertainty, doubt, and marginalization. She is particularly interested in understanding the link between self-advocacy and collective action.

Advancing Food Safety Technology: From Cave Dwellers to the Modern Home Kitchen
Ken Lee

Great food enables great human achievement. When humans discovered how to cook, we distinguished ourselves from all other life forms, giving us the time and energy to build an advanced society. Cave dwellers used trial and error to figure out what food practices were safe. These were limited to cooking, fermentation, salting, and dehydration. Those who got it right survived, and those who did not perished.

The idea of cooking fresh food over fire has not changed; it just moved from the cave to the kitchen. Cooking makes food safe but does not preserve it. In 1795, Napoleon Bonaparte desperately needed to feed his troops through winter and offered an enticing prize of 12,000 francs for a solution. A French confectionary chef, Nicholas Appert, won the prize by cooking food in corked containers and keeping the troops fed. Chef Appert accomplished this by trial and error, decades before another Frenchman, Louis Pasteur, discovered food pathogens.

Several thousand years after the time of cave dwellers, food and survival remain inextricably linked, but food safety practices are no longer done in isolation. Today, we have a remarkable shared connection known as the Internet that gives us unprecedented food awareness. Food technologies have been slow to evolve to date, but in the coming years social and data connections will have an accelerating impact on food safety. Global food needs and a new menu of emerging food technologies can create the next green food revolution.

The Smart Kitchen

Today, a primary technology for preserving food remains heating foods in sealed containers. The now-sophisticated science of thermal processing succeeds in making foodborne illness from canned food an extremely rare event. Tomorrow, the primary technology for safe food will not be this Napoleonic-era discovery. We are on the eve of a revolution in emerging food technologies that makes food safe with minimal heat and better taste outcomes.

There has never been a foodborne illness in space as all food ever orbited was made safe by food irradiation. Gamma rays from cobalt, X-ray machines, or accelerated electrons from an e-beam device excel in making a fresh food free of harm. Extremely high pressure processing can shuck a fresh oyster and cleanse it of deadly *Vibrio* bacteria. This same pressure process provides an array of new fresh foods in today's grocery that are safe and tasty. Pulsed electric field technology allowed the Genesis Juice Corporation to sell fresh, unheated but safe juices. Innovations such as pulsed light, plasma microwave, gaseous or aqueous ozone, or perhaps vaporized hydrogen peroxide will have a major food safety impact in the coming years, rivaling the impact of Chef Appert more than 200 years ago.

Home food preparation remains a leading source of foodborne illness, yet the home kitchen is remarkably dumb. Smart appliances are still in their infancy but have the potential to revolutionize food preparation. The goal to make all food both harmless and enjoyable is within reach. When *Scientific American* magazine asked about the kitchen of the future a decade ago (The Vigilant Kitchen, *Scientific American*, September 2007, p. 117), I predicted the home kitchen could become the safest link in the food chain. Here are a few examples of home appliances with great potential to get smart and make our homes the safest place to eat.

The microwave oven, since it was first sold in 1946, has a clock controlling cook time. That is silly, as we want to know the final temperature and if the food is safe. Instead of a time endpoint, the microwave can have a food safety outcome. An RFID or code on the food itself can tell the oven what to do to achieve the right internal temperature for the best safety and best flavor. The oven can be even more intelligent with online access to a continuously updated data on safe food. If the home owner has a recalled food ingredient, this smart oven will reject it.

We need not rely on a smart cooktop or smart microwave to advance food safety. The home refrigerator, since it was introduced by Frigidaire in 1923, has a simple thermostat controlling it. That is questionable, as we need to know the food temperature history and how long before food goes bad. The smart refrigerator senses individual food temperatures and time histories, identified by digital tags that allow trace-back to the original farm or factory. The "best if used by" date will be a national database alerting consumers if the storage conditions required for each food were met. Perishable or frozen items that get warm or defrosted are flagged by this smart appliance to prevent inadvertent food illness. The illumination when we open the door can be paired with pulsed light technology when we close the door, to eradicate microbiological contaminants.

Water treatment impacts both microbiological and chemical food safety. Today, we depend upon an aging and sometimes inadequate community water infrastructure to deliver a safe supply. Real time monitoring of community and home water quality in tomorrow's smart kitchen could provide fresh water without contaminants. Ozone, replacing risky chlorine, can free water of microbiological pests. Smart filters can respond directly to chemical hazards. Water can be tailored to the taste and health preferences of the home owner. Coffee lovers can enjoy water known to make the perfect brew. Health conscious consumers can hydrate with beverages tailored to enhance desired health outcomes. The presence of microorganisms, if any, will be probiotic, intentional, and tailored to the individual.

The smart kitchen is an integrated system. Countertop lighting may have a night ultraviolet cycle that kills surface bacteria when no one is present. Trash containers may measure food waste and inform the next grocery purchase. Newer food technologies, such as ultra-high pressure processing, pulsed electric fields, and plasma microwave, can empower the consumer with control of food from farm to fork and make the accident of food poisoning a historical footnote.

Great human achievement enables great food. Connected people and connected gadgets will find their home in the innovative kitchen, serving up some very appealing, safe, and enjoyable food.

Dr. Lee is Director of Food Innovation at The Ohio State University, advancing the human condition with food. Lee was twice elected Chair of the Senate Steering Committee that sets the University agenda. Lee served 15 years as department chair. He was on the Board and chaired several initiatives of Institute of Food Technologists (IFT). He taught the first course at University of Wisconsin-Madison, broadcast live on cable TV. Dr. Lee was selected as an American Council for Education leadership Fellow for the Wisconsin University System in 2009. He advances food commercialization as the Principle Investigator of a $3 million Third Frontier Award. He has published 75 scholarly papers and, in December 2001, he delivered the Ohio State Commencement address. He won the 2007 IFT Carl R. Fellers award and the 2014 IFT Harold Macy award and is past president of the food science honorary Phi Tau Sigma. He was elected a Fellow of the American Association for the Advancement of Science in 2015.

Learning from Today to Ensure Safe Food Tomorrow
Gina Nicholson

Fifty years ago, people became ill and died without health care providers ever considering foodborne pathogens as a source of illness. Today—and in the future—health care professionals and food safety scientists must have technology to quickly determine the source of a foodborne illness outbreak, stop food distribution, and conduct immediate recalls.

Changes in dietary preferences, a growing population, and environmental change will add to the challenges of keeping food safe now and into the future. Production techniques such as hydroponics and vertical growing will likely increase worldwide as people strive to grow food in nontraditional settings, such as along walls and inside converted manufacturing/warehouse facilities. These techniques will be essential to feeding the world population, which is projected to grow to 9.6 billion by 2050. The situation becomes even more challenging in the face of diminishing water resources and decreased tillable acreage.

We can learn from today's food safety challenges to improve technology to ensure safe food in the future.

Today's Lessons and Trends

Developed countries are not immune from foodborne illness resulting from poor sanitation. Americans are eating healthier by consuming more fresh fruits and vegetables to achieve healthy weights and prevent life-threatening disease. Increased demand for fresh produce is resulting in more people planting gardens and growing foods on patios and along walls in their homes. This trend is spilling over into restaurants as patrons demand more local produce.

Vertical production, a method of growing food on poles and stacking grow boxes, is being used to maximize the amount of food produced in a minimal space. In some areas, communities are converting abandoned manufacturing or warehouse spaces into greenhouses and employing vertical growing practices to raise produce for local residents. While this type of production can yield fresh, delicious produce, foodborne-disease-causing bacteria can develop without adequate food safety protocols. In order to gain all of the health benefits of eating fresh produce, it must be grown, harvested, and prepared in a clean environment.

Consumers and restaurants often have a false sense of security regarding locally grown food—perceiving it as higher quality, better tasting, and *safe*. This is not necessarily the case, which is why food growers must implement food safety practices at every step of the growing, harvesting, and distribution process. The local foods movement has made traceability more important than ever. If a foodborne illness event occurs, investigators must be able to track the food to its source. Even though consumers and food businesses purchase from a local cooperative, produce may be provided by dozens of growers.

Healthy and Safe Produce

The challenges with fresh produce emerged when one of the worst *Listeria* outbreaks in recent years occurred in Colorado in 2011. Almost 150 people got sick and 33 people died from cantaloupe contaminated with *Listeria* bacteria. Investigators tracked the source to an unsanitary dump truck used to discard melons parked near the packing shed (Neuman, 2011). Inspectors also discovered pools of water in walkways and along drains, providing breeding grounds for bacteria. Washing and sorting equipment was purchased from a potato operation and could not be properly cleaned or sanitized for melons.

In addition, the farm did not follow FDA guidelines for cooling melons and packed warm melons from the field in boxes that were then refrigerated. This method of cooling had the potential to produce condensation, which promotes *Listeria* growth. Every grower must implement proper sanitary measures and employ good agricultural practices developed by the food industry, producer organizations, governments, and nongovernment organizations. Failure to do so could result in local and regional foodborne illness outbreaks and long-term health consequences for those individuals affected.

Frozen Foods

Trends toward healthier eating have created food safety issues within the frozen food industry. Consumers are increasingly eating frozen foods raw that were never intended for consumption without thorough cooking. For example, health-conscious people often add frozen fruits and vegetables to salads and mix them into smoothies without cooking. The frozen food industry should have been able to predict this consumer trend and prepare for it by increasing the food safety standards for pathogen tolerance of frozen food production. However, the only standards that were changed were the consumer cooking instructions on the packaging.

The year 2016 saw a large-scale voluntary recall of frozen fruits and vegetables marketed under 42 brand names. The recall involved 350 frozen foods, with 8 illnesses and 2 deaths (Mele, 2016). It took the loss of lives, health, and negative economic impact for the frozen food industry to begin changing its food safety standards.

Raw Flour

Raw cookie dough and other food dough were identified as sources for *Escherichia coli* outbreaks. Thirty-eight people became infected with an outbreak strain of *E. coli* in 20 states that was traced to flour produced at a General Mills facility in Missouri. All of the people affected reported using flour in the week before they became ill or eating or tasting homemade dough or batter (FDA, 2016).

Wheat and other grains are not treated to kill bacteria that might come from animals, specifically birds and rodents, which defecate on the grain before it is milled into flour. The expectation has always been that the flour used to make food will be cooked to a high-enough temperature to kill foodborne pathogens that may remain in the product.

Innovative Consumer Demands

Americans' demand for healthy, convenient food has resulted in food delivery services that send consumers a box of pre-portioned meal ingredients and recipes for an entire week. These foods are nutritious and appealing but the question arises as to whether the foods are stored at the proper temperature when delivered. Do delivery personnel leave food packages on the porch during the hot summer until the consumer returns?

Home-delivered food must be accompanied by ice packs or contained in insulated coolers capable of keeping the product safe. In the future, drones and self-driving vehicles may be used to make home food deliveries; food packages may include computer chips to monitor the product temperature and indicate (with a color change or a message on the recipient's cell phone) if the food becomes unsafe for consumption.

Food printing will likely burgeon in popularity as healthy 3D printed foods (pasta, chocolates, and dough-based foods) become available. Home cooking machines have the capability to prepare foods such as lasagna. The consumer places the ingredients in the machine and returns home to find prepared hot lasagna ready for the family meal.

The food industry must consider various issues relative to this type of technology. If the machine breaks, will ingredients such as ground beef cook to the proper temperature? How is the machine cleaned and sanitized, and can it be broken down for cleaning? 3D printer users must be able to prevent food-borne illness and remove allergen proteins that can contaminate foods that the printer next prepares.

Safe Food Tomorrow

Food safety will continue to be a key issue during the coming decades, with the greatest challenge relative to developing technology to keep the world food supply sufficient and safe. Consumers will need new skills and equipment in their homes while producers, processors, and distributors will require new technology to keep food safe from harvest through consumer purchase.

Technology in the Laboratory

Pathogens are resilient and have the ability to survive even extreme conditions. When a foodborne illness event occurs, investigators and food scientists need technology to conduct pathogen and allergen tests and receive instant results. These results enhance traceability and minimize their spread. Today's technology takes days—tomorrow's technology will take seconds.

This instant testing technology will not only facilitate quick and efficient foodborne illness outbreak investigation and detection of foodborne illness in sick consumers but will also allow safer food to enter commerce and reduce waste of perishable foods in warehouses waiting for laboratory test results. Instant testing technology will also assist with identification of food fraud and intentional contamination at nations' borders. Many scientists are presently working to develop this technology.

Technology in the Home

Consumers of the future will likely benefit from technology allowing them to test and instantly confirm their food is safe before they eat it. Smart phones or gadgets will be equipped with instant foodborne pathogen and food allergen testing features for use prior to consuming a meal, whether at home or away.

Home chefs may rely on computers to prepare their meals and must have the technology to properly clean and sanitize the equipment so it is ready to prepare the next meal. Future food preparation equipment will probably be self-cleaning, conserving water. Skillets, utensils, and other equipment may well incorporate antibacterial and antiviral materials to help keep food safe. Knives and plates, for example, may be manufactured with resins that incorporate these properties.

Technology in the Industry

In the future, food-processing facilities may employ virtual auditors to replace onsite food safety experts. A worker may wear glasses with a camera and video system capable of recording production and handling processes so recommendations can be made. A restaurant manager may have a holographic projection of a third party auditor or regulator accompanying him or her during an onsite audit/inspection. Headsets will allow both the manager and off-site food safety expert to identify and discuss processes and areas needing correction.

With all of the technology that is likely to evolve during the next 50 years, the food safety industry will require a growing number of qualified food safety specialists capable of and committed to developing new technology. Educators of today must encourage their students to pursue careers in the food safety industry and to obtain strong math, science, and technology backgrounds.

While technology will likely provide the food safety industry the greatest potential to prevent foodborne illness and save lives, food safety scientists must be able to look at the big picture and consider how technological investments will impact food companies' bottom line. State-of-the-art technology will continue to be expensive, and food safety scientists must understand what motivates food companies and be prepared to encourage them to make investments in technology that will help ensure a safe food supply.

References

FDA. 2016. Gold Medal, Gold Medal, Wondra, and Signature Kitchens Flour Recalled Due to Possible E. Coli 0121 Contamination. http://www.fda.gov/Safety/Recalls/ucm504235.htm

Mele, Christopher. 2016. Huge Recall of Frozen Fruits and Vegetables after Listeria Outbreak. *The New York Times*, May 22. http://www.nytimes.com/2016/05/23/us/listeria-outbreak-frozen-fruits-and-vegetables-recall.html?_r=0

Neuman, William. 2011. Listeria Outbreak Traced to Cantaloupe Packing Shed. *New York Times*, October 20. http://www.nytimes.com/2011/10/20/business/listeria-outbreak-traced-to-colorado-cantaloupe-packing-shed.html

Gina Nicholson, RS/REHS, is Executive Director of Savour Food Safety International, assisting companies in developing long-term food safety culture and behavior change programs. She helps companies with new products/technologies from ideation to commercialization. As owner/operator of her own organic bakery, Manager Health Promotions at Columbus Public Health, Senior Manager Food Safety & Quality at The Kroger Co., to Global Director Retail Food Services at NSF International, Gina has spread her knowledge of and innovative approach to food safety to organizations small and large. An active member with STOP Foodborne illness, Conference for Food Protection, International Association for Food Protection, Food Safety Summit, and Food Safety Consortium and contributor for Food Safety Magazine *and* Food Safety Tech, *Gina attended Ashland University (BS Biology). Gina is a Registered Sanitarian and Registered Environmental Health Specialist.*

Whole Genome Sequencing—Implications for the Food Industry
Melinda Hayman

Whole Genome Sequencing (WGS), sometimes also referred to under the wider umbrella of "next generation sequencing," has gathered a lot of steam in the food safety arena in a very short time. This is largely due to the efforts of the FDA and the Centers for Disease Control and Prevention (CDC).

Every living thing contains genetic material. DNA can be read, or "sequenced," providing a map, or fingerprint, of that organism. Sequencing technology has existed for quite some time; we have been able to replicate smaller sections of DNA for more than 50 years. However, sequencing a whole genome has been much more difficult because of the massive amounts of data involved. Genomes of microorganisms were first sequenced in 1995, but it wasn't until 2003 that the first human genome was sequenced. These first attempts were major undertakings that were incredibly expensive and time consuming.

Over the last few years, sequencing technology has evolved, allowing for cheaper and faster approaches for use in a more routine capacity.

So how is this technology used by regulatory agencies for food safety? DNA testing can tell if two humans are related, and similarly WGS can tell if two bacterial isolates are related (i.e., come from the same ancestor). If a person becomes ill from eating a food contaminated with pathogenic bacteria and a bacterial culture is collected, the culture will go to the CDC or a State Health Laboratory. The genetic sequence for pathogens such as *Listeria monocytogenes*, *Salmonella* spp., or pathogenic *E. coli* can be identified using this technology; currently, CDC sequences every *L. monocytogenes* isolate they receive during investigations. Additionally, during inspections of food-processing facilities, the inspector may collect bacteria from foods and the processing facility's environment or equipment. Sequences from these organisms go into a database, as do the sequences obtained from patients with foodborne illness. The fingerprints of each organism are compared, and the database can show if other people have become sick from the same bug, and if the bug has been isolated from a specific food or manufacturing facility. In this way, CDC and FDA can more rapidly identify and stop outbreaks of foodborne illness than in the past.

This technology has been used to detect a number of outbreaks, some of which may not have been solved using pulsed field electrophoresis (PFGE analysis), the previous subtyping tool used for outbreak investigations. Examples include an outbreak of listeriosis involving two people who ate stone fruit (2014), as well as an outbreak associated with ice cream (2010–2015).

Another benefit of WGS is that one work flow can replace a number of currently existing individual tests. For example, regulatory agencies may test bacterial isolates for antimicrobial resistance, serotype, and PFGE type. In some countries, WGS has replaced all of this testing, while in others side-by-side testing is being conducted with the aim of eliminating much of the historical testing. This should also reduce the cost and time of testing.

One of the current questions in this field is—how can this tool be used by the food industry? While it has worked quite well in the regulatory space, there are still a number of issues that need to be worked out before it will be widely implemented by the food industry. Some of these issues are discussed below.

1. **Purpose of testing.** Much of the current food industry testing is to determine the presence or absence of a pathogen, or indicator, or levels of an indicator. In many cases, a decision on product disposition is made based on the results of the screening test (i.e., without confirmation).

2. **Cost.** Although the price is decreasing significantly, WGS still exceeds the cost of performing the types of routine testing the food industry typically conducts. To bring WGS technology in-house requires a significant initial investment in both the sequencing and analysis equipment.

3. **Lack of standard methodology.** This provides a major hurdle. Currently, if you want to test for presence of *L. monocytogenes* in a food, you can go to many different sources and find an established method. The FDA and USDA provide easy access to methods that are considered the gold standard, which can be easily replicated and conducted in most labs. There is nothing equivalent to WGS. That is, there is no standard procedure on how to extract DNA, cut and replicate the DNA, and run the sequencing. This means that someone with a high level of expertise in molecular biology is needed to design and oversee the testing. It can also make it difficult to compare results.

4. **Lack of bioinformatics expertise.** The data analysis is complex and may require using a number of different, complex tools to trim, assemble, and analyze the data. Analysis of WGS data requires staff, or access to experts, with bioinformatics expertise. People with this training and expertise are few and in high demand.

5. **Lack of regulatory guidance.** This may be the biggest hurdle. Without procedures in place to guide the industry on the regulatory implications of the data, there is much hesitation to collect it.

Consensus within the scientific community is that WGS is an exciting technology and that incredible strides have been made in this field in a short period of time. It's been a game changer in the field of food safety. Implementation by the food industry will continue to take some time as some of the remaining issues are ironed out. However, it's a topic that every food safety professional should keep a keen eye on.

Dr. Melinda Hayman is a food microbiologist specializing in food safety. Melinda received her PhD in Food Science from the Pennsylvania State University and a BS Honors in Microbiology and Biochemistry from the University of Sydney. For both degrees, her research project focus was inactivation of Listeria monocytogenes by high pressure processing. She authors food safety publications and designs and provides food safety education. Melinda also serves as a delegate to the Codex Committee on Food Hygiene and is the staff liaison for the GMA Microbiological Safety Committee.

The safety of the food supply has been shaped by many people and multiple organizations. The profiles below are not comprehensive because there are certainly people and organizations missing from this list. However, these profiles do offer a synopsis of how modern-day food safety has been affected by the work of a broad range of individuals and groups.

Individuals

Some of the most influential people are historical figures who contributed to contemporary food safety because of their work on seemingly unrelated issues. For example, Rachel Carson was a botanist who called attention to how pesticides were affecting bald eagle populations. The concerns she raised built the framework for modern movements against the overuse of chemicals in the food supply. Upton Sinclair wrote a seminal book about the plight of workers in the meat-packing industry at the turn of the century and influenced the first food safety legislation in the United States. Theodor Escherich was working to understand why children were suffering

Matt Ohloff, Iowa regional organizer for Food and Water Watch, speaks in favor of GMO food labeling, on the Capitol steps in Des Moines, Iowa, on April 3, 2013. On July 29, 2016, President Obama signed a law requiring the U.S. Department of Agriculture to establish rules for labeling GE products. The law is controversial because it restricts states' abilities to require their own labeling and relies on digital labels that could limit access. (AP Photo/MacKenzie Elmer) *from diarrhea, and he identified one of the leading pathogens of foodborne illness today. The people below are notable because their work either directly or indirectly affects food safety.*

Rachel Carson (1907–1964)

Rachel Carson grew up on a 65-acre parcel of land 15 miles north of Pittsburgh, Pennsylvania. Her father, an aspiring real estate developer, bought the parcel with the intention of subdividing it, but Pittsburgh grew in another direction, which kept the land mostly undeveloped. Carson spent her childhood roaming the countryside and writing stories. At the age of 10, she won a prize for a story from *St. Nicholas Magazine*.

In college, Carson majored in English until her junior year, when her love of nature won out and she switched to zoology. After college, she went to work for the Bureau of Fisheries (now part of the Department of Fish and Game), writing radio scripts about fishery and marine life. In 1936, Carson took the civil service exams for Junior Aquatic Biologist. She scored higher than everyone else who applied and became the first female biologist ever hired by the Bureau of Fisheries. She had many duties but continued to write, eventually becoming the editor in chief of the Information Division. On the advice of her boss, Carson submitted one of the pieces she had written for the Bureau to *Atlantic Monthly*. The magazine accepted the story, and she began to write for publication. Her first book, *Under the Sea-Wind,* was published in 1941.

In 1945, the pesticide dichlorodiphenyltrichloroethane (DDT) became available for civilian use. It had been used during World War II in the Pacific Islands to kill malaria-causing insects and as a delousing powder in Europe. Considered a wondrous substance by many, the inventor of DDT was awarded the Nobel Prize. As part of the commercialization process, many DDT tests were conducted. Carson had observed a series of tests near her home in Maryland and approached *The Reader's Digest* proposing an article about the tests. The magazine did not think the subject merited an article, and Carson returned to her other writing.

Carson's next book, *The Sea Around Us*, was published in 1951. It described the origins and geologic aspects of the sea. It won the John Burroughs Medal and the National Book Award and stayed on the *New York Times* best-seller list for 81 weeks.

In 1958, Carson received a letter from her friend Roger Owens Huckins. Huckins owned a private bird sanctuary in Duxbury, Massachusetts. One day, he had found dead and dying birds a few days after a massive, unannounced spraying of DDT. Carson began researching DDT, spending four years consulting with biologists and chemists and reviewing massive amounts of data and documentation. She wrote *Silent Spring*, carefully describing how DDT entered the food chain and accumulated in the fatty tissues of animals, including humans, causing cancer and genetic damage. She concluded that DDT and other pesticides had irrevocably harmed birds and animals and had contaminated the entire world food supply.

Silent Spring was first serialized in *The New Yorker* in 1962. Readers all over America became alarmed, and the chemical industry responded sharply. Ironically, this response only drew more attention to Carson's work. Carson had meticulously documented her findings; the book included 55 pages of notes and a list of experts who had read and approved the manuscript. President John F. Kennedy instructed the President's Science Advisory Committee to examine the issues raised in the book. The committee's report supported the conclusions of the book and vindicated Carson. *Silent Spring* became a best seller. DDT received close scrutiny from the U.S. government and was eventually banned. Carson died of breast cancer in 1964.

Ann Cooper (1953–)

Ann Cooper dropped out of high school to become a ski bum. She hitched a ride to Telluride, Colorado, and took a job in a restaurant to support her lifestyle. Eventually, she started a baking business with another woman. At 26, she decided to make a career of cooking and entered the Culinary Institute of America, where she graduated with honors. She cooked for various restaurants and the Holland America Cruise Line before working for the Putney Inn in Vermont. It was there that she became interested in sustainable agriculture and food safety issues. She has authored four books related to food safety and after *Bitter Harvest* was published in 2000, she was approached by the Ross School in East Hampton, New York, to become their chef. Although she didn't see herself as a "lunch lady," she was intrigued by the opportunity to bring the principles of sustainable agriculture to the next generation. Using the mantra "Regional, Organic, Sustainable, and Seasonal," she transformed the menu to include natural, unprocessed ingredients that were about 65 percent organic. Cooper hoped that other student cafeterias would follow her example, but most thought it could only be done at a private school such as Ross.

In 2005, Cooper took a position with the Berkeley, California, School District and transformed the school lunch program. Ann argued that school lunches are a social justice issue in a 2007 TED talk because of the impact that they have on student achievement. She speaks out against antibiotics, growth hormones, and pesticides in foods and is in favor of organic, local, and sustainable food. In 2009, she became the Director of Food Services for the Boulder Valley School District, Boulder, Colorado. There is now a salad bar in every school cafeteria in the district, and all meals are scratch made rather than reheated or processed. Through her works with schools, she has become known as the "Renegade Lunch Lady." In 2009, she also founded the Food Family Farming Foundation, now known as the Chef Ann Foundation (CAF). The Lunch Box is a free resource from CAF and offers support for schools making changes to their programs.

Cooper sits on the U.S. Department of Agriculture (USDA) Organic Standards Board and is advocating an increase in funding for the national school lunch program so that money is available to bring higher-quality food to children. She is also a member of the Women's Chefs and Restaurateurs and on the advisory board of the Real Foods for Kids.

Ronnie Cummins (1946–)

Ronnie Cummins has been an activist since 1967 in a variety of movements, including human rights, antiwar, antinuclear, labor, and consumer issues. In the early 1990s, Cummins turned his attention to food safety, sustainable agriculture, organic food standards, and genetically modified foods. He has been director of the Beyond Beef Campaign, the Pure Food Campaign, and the Global Days of Action against Genetic Engineering. Cummins is the national director of the Organic Consumers Association, a nonprofit public interest organization working to build a healthy, safe, and sustainable system of food production and consumption in the United States and the world. In 1998, Cummins organized the Save Organic Standards Campaign to pressure the USDA to strengthen the regulatory definition of what is meant by the term "organic." In 2000, the USDA announced that foods could not be labeled "organic" if they had been genetically modified.

A frequent writer, Cummins contributes to the *Huffington Post*, *Alternet*, and *Truthout* and other publications considered alternative media. He is a coauthor of *Genetically Engineered Food: A Self Defense Guide* (2004), which helps consumers avoid genetically engineered products at the grocery store.

Nancy Donley (1954–)

Nancy Donley lost her son Alex to hemolytic uremic syndrome (HUS) that he contracted from eating a hamburger tainted with *Escherichia coli* O157:H7. Alex was 6 years old and died quickly, just four days after eating the meat. Donley, who had never been involved in any political organization before, heard about Safe Tables Our Priority (STOP) from a pediatrician who treated her son.

She quickly joined and began lobbying for STOP. With the determination that netted her a degree in marketing after eleven years of night school, Donley, along with Mary Heersink and others at STOP, pursued legislation and policy changes that have improved the safety of the U.S. food supply. STOP is largely credited with effecting the 1997 USDA policy change requiring Hazard Analysis and Critical Control Point (HACCP) procedures and microbial testing on meats. STOP continues to work on food safety issues with special focus on food safety issues that affect children.

For many years, Donley was the unpaid president of STOP in addition to her job as a real estate broker. She has served on the National Advisory Committee on Meat and Poultry, won the Golden Carrot Award from the Consumer Federation of America, and was honored as the first recipient of the STOP Foodborne Illness Legacy Tribute. In 2015, she decided to step away from being the key spokesperson for STOP.

Theodor Escherich (1857–1911)

E. coli is named for Theodor Escherich, who was a pediatrician and clinician with a strong desire in helping children avoid disease. His interest in microbiology began with study of *Vibrio cholerae*, the bacteria that causes cholera, and carried forward as he earned his medical degree. By all accounts, he was a compassionate doctor who was very concerned with the lack of attention paid to children suffering from intestinal illness. When he isolated bacteria in numerous stool samples, he concluded that this was a likely cause of the distress. At first, the bacteria was called *Bacillus coli commune* (the common colon bacteria), but the name was eventually changed in tribute in 1958. He wrote one of the most influential books about pediatric illness of the time, *The Bacteria of the Intestines of the Infant.*

Some strains of *E. coli* are the most important and often deadly foodborne pathogens today. It is also considered a "model organism" because of the ability to study it in the laboratory. The bacterium is often referred to as one of the most understood organisms on earth because of the magnitude of research since its discovery more than a century ago. Several researchers have won Nobel Prizes for their research with *E. coli*, including biochemist Paul Modrich, who won the award in 2015.

Escherich's commitment to the welfare of children was a pivotal moment in understanding intestinal diseases. He is considered the first pediatric infectious disease physician by many, as well as one of the most influential people who shaped modern microbiology. In addition to being a doctor and researcher, Escherich was a skilled administrator. He was the Chair of Pediatrics at the University of Vienna and the Director of the St. Anna Children's Hospital in Vienna. He helped establish the Austrian Society for Children's Research and the Association of Pediatricians in Vienna. He was instrumental in the design of the Children's Hospital in Vienna, although a few days before it was set to open, he died of an apparent stroke. He was only 53 years old.

Patricia Griffin (1949–)

Patricia Griffin graduated from the University of Pennsylvania School of Medicine and completed her internship at the University's medical center and her residency in gastroenterology at Brigham and Women's Hospital in Boston. After completing a variety of research fellowships in gastroenterology, Griffin went to work for the Epidemic Intelligence Service of the Centers for Disease Control and Prevention (CDC).

As an officer in the Epidemic Intelligence Service, Griffin did extensive fieldwork throughout the United States as well as in Thailand, Kenya, Lesotho, Brazil, Guatemala, Zambia, and Japan. In the 1980s, she became intrigued by *E. coli* O157:H7 and began conducting research. In 1983, another scientist, Mohamed Karmali, proposed that HUS was linked to exposure to *E. coli* O157:H7. The syndrome was first recognized in 1955, and many possible causes had been proposed. Griffin began calling pediatric nephrologists to ask them to look for the pathogen in their patients' stools. Although doctors were not very receptive to looking for *E. coli* O157:H7, Griffin persisted because she believed that the pathogen was an important cause of bloody diarrhea.

In 1987, Marguerite Neill and Phillip Tarr did a study in Seattle showing that most cases of HUS were related to *E. coli* O157:H7. Griffin then directed the CDC's efforts to control the disease, informing physicians of the connection to *E. coli* O157:H7, working with labs to test for the pathogen, and following up on cases around the country. In 1993, when the western states' epidemic occurred, Griffin had the knowledge of the disease and the skills of an epidemiologist to identify the probable cause of the outbreak. Griffin and members of STOP campaigned successfully to make infection with *E. coli* O157:H7 a disease that must be reported to health departments. Griffin is now chief of the Enteric Diseases Epidemiology Branch at CDC and an adjunct professor of Medicine and Public Health at Emory University and has written extensively about *E. coli*.

Fritz Haber (1868–1934)

Fritz Haber was born into a prominent family in Breslau, Germany. He attended a classical grammar and high school, St. Elizabeth's, and while there he did many chemistry experiments. He earned degrees at the University of Heidelberg, the University of Berlin, and the Technical School at Charlottenburg. After university, he went to work in his father's chemical business and took some other short-term positions before settling as a professor of chemical technology at Karlsruhe University. At Karlsruhe, he worked on many different chemical processes—inventing the glass electrode, finding ways to combust carbon monoxide and hydrogen (although not in commercially viable ways), and studying the flame in Bunsen burners.

Because there was such a commercial need for a source of nitrates (Germany was importing 33% of its nitrates from Chile) for enriching the soil, Haber worked intermittently on the problem of converting nitrogen from the atmosphere into ammonia which could be utilized by plants. (Nitrogen is very stable in the form N_2 [two nitrogen atoms bonded together], but to be available for use by plant cells, it needs to be able to combine one atom at a time.) Haber had all but given up on the problem when a fellow scientist, Walther Nernst (a prominent chemist who won the Nobel Prize in 1920), publicly attacked his research methods at a scientific meeting. Haber became morose and then obsessed with finding a way to solve the problem.

Haber succeeded in 1905, finding the right combination of temperature, pressure, and a metal catalyst, and shortly thereafter, Bosch found a way to make the process commercially viable. This discovery allowed the Germans to become independent of Chile's nitrate supply. Nitrate chemical fertilizers have become so important that they allow the earth to support approximately 40 percent of the population that would otherwise not exist.

Haber believed strongly in the maxim "A scientist belongs to his country in times of war, and to all mankind in times of peace." This maxim led Haber to work diligently for the German war effort during World War I. Haber had the idea of using poison gas to break the stalemate when both sides were stuck in the trenches, and he directed the first gas attack in military history. For this reason, many protested when Haber won the Nobel Prize for fixing nitrogen in 1918.

After World War I, Haber invented the firedamp whistle for protection of miners and made other important chemical discoveries. He also tried to extract gold from seawater, with the idea that Germany could use the process to pay its war reparations. In 1933, the Nazis were coming to power, and they forced all of Haber's Jewish colleagues to resign from the Institute at Karlsruhe. Haber, also a Jew, resigned in solidarity with his colleagues. He died shortly thereafter, in 1934.

Mary Heersink

Mary Heersink led a typical suburban life as a mother until 1992, when one of her sons ate undercooked hamburger at a Boy Scout outing and developed hemolytic uremic syndrome (HUS). HUS is a complication that can develop from poisoning by *E. coli* O157:H7. Marnix Heersink, Heersink's husband and an ophthalmologist, probably saved his son's life by researching HUS and connecting his son's doctors to a hematologist familiar with the disease. Although Damion Heersink's case was severe, he made an impressive recovery.

During the five weeks Damion spent in the hospital, Mary Heersink began to research the cause of the illness. She read widely about the syndrome and its causes and became infuriated that the USDA standards and procedures were not sufficient to prevent tainted meat from entering the food supply. She began to network with other parents of children suffering from HUS, faxing medical articles to the parents of sick children, and formed STOP with other victims of foodborne illness.

She worked tirelessly for STOP, appearing before commissions, traveling overseas to investigate other countries' practices, meeting with USDA officials, and giving interviews to the news media. She also authored a book, *E. coli O157: The True Story of a Mother's Battle with a Killer Microbe.* Largely through the efforts of Heersink and the other parents of STOP, the USDA changed the meat-handling laws in 1996, which went into effect in 1997, to incorporate HACCP, which requires microbial testing and performance standards for fresh and processed meats and poultry.

Sir Albert Howard (1873–1947)

Sir Albert Howard, now considered the father of modern organic agriculture, was an agricultural researcher in England in 1905. He was sent to Bengal in 1905 to establish an agricultural research base. Although his mission was to help indigenous people, he learned more about agriculture from them than they from him in the 25 years he was there.

Howard observed that the healthiest plants and animals were raised using the most traditional farming methods and that healthy plants and animals started with rich soils. He considered pests to be "nature's professors" of good husbandry because they were indicators of bad management and they were the best way to identify mistakes and apply corrective management. He believed that diseases in plants, animals, and people could all ultimately be traced to the health of the soil.

While in India, he refined the native techniques into what is called the "Indore" method of composting, named for the region where he developed the method. In the method, piles or pits of manure are layered with dry matter to facilitate aeration, and then the piles are physically turned every month or so. This causes aerobic decomposition via passive aeration. The rural Chinese have a similar technique. This technique spread to British tea and coffee plantations throughout Africa, Asia, and the Caribbean, and it's the first thing that agricultural volunteers with the Peace Corps are taught.

To test his beliefs that good husbandry would prevent disease, Howard designed some experiments in which he raised livestock in as healthy a manner as possible and then exposed the livestock to diseased cattle to see what would happen. One of the diseases he exposed them to was foot and mouth disease, a highly contagious disease that has caused massive destruction of cattle in the United Kingdom. Howard found that almost none of his cattle became infected with foot and mouth, which led him to believe that foot and mouth disease is a disease of malnutrition.

In 1940, he wrote *An Agricultural Testament*, which summed up his beliefs about sustainable agriculture and is considered by some to have launched the organic farming agricultural movement. The book covers the nature and management of soil fertility and describes composting.

Fred Kirschenmann (1935–)

Fred Kirschenmann grew up on the North Dakota farm his father started in 1930. As an adult, he left the farm and became a professor of religious history. While teaching in 1970, he was very impressed by a student's essay about how farming with heavy nitrogen fertilizers was causing deterioration of the soil. Six years later, in 1976, Kirschenmann's father, Ted, suffered a heart attack. Fred offered to come home and run the farm provided he could convert it to organic agriculture.

All of Kirschenmann's neighbors thought organic farming wouldn't work, but he persisted. Using a variety of techniques, including crop rotation, composting cattle manure to use as fertilizer, planting legumes to build the soil, and not planting sunflowers in the blackbirds' flight path, Kirschenmann was able to make the farm a commercial success. He continues to manage the 1,800-acre certified-organic farm in North Dakota. In 2000, Kirschenmann gave up day-to-day management of the farm and returned to academia at Iowa State University, where he directs the Leopold Center for Sustainable Agriculture. The research and educational center, funded by Iowa fees on nitrogen fertilizer and pesticides, develops sustainable agriculture practices that are both profitable and conserving of natural resources. In 2006, he was appointed to the National Commission on Industrial Farm Animal Production operated by the Johns Hopkins School of Public Health and funded by Pew Charitable Trusts.

Dr. Kirschenmann has received numerous awards for his work in sustainable agriculture, including the James F. Beard Leadership award in 2011 and the Sustainable Agriculture Achievement Award in 2012. In 2010, his ecological farming philosophy was published in a book called *Cultivating and Ecological Conscience: Essays from a Farmer Philosopher.*

Alice Lakey (1857–1935)

Alice Lakey was born in Shanesville, Ohio. Her father was a Methodist minister and an insurance broker. Alice's mother died when Lakey was 6 years old. She attended public school until the age of 14, when her father hired a private tutor for her. Lakey had a talent for singing and moved to Europe, performing on many occasions in the United Kingdom. After nearly 10 years of living abroad, she returned to the United States for health reasons. A few years after her return, she and her father moved to Cranford, New Jersey. She was active in many civil causes in Cranford, including successfully encouraging the city fathers to establish a school, fire department, and baby clinic.

When her father became ill, Lakey was unable to find unadulterated foods for him or herself. She joined the Domestic Science Unit of the Village Improvement Association and became president shortly thereafter. In 1903, Lakey wrote to Secretary of Agriculture James Wilson to get literature and a recommendation of someone who could speak to the club. He suggested Harvey Wiley, then a chemist for the USDA and the most active government worker interested in food purity issues. Wiley was actively trying to improve food standards. The connection with Wiley may have been what inspired Lakey to work on her goals at the national level; in 1904, she persuaded the Cranford Village Improvement Association and the New Jersey Federation of Women's Clubs to petition Congress to enact the pure food and drug bill.

In an effort to broaden support for the bill, Lakey approached the National Consumer's League to support the pure food cause. The League decided to investigate the conditions under which food was prepared and the working conditions of the food workers. Lakey was appointed to head the investigation committee in 1905. The committee became known as the Pure Food Committee. The group created an activist network of the nation's pure food, drink, and drug advocates, forming a coalition of members from many organizations. Using the information from the Pure Food Committee, the League was able to articulate definite consumer objectives and speak with authority for U.S. consumers.

Lakey and Wiley met with President Roosevelt in 1905 to urge his support for the pure food bill. Roosevelt told the pair that he would support the bill if they obtained signed letters to Congress. Lakey and others influenced over one million women to write letters supporting the bill.

After the bill passed in 1906, Lakey continued to work for pure food issues, pressuring Congress to fund the agency to enforce the act and to pass the pure milk bill. She continued this work until 1919, when her father died and she took his place as the manager of the trade journal he founded, *Insurance.*

Lakey was the first woman to be listed in *Who's Who* and was named to the National Academy of Social Sciences for her work. She died of heart failure in 1935.

Antoni van Leeuwenhoek (1632–1723)

Antoni van Leeuwenhoek was a Dutch tradesman with no higher education. Nevertheless, he became interested in microscopes and began making his own. The microscopes of the day were compound (made of more than one lens, similar to microscopes of today), but they only magnified objects 20 to 30 times. Leeuwenhoek ground his own lenses and made microscopes by mounting the lens in a hole in a brass plate. The specimen was mounted on a sharp stick in front of the lens. The position and focus was adjusted with two screws. As the microscope was very small, approximately 3 to 4 inches, it had to be held close to the eye and was difficult to use.

However, using his well-made lenses and special lighting techniques that he never revealed, Leeuwenhoek was able to magnify objects over 200 times. He took great interest in looking at objects with his microscope and discovered bacteria, free-living and parasitic microscopic protists, sperm cells, blood cells, microscopic nematodes, and rotifers, as well as many other organisms.

The prevailing theory of the time was that low forms of animal life could appear spontaneously. Leeuwenhoek studied the weevils in granaries and was able to show that weevils are grubs hatched from eggs deposited by winged insects and not bred from wheat. At one point he examined the plaque from his teeth and was disturbed at the abundant life living in his mouth. In 1673, Leeuwenhoek started writing to the Royal Society of London, describing his discoveries. Not much of an artist, he hired an illustrator to draw the microbes he saw. Although he had no formal scientific training, the Royal Society was so pleased with his discoveries that they made him a full-fledged member.

Leeuwenhoek continued working up until shortly before his death in 1723. He is considered the father of microbiology.

Stuart Levy (1938–)

Stuart Levy graduated from Williams College and went on to attend the University of Pennsylvania Medical School. After receiving a Public Health Service fellowship, he took a year off from medical school to study radiation genetics in Paris. While there, he learned about the work of Tsutomu Watanabe at Keio University in Tokyo. Watanabe was just starting to discover transferable bacterial resistance to antibiotics. Levy went back to medical school but took several months off after his third year to study in Tokyo with Watanabe. He graduated from medical school in 1965, completed a residency at Mount Sinai Hospital in New York, and did postdoctoral research at the National Institutes of Health.

Levy continued to study bacterial resistance. Some bacteria become resistant by acquiring resistance from other bacterial cells, but Levy was interested in how specific mutations in the bacterial cell cause it to develop pumps in its outer membrane to pump antibiotics, biocides, and other substances that would endanger the bacteria out of the cell. This process is called efflux. Levy and his team discovered the first antibiotic efflux mechanism that used ATP (adenosine triphosphate) for pumping and efflux protein for tetracycline. (ATP is generated in the mitochondria of cells and is a high-energy compound that cells use for processes that require energy.)

Levy is the Director of the Center for Adaptation Genetics and Drug Resistance at Tufts University and president of the Alliance for the Prudent Use of Antibiotics, which was established in 1981 to promote appropriate use of antibiotics in agriculture and in human use. He has authored hundreds of papers and books, including the influential *Antibiotic Paradox: How Misuse of Antibiotics Destroys Their Curative Powers*. He founded Paratek Pharmaceuticals, where he is working on ways to modify tetracycline to circumvent resistance mechanisms, thereby making the drug effective again, and also looking at ways to make drugs that could control the "master switch" present in many gram-negative bacteria that confers multiple antibiotic resistance in such bacteria as *Salmonella*, *E. coli*, and *Shigella*.

Joseph Baron Lister (1827–1912)

Joseph Lister is considered the father of modern surgery and the founder of antiseptic surgery. His interest in surgery started when he was very young, under the influence of his Quaker father, who was himself a medical trailblazer. He was appointed a Professor of Surgery at the University of Glasgow when he was 33 years old.

During the time Joseph Lister was working as a Professor of Surgery at the University of Glasgow, the commonly accepted reason why infections occurred was "miasmas" or something in the air. The worse infections were occurring in surgical wards, and there was a movement gaining momentum to stop surgeries altogether because of this. Lister was intrigued by the work of Louis Pasteur, who showed that microbes could be destroyed with heat and other techniques. He questioned whether Pasteur's methods could apply to pathogens that caused human infections.

Since Lister believed in the "germ theory" of disease, he tried using carbolic acid to clean wounds in the surgical ward and found great success in stopping the spread of infection. At the time Lister started raising questions there were no sanitary protocols for surgery. Surgeons were not even washing their hands between patients. Lister was one of the first to require his surgeons to wash their hands and wear gloves and other protective equipment during operations. Since infections sharply declined as a result of his requirements, he is credited with pioneering antiseptic methods during surgery.

He received many honors after his death, including two postage stamps bearing his likeness, a public monument in London, and the renaming of the British Institute of Preventive Medicine to the Lister Institute of Preventive Medicine. He is known as the father of antisepsis. Perhaps he is more well known for the mouthwash Listerine being named in his honor and from the foodborne perspective, one of the most important pathogens, *Listeria*. Joseph Lister did not discover the gram-positive, rod-shaped bacteria, but it was named in his honor in 1940.

Howard Lyman (1938–)

Howard Lyman was born in Montana and grew up on his family's organic dairy farm with his brother, Dick. He attended Montana State University, studying agriculture, including the business aspects of running a farm and using chemical fertilizers to boost productivity. After college, Lyman joined the army. Lyman liked the army, but his brother was dying of Hodgkin's disease and their father was getting too old to run the farm by himself, so Lyman returned home to run the farm.

Lyman decided that the organic dairy operation was not profitable enough, so he converted to chemical-based farming techniques. Although he increased his acreage 40-fold and increased his crop yields dramatically, it was almost impossible to make the farm profitable; the chemicals were expensive to use, and each year he had to use more chemicals and antibiotics to achieve the same result. The $5-million-a-year operation was taking a profound toll on the farm. The soil, once rich, loamy, and worm-filled, was crumbly and thin as sand. The worms were gone and the trees were dying.

In 1979, Lyman was diagnosed with a tumor on his spinal column. Facing probable paralysis, Lyman committed himself to restoring his family's farm to the way it was. During his long recuperation, he planned a strategy. He began using integrated pest management techniques that do not rely solely on pesticides. Lyman ran for Congress in 1982. Toward the end of the campaign, the bank foreclosed on his farm. Lyman lost the election by a small margin and was forced to sell off most of his holdings. In 1983, he began working for the Montana Farmer's Union and went to Washington, D.C., as a lobbyist for them in 1987. While in Washington, Lyman successfully lobbied for the National Organic Standards Act and for funds to finance the act's administration.

In 1990, Lyman became a vegetarian for environmental, humanitarian, and health reasons; currently, he is a vegan and consumes no animal products at all. He served as president of the International Vegetarian Union and was invited to appear on the *Oprah Winfrey Show* in 1996. While on the show, Lyman discussed ruminant-to-ruminant feeding (the practice of sending leftovers from the slaughter process to rendering plants and feeding the rendered animal protein to cattle) and its link to mad cow disease. After the show aired, Lyman and Winfrey were sued for food disparagement by a group of Texas cattle ranchers. The jury decided in favor of Lyman and Winfrey in 1998.

Since the suit, Lyman founded Voice for a Viable Future, a campaign to educate people about sustainable agriculture and the dangers of current methods of food production. His book *Mad Cowboy: Plain Truth from the Cattle Rancher Who Won't Eat Meat* was published in 2001, followed by *No More Bull!: The Mad Cowboy Targets America's Worst Enemy: Our Diet* in 2005.

Bill Marler (1958–)

In 1993, the first case of *E. coli* 0157:H7 was linked to hamburgers from Jack-in-the-Box restaurants in Seattle, Washington. This was Bill Marler's entrance into the world of litigation related to food safety. Bill's law firm, Marler Clark, handled the case and was involved in one of the largest foodborne illness settlements to date. Since that time, Bill Marler has become one of the nation's leading lawyers handling foodborne illness cases.

He went to law school at the University of Washington with plans to use his law degree for a career in politics. At age 19, he was the youngest person ever elected to the Pullman, Washington City Council, but the 1993 outbreak changed his life. He got involved with the case against Jack-in-the-Box because he was astonished that hamburger could be so dangerous and was hired by the family of the young girl who was the prominent victim of the outbreak.

Marler is outspoken about foodborne illness and assigning blame to industry and regulatory agencies for not monitoring the safety of the food supply. While he focuses on litigation, he is also involved in education and philanthropy. Through several websites and blogs, Marler provides commentary and advice on keeping food safe, protecting business interests, and seeking justice for suffering from unknowing exposure to pathogens. He is also advises against consuming products such as raw milk, seed sprouts, and oysters. His law firm supports websites such as Real Raw Milk Facts, which is dedicated to providing objective information about the risks of consuming raw milk.

Helen McNab Miller (1862–1949)

Helen McNab Miller was born in Zanesville, Ohio, and studied at Stanford University, the University of Nevada, and the University of Missouri. A home economist at the Agricultural College in Columbia, Missouri, Miller had a strong professional interest in food purity issues.

As a member of the General Federation of Women's Clubs (GFWC), she was known as an energetic club woman and became chair of the pure food subcommittee. As part of her work as a home economist, she worked with many government officials and committees on pure food, drink, and milk issues. This government experience was rare among women at the time and gave Miller a unique ability to help the club set and accomplish politically viable goals. Miller advocated firm but fair legislation. She was described as an accomplished speaker with a carefully modulated voice.

When President Roosevelt told Alice Lakey and Harvey Wiley to produce letters to Congress in support of the pure food legislation, Miller was assigned the task of soliciting letters from the Midwestern United States. At the GFWC biennial convention in St. Paul in June 1906, Miller requested that each delegation send telegrams to their representatives in the House and Senate, the Speaker of the House, and President Roosevelt urging swift passage of the pure food bill. After Miller read a summary of the terrible state of food, drugs, and alcohol in the United States, the telegrams poured into Washington.

After the bill passed, Wiley named Lakey and Miller as outstanding leaders of the crusade. Miller continued to work on food purity issues, securing the passage of the pure milk bill in Missouri in 1907. She later moved to Kalispell, Montana. Little is known about the remainder of her life.

Marion Nestle (1936–)

Marion Nestle attended high school in Los Angeles and then went to the University of California, Berkeley. She was always interested in food, but at the time, the only way to study food was by studying agriculture, so she chose to earn a bachelor's degree in microbiology, a master's degree in public health, and a doctorate in molecular biology. She started her career in academia at Brandeis University on the biology faculty but after being assigned to teach a nutrition class to undergraduates, her interest in nutrition led her to a 10-year stint at the University of California, San Francisco, as the associate dean of the School of Medicine, where she taught nutrition to medical students, residents, and practicing physicians.

In 1986, she became senior nutrition policy advisor in the U.S. Department of Health and Human Services and editor of the 1988 *Surgeon General's Report on Nutrition*. As the Paulette Goddard Professor in the Department of Nutrition, Food Studies, and Public Health at New York University, Nestle is a frequent and outspoken member of U.S. government panels that make decisions about dietary guidelines, is a member of the Food and Drug Administration (FDA)'s Food Advisory Committee, and has served on the board of the Center for Science in the Public Interest.

Nestle has been able to use her insights about how policy is made to advocate for safer and more nutritious food for consumers. She has a particular talent for making food safety and nutrition information understandable to the average consumer and has written several books, including two editions of *Safe Food: The Politics of Food Safety*. She believes that a locus of public health, public policy, and journalism will be needed to combat obesity and promote sustainable agriculture.

Michael Osterholm (1953–)

After earning his Ph.D. at the University of Minnesota, Michael Osterholm went to work for the Minnesota Department of Health. He worked in various positions, becoming the state epidemiologist in 1985; in this position, Osterholm improved the level of surveillance in Minnesota, creating a reporting system more advanced than systems in most other states. He led many investigations of outbreaks of foodborne disease and did extensive research in epidemiology. His team was first to call attention to the changing epidemiology of foodborne illness.

While Osterholm was the chair of the Emerging Infections Committee of the Infectious Disease Society of America,

Osterholm became an expert not only in foodborne illness but also in biological terrorism and antimicrobial resistance. He currently serves as the director of the Center for Infectious Disease Research at the University of Minnesota, where he is also a professor in the School of Public Health. He is a nationally recognized expert in infectious disease with specific emphasis on food safety and bioterrorism and has served on numerous panels and committees, including the Task Force on Antibiotic Resistance in the American Society of Microbiologists and the Institute of Medicine Committees on Emerging Microbial Threats in the 21st Century and Food Safety, Production, and Consumption.

Louis Pasteur (1822–1895)

Louis Pasteur, the son of a tanner, spent his boyhood in France drawing. It was not until later that he developed an interest in science, earning a bachelor's degree in science in 1842, followed by master's and doctorate degrees in 1845 and 1847, respectively.

In 1854, Pasteur became dean of the new science faculty at the University of Lillie. As dean, he introduced programs to bridge science and industry, including taking his students to factories, supervising practical courses, and starting evening classes for young workmen. Perhaps because of the connections he made to industry, a businessman inquired about producing alcohol from grain and beet sugar. This inquiry began his study of fermentation.

In 1857, Pasteur found fermentation was the result of the activity of minute organisms. If fermentation failed, it was because the necessary organism was missing or unable to grow properly. As he continued his research, Pasteur proved that food decomposes when placed in contact with germs present in the air. He discovered that spoilage could be prevented if the microbes already present in foodstuffs were destroyed and the sterilized material was protected against later contamination.

A practical man, Pasteur applied his theory to food and drinks, developing a heat treatment called pasteurization. He was able to aid the French wine industry by solving the problem of wine going sour when it was transported, and his process eliminated the serious health threats of bovine tuberculosis, brucellosis, and other milk-borne diseases.

Pasteur's interest in bacteria also led him to study diseases. After he had determined the natural history of anthrax, a fatal disease of cattle, he concluded that anthrax was caused by a particular *Bacillus*. He suggested giving anthrax in a mild form to animals to inoculate them against a more severe reaction. He tested his hypothesis on sheep, inoculating 25 with a mild case of anthrax. A few days later he inoculated the same 25 plus 25 untreated sheep with a virulent strain of the bacteria. As Pasteur believed would happen, the 25 sheep who had been vaccinated survived, but the 25 who were given the virulent bacteria died. Pasteur is credited with developing vaccines for chicken cholera, smallpox, and rabies before his death in 1895.

Michael Pollan (1955–)

Published in 2006, *The Omnivore's Dilemma* is one of the most important books about food in recent years. Michael Pollan paints a compelling picture about how the way we eat is leading us into a future with serious ecological consequences. Since this book was published, Pollan has become a celebrity, speaking and writing about food and nutrition. He has appeared in numerous documentaries and talk shows, including *The Colbert Report* and *Oprah*. In 2010, *Time Magazine* named Pollan one of the 100 most influential people; Pollan has received numerous high profile awards.

Pollan's focus on food grew from his interest in how humans relate to nature. His arguments in favor of sustainable agriculture and simplifying eating include making choices for foods with no more than five ingredients. Pollan's rules for eating also include never eating anything that won't eventually rot.

This means that processed foods should not be part of the diet because they are so unnatural that they will never spoil.

Pollan is not a food safety expert; rather, he is a journalist focusing on food issues and is a contributing writer to the *New York Times Magazine*. He has a master's degree in English from Columbia University and extensive experience in journalism. He is a Professor of Journalism at UC Berkeley's Graduate School of Journalism. He has written eight books, including *Omnivore's Dilemma*, *In Defense of Food*, and *Cooked: A Natural History of Transformation*. In 2016, Pollan created a Netflix documentary series, *Cooked*.

Stanley Prusiner (1942–)

Stanley Prusiner was born in Des Moines, Iowa, and went to the University of Pennsylvania, where he earned a bachelor's degree in 1964 and a medical degree in 1968. He started a residency at the University of California, San Francisco (UCSF) in neurology, intending to enter private practice after graduation. One of his patients died of Creutzfeldt-Jakob disease, and Prusiner decided to stay at UCSF instead of entering private practice.

Over the course of his research, Prusiner determined that an abnormal protein, which he dubbed a prion (for proteinaceous infectious particle), caused the CJD that killed his patient. The prion was a previously unrecognized infectious agent, different from bacteria, viruses, and parasites. A prion is a protein that has the same amino acids as a normal protein but is shaped differently. It is the different shape that Prusiner believes causes certain brain disorders, including other spongiform encephalopathies like kuru, a disease of human cannibals, scrapie in sheep, and bovine spongiform encephalopathy (BSE). In 1984, Prusiner and his group identified 15 amino acids at the end of the prion protein. This discovery was enough for other labs to identify the gene for producing the prion protein in both healthy and infected mice and hamsters.

In 1992, Prusiner, with Charles Weissmann of the University of Zurich, was able to show that lab mice stripped of the prion gene became immune to prion-linked diseases. Although some scientists didn't believe that the deformed prion was the infectious agent, in 1997 Prusiner was awarded the Nobel Prize for Medicine or Physiology. He continues to do research on prions as the director of the Institute for Neurodegenerative Diseases at the University of California, San Francisco. In addition, Prusiner founded and is chairman of InPro, a biotechnology company that has commercialized prion disinfectant and diagnostic products (such as tests for BSE and scrapie) that he developed in his lab at UCSF. In 2014, Prusiner published *Madness and Memory: The Discovery of a New Biological Principle of Disease*, which chronicles his research with prions.

Milton J. Rosenau (1869–1946)

Milton Joseph Rosenau's book *Preventive Medicine and Hygiene* (1913) was the first to focus on diseases spread from person to person and through the environment. He strongly believed that the only way to prevent diseases from spreading was through understanding modes of transmission. His book, which became a staple in public health programs, led to Rosenau being referred to as the "father of preventive medicine" in the United States.

Rosenau was born in Philadelphia and earned his medical degree from the University of Pennsylvania in 1889. He worked for the U.S. Marine Hospital Service as a quarantine officer and directed the MHS Hygienic Laboratory. During his time with MHS, he wrote the book *The Milk Question* (1912). A significant portion of Rosenau's early work was focused on milk sanitation, specifically improving the use of pasteurization; he believed the safety of milk was one of the most important public health issues. He is credited with modifying Pasteur's heat treatment process in a way that made milk more palatable. As such, he was instrumental in enhancing the safety of the country's milk supply.

Rosenau had a long career in public health. He was both a practitioner in the U.S. Public Health Service and an academician at the Harvard Medical School. He created the School of Public Health at the University of North Carolina (UNC)– Chapel Hill and was its first dean; he remained at UNC until his death in 1946. Rosenau Hall at UNC–Chapel Hill houses the Gillings School of Global Public Health.

Joel Salatin (1957–)

Joel Salatin is a third-generation organic farmer. His parents farmed in Venezuela until they lost their farm for political reasons and then returned to their native United States. In 1961, they purchased 550 acres that had been a tenant farm in Swoope, Virginia. While in high school, Salatin began raising chickens following a "pastured poultry" model. Believing that the land and the animals can occupy complementary niches, Salatin modified and refurbished some old rabbit cages and put chicks in the cages. As chicken manure collected underneath the cages, Salatin moved the cages to other areas of the farm.

Salatin uses his animals to enrich the soil and transformed his farm "Polyface Farm" into a thriving, sustainable, and profitable enterprise. His animals move around continually so they do not overgraze and exhaust the soil, and he employs innovative strategies to make his animals do the work. For example, during the winter, he feeds his cows hay in the barn, and instead of mucking out the barn, layers their straw bedding with wood chips and leaves to minimize leaching and vaporization. He also throws some whole corn in the layers. Over the winter, the corn ferments. In the spring, Salatin moves the cows out to the pasture and moves the pigs into the barn. The pigs root for the fermented corn, thereby aerating the compost pile and initiating aerobic decomposition. Salatin has spared himself the labor of moving the manure out of the barn and instead gets the pigs to help him finish the compost. Strategies like these help Salatin save on equipment and fossil fuels while improving overall livestock health.

Salatin also prides himself on the taste of the products his farm produces. People drive from miles around to purchase eggs, chicken, and other products that are considered to be flavorful because of the animals' varied diet and exercise. He also sells to buying clubs and restaurants that pay a premium for his products because of consumer demand. Salatin calls this "relationship marketing." He sees himself in relationships with the people who purchase his products. Salatin has written several books about organic agriculture.

Daniel Salmon (1850–1914)

Daniel Salmon received the first Doctorate in Veterinary Medicine awarded in the United States, from Cornell University in 1876. He was pivotal to understanding animal diseases, especially those in food animals such as cattle and hogs. His research was mainly focused on lung diseases in cattle, and he is credited with eliminating contagious bovine pleuropneumonia from the United States. He was the first director of USDA's Bureau of Animal Husbandry and remained its leader for 21 years.

Salmonella bacteria are named after Daniel Salmon because it was discovered in his lab, although not by him. His laboratory assistant, Dr. Theobald Smith, is credited with discovering the bacterium, but Salmon took the naming rights. This created friction between the two, as Smith was angered by the lack of credit for the work he did. Historical records suggest this was the classic case of a senior researcher taking credit for work completed by their assistants. Smith went on to a brilliant career in microbiology and appears to have been more well respected by his peers than Salmon ever was.

Salmon is credited with creating the first procedures for meat inspection in the United States and for establishing policies to minimize the spread of disease from cattle being imported into the country. He was also president of the American Public Health Association and the American Veterinary Medical Association. He resigned from the USDA because of questions surrounding a partnership he had with a company that manufactured meat inspection labels. Even though this scandal marred his career at USDA, he remains an important historical figure in food safety.

Upton Sinclair (1878–1968)

Upton Sinclair was born in Baltimore, Maryland. Although both his parents came from middle- and upper middle-class backgrounds, his father was an unsuccessful salesman. His lack of success propelled the family into poverty. Sinclair lived in bug-ridden boarding houses with his parents and later alternated between this environment and Baltimore society with his mother's well-off relatives. Sinclair's father turned more and more to alcohol, and Sinclair was often sent to bars to retrieve his father. The contrast between his luxurious existence with his relatives and the poverty he saw with his parents led to a great social awareness and a desire to increase social justice. After completing college at 18, he became a hack writer of young men's adventure stories. He was interested in social issues, however, and his early serious novels began to show evidence of his conversion to socialism.

In 1904, Sinclair was commissioned by a widely circulating socialist weekly, *Appeal to Reason*, to investigate labor conditions in the Chicago stockyards. With a $500 stipend, he spent seven weeks in Chicago and returned to Princeton, New Jersey, to write *The Jungle*. The novel documented alarmingly unsanitary conditions in the Chicago stockyards and the hard life of the immigrants who worked there. In 1905, it was serialized in *Appeal to Reason*. Although enormously popular in serial form, Sinclair had a difficult time getting the novel published in book form. It was rejected by several book publishers, and Sinclair prepared to publish it himself. Doubleday finally agreed to publish it if the conditions Sinclair wrote about could be adequately documented. They sent a lawyer to Chicago, who was able to substantiate Sinclair's findings.

In 1906, *The Jungle* was published. Within two months, it was selling in the United Kingdom and had been translated into 17 languages. People were outraged at the lax standards for processing meat. The publicity that Sinclair created was enough to get the pure food and drug bill and the beef inspection bill passed. This legislation had originally been proposed in 1902, but it took public sentiment and pressure from President Roosevelt to get the bills passed in 1906.

In Sinclair's later life, he continued to write novels about a variety of social issues. He ran for state office in California, running for governor in 1934 with the slogan "End Poverty in California." He was narrowly defeated and retired from politics. Although Sinclair wrote about many social issues, he is best known for *The Jungle*; he had more impact on the food safety issue than any other issue he was concerned about.

Theobald Smith (1859–1934)

Theobald Smith was a brilliant microbiologist who made some of the most significant contributions to understanding how disease spreads to people from insects and animals. He was the only son of German immigrants in Albany, New York. He earned a scholarship to attend Cornell University and after graduating with honors, went on to earn an M.D. from Albany Medical College. He chose to pursue a career in medical research rather than clinical practice and took a job with the new USDA Bureau of Animal Husbandry after graduation.

Daniel Salmon was the head of the Bureau. He assigned Smith to work on swine diseases, but Smith eventually turned his attention to Texas cattle fever and published *Investigations into the Nature, Causation and Prevention of Texas or Southern Cattle Fever* in 1893. His conclusion on the cause of this disease that was severely affecting cattle was a parasite spread by a tick. His discovery and publication is credited with saving the cattle industry from ruin at the time.

Smith is known to have discovered the *Salmonella* bacteria species, although Daniel Salmon took credit for this discovery. This created animosity between the two, and Smith left the Bureau in 1895 to take positions at Harvard and with the Massachusetts State Board of Health, the nation's first public health department. Smith finished his career as the director of the animal pathology laboratory at the Rockefeller Institute for Medical Research in Princeton, New Jersey.

He is described as the first American to be prominent in the field of microbiology. His work was monumental in understanding pathogens in water, milk, and food. Smith's impeccable research accomplishments are likely the most important reason that medical science is seen as an important contributor to public health.

John Snow (1813–1858)

John Snow was born to working-class parents in York, England. He apprenticed to be a doctor in Newcastle at the age of 14. Even as an apprentice, he was known for his keen observations and the extensive notebooks he kept filled with scientific theories and observations. When he was 18, a cholera epidemic struck England, killing 50,000 people. Dr. Hardcastle, Snow's supervising doctor, was overwhelmed with patients and sent Snow to help the coal miners in a nearby town. But Snow had only bloodletting, laxatives, and brandy as available treatment options, and these had no effect.

At 23, Snow entered the Hunterian School of Medicine in the Soho area of London. After medical school, Snow started a practice in Soho instead of returning to his hometown, as was the traditional way to start a practice. As a result, his practice grew slowly. He occupied his time doing medical research, studying respiration, asphyxiation, and carbon monoxide poisoning. In 1846, news of the medical value of ether to induce unconsciousness reached England, and Snow was intrigued about the possibilities for surgery. Snow began a systematic study of many species of animals and human surgery patients using precise doses of ether and chloroform to determine safe levels of use. He became the leading practitioner of anesthesiology in his day and even anesthetized Queen Victoria in 1853 for the birth of her eighth child.

Aside from his considerable contributions to anesthesiology, Snow is also considered the father of epidemiology. Another major cholera epidemic broke out in London in 1848. Snow was convinced that cholera was waterborne and caused by tiny parasites in the water and not by the poison gases (called miasmas at the time) that most scientists and policy makers believed caused the disease. Although the discovery of the microscope in the 1600s showed that microscopic life existed, the germ theory was not well established until the 1860s, when Louis Pasteur conducted his experiments.

Snow did not have the means to show the cause of the disease, so he systematically traced the path of the disease. Snow collected data on where the cholera victims lived, where they got their water, and other factors. He published the results in the pamphlet "On the Mode of Communication of Cholera." So as not to antagonize his readers, Snow downplayed the parasite theory and instead indicated the cause was an unknown poison that could multiply in water. The pamphlet was largely ignored, so Snow gave lectures to try to generate support for his ideas, while continuing to gather data that showed how the pattern of disease was linked to particular water supplies. By the time the epidemic had run its course, 50,000 people were dead throughout Great Britain.

When cholera reemerged in 1853, Snow traced water supplies from two water companies that drew their water from the Thames. One of them was near an area of sewage outflows, and one was upstream of the sewage outflows. During the same epidemic, Snow noted that many of the cases occurred near the Broad Street pump. He was able to convince officials to remove the pump handle, even though they did not believe the water causing the disease. Later, he was vindicated when it was determined that sewage from a nearby cesspool was leaking into the well supplying the pump. Snow's ideas were still not well accepted when he died of a stroke in 1858, but he is revered today as the father of epidemiology and his methods and story are the foundation of public health.

David Theno (1950–)

David Theno grew up in rural northern Illinois, raising farm animals. Although he was planning to be a veterinarian, he found himself enjoying the blend of science and business in the Animal Sciences and Foods Group at the University of Illinois. When he was invited to stay for a doctorate degree within the group, he skipped veterinary school and earned a Ph.D. in muscle biology in 1977. As a food professional implementing new technologies, Theno earned the reputation as an effective problem solver. Within a few years, he was working at Armour Foods as the director of product quality and technology, where he applied a troubleshooter's eye to continually making food processing safer. While at Foster Farms in the 1980s, Theno developed and implemented the first comprehensive HACCP system in the poultry industry and was able to decrease *Salmonella* counts to less than one-third the counts at other plants.

Theno started a consulting business, designing and implementing HACCP systems for companies all over the country. When tainted hamburger served at Jack-in-the-Box restaurants in 1993 sickened hundreds and killed four toddlers, Theno was asked to take over food safety operations. By 1994, Jack-in-the-Box, under Theno's direction, had implemented HACCP standards that exceeded the Model Food Code of the FDA.

Theno is currently the CEO of Gray Dog Partners, Inc., which is a consulting firm specializing in food safety and restaurant operations. He also has been active in the USDA's National Advisory Committee on Microbiological Criteria for

Foods, the National Cattlemen's Beef Association's Beef Industry Food Safety Council, and the National Livestock and Meat Board's Blue Ribbon Task Force for "Solving the *E. coli* O157:H7 Problem." In 2016, he was hired by Chipotle to help them manage a series of outbreaks.

Harvey Wiley (1844–1930)

Harvey Wiley was born in a log cabin on a frontier Indiana farm. His father, Preston Wiley, was a teacher at a subscription school. Wiley began going to school at age 4 and learned to read through his father's instruction. He attended Hanover College and served in the army during the U.S. Civil War. Wanting to become a doctor to help people, Wiley enrolled in medical school, where he became interested in preventative medicine. He believed that an essential part of living a healthy life was eating healthful food. He also believed that moderate eating was important for health.

Wiley demonstrated a talent for analytical chemistry in college and medical school and never practiced medicine. He earned a doctorate degree in chemistry from Harvard University and became a researcher and professor at Northwestern Christian College and Purdue University. At Northwestern Christian, Wiley taught chemistry with student labs, something novel at that time. At Purdue University, Wiley became the state chemist for Indiana and studied the syrup and sugar produced by the hydrolysis of cornstarch. This corn sugar was frequently used as a cheap adulterant for cane and maple syrup products. At that time, there were no regulations requiring accurate labeling of contents. Wiley lobbied the Indiana state legislature to require manufacturers to label contents.

In 1883, Wiley was offered an appointment with the USDA as a chemist. He was hired to help establish a U.S. sugar industry, but he continued to be interested in food purity issues. Mainly through his work, pure food bills were introduced in Congress throughout the 1880s and 1890s, but none passed.

One of the leading chemists of the day, he helped found the Association of Official Analytical Chemists in 1891, which still offers an award in his name.

In 1902, Wiley organized a volunteer team of healthy young men called "The Poison Squad," who volunteered to eat all their meals in Wiley's special kitchen. Wiley gave the men large doses of the preservatives and adulterants in common use at the time to determine what ill effects they might cause. Testing one substance at a time, Wiley was able to demonstrate the unhealthful effects of many substances.

The Poison Squad garnered considerable publicity. Upton Sinclair's book *The Jungle* came out in 1906, exposing the unsanitary conditions in the nation's meat packing plants. The steady pressure from Wiley, coupled with increasing public pressure, led to the passage of the Pure Food and Drug Act of 1906. Wiley was appointed to oversee the administration of the act and stayed in government service until 1912.

Recruited by *Good Housekeeping* in 1912, Wiley set up the magazine's Bureau of Foods, Sanitation, and Health. He lobbied for tougher government inspection of meat, pure butter unadulterated by water, and unadulterated wheat flour, which growers were mixing with other grains. At *Good Housekeeping*, his bureau analyzed food products and published its findings. They gave the *Good Housekeeping* "Tested and Approved" seal to those products that met their standards of purity.

Before his death in 1930 at the age of 86, Wiley authored a number of books; contributed to the passage of the maternal health bill, which allocated federal funds for improved infant care; and helped secure legislation to keep refined sugar pure and unadulterated.

Craig Wilson (1948–)

Craig Wilson was working at Frigoscandia in Redmond, Washington, in 1993 when four children died and many more got sick from eating tainted hamburger at Jack-in-the-Box restaurants. Some of the children were friends of his own children. Frigoscandia manufactures equipment for a variety of applications, including food processing. Wilson understood the mechanism of the *E. coli* O157:H7 poisoning: bacteria that are often present in the gut of cows had gotten onto the carcass during processing and had tainted pounds of hamburger when the carcass was ground up. *E. coli* O157:H7 is so virulent that as little as one bacterial organism can cause illness. If bacteria from one animal contaminate a carcass, it can affect thousands of pounds of meat, because hamburger is processed in such large batches.

Wilson decided that what was needed was a better way to treat carcasses so that even if some bacteria got onto the carcass, the bacteria could be killed before the meat was ground up. Wilson came up with the idea of steaming the carcasses in a quick burst. The process would be long enough to kill any bacteria contaminating the surface but not long enough to cook the meat.

Wilson approached one of Frigoscandia's customers, Cargill, one of the largest meat processors in the world. Cargill's Jerry Leising worked with Wilson, and together they approached Randy Phebus at Kansas State University. The three of them were able to turn Wilson's idea into a commercially viable process. Wilson stayed at Frigoscandia until 1998, when he joined Costco as the director of food safety.

At Costco, Wilson has involved the entire company in food safety. Every Costco employee must take a basic food safety training course, and managers take a 22-hour home-study course followed by a 4-hour in-house training and exam. Costco's food safety manual is online so that every department has access to the manual should a food safety question arise. Wilson has taken care to make sure that every section of the manual is understandable to the high school graduates that Costco hires. In many cases, Costco uses more stringent standards than the U.S. government requires. Costco maintains a quality assurance laboratory in Washington State, where the microbiological quality of food product samples is tested from all over the country. Food quality specialists also do thorough audits of their vendors to ensure that safety is a priority.

Organizations

Many organizations around the world are working to improve food safety at local, national, and international levels. Most local, regional, and national governments have agencies that specifically promote food safety by making and enforcing laws and regulations. Nonprofit organizations worldwide are committed to food safety improvements, although they don't always agree about how improvements should be accomplished. For some of the organizations listed here, food safety is their primary focus. For others, food safety fits in with their general focus on consumer, humanitarian, or environmental issues. There are also many trade organizations promoting specific foods and include food safety as part of their mission. Most of these organizations have websites that can be found by entering the specific food item and the word "board" or "commission" in a search engine (e.g., "egg board").

Nonprofit, Trade, and Professional Organizations

Academy of Nutrition and Dietetics

The American Dietetic Association was founded in 1917 and changed its name in 2012 to the Academy of Nutrition and Dietetics. The Academy is the primary professional organization of U.S. dieticians, representing more than 100,000 credentialed practitioners; about 70 percent of its members are registered dieticians or registered dietician nutritionists. Although the emphasis is on nutrition in general, food safety is an area of interest. The association publishes *The Journal of the Academy of Nutrition and Dietetics.*

Alliance for the Prudent Use of Antibiotics

The Alliance for the Prudent Use of Antibiotics (APUA) is located at Tufts University Medical School. The Alliance conducts research and surveillance projects to define resistance patterns and trends in antibiotic prescriptions and develops strategies to curb antibiotic resistance and improve antibiotic use. Although much of the organization's efforts are directed toward overuse in humans, APUA also has a research and educational program about animal agriculture. The APUA has 65 international chapters; one of its programs provides technical assistance and small research grants to research teams in developing countries for work on antimicrobial resistance.

American Council on Science and Health

The American Council on Science and Health (ACSH) was founded to ensure science is used to inform decisions that affect the environment and public health. The organization is in direct opposition to groups such as the Environmental Working Group and the Center for Science in the Public Interest. The ACSH is funded from private foundations, corporations, donations, and sales of publications. The Council publishes reports, opinions, and blogs on a wide variety of food, health, and environmental topics.

American Public Health Association

The American Public Health Association (APHA) has more than 50,000 members representing dozens of occupations in public health. The APHA helps set public health standards, works with national and international health agencies to improve health worldwide, and provides public health professionals with resources for professional exchange, study, and action. Two of these practice sections have particular application to food safety: the Food and Nutrition Section contributes to long-range planning in food, nutrition, and health policy; and the Epidemiology Section works to disseminate new scientific information to improve development, implementation, and evaluation of policies impacting public health. The APHA publishes the refereed *American Journal of Public Health* and the newspaper *The Nation's Health*.

Association of Food and Drug Officials

Established in 1896, the Association of Food and Drug Officials (AFDO) is one of the oldest nongovernmental organizations involved in food safety. Today, it is an international organization devoted to streamlining regulation and resolving public health and consumer protection issues related to the regulation of foods, drugs, medical devices, and consumer products. Members include local, state, and federal regulators, as well as representatives from academia and industry. The AFDO works to bring together regulators, industry, trade, and consumer organizations to design regulations. The AFDO publishes a *Directory of State and Local Officials* on their website.

Association of Public Health Laboratories

The APHL is comprised of close to 800 member laboratories involved in analyzing specimens to support public health decision making. Key programs of the APHL include developing laboratory standards, assisting in outbreak detection, and training member laboratories on state-of-the-art techniques. In 1996, the APHL cofounded the nationwide foodborne disease surveillance network PulseNet. The APHL is also currently involved in sequencing the genome of the *Listeria* bacteria, which is a leading cause of foodborne illness.

Association of State and Territorial Health Officials

The Association of State and Territorial Health Officials (ASTHO) represents administrators of public health agencies and professionals in all 50 states, U.S. territories, and the District of Columbia. Its history traces back to the late 1800s with the National Conference of State Boards of Health; however, it was incorporated in 1942. The ASTHO has a wide range of programs designed to assist state agencies with implementing public health laws and regulations. In addition, it has a series of policy and position papers on numerous public health issues, including environmental health. As a result of the passage of the FSMA, the ATSHO reconvened its Food Safety Advisory Group to contribute to implementing the law.

Center for Food Safety

The Center for Food Safety (CFS) was established in 1997 and focuses on protecting the environment and human health from industrial food production. The CFS uses litigation as a significant means to accomplish their goals; in particular, one of their main issues is eliminating existing and fighting against new genetically modified organisms. The CFS has offices in Washington, D.C., and San Francisco, CA. The CFS offers free membership and encourages members to be active and fighting against genetically modified organisms, pesticides, and many other food issues.

Center for Science in the Public Interest

The Center for Science in the Public Interest (CSPI) is a non-profit education and advocacy organization with a focus on improving the safety and nutritional quality of the food supply. Some of the organization's projects include working to reduce antibiotic use in animals, calling for stronger international food safety rules, monitoring new additives, encouraging consumers to consider the impact of their food choices on the environment, and working to reduce soda consumption in children. The CSPI has more than 900,000 members and produces the *Nutrition Action Letter*, which keeps its members abreast of food safety and nutrition issues.

Consumers Union

Since its founding in 1936, Consumers Union has been a highly regarded nonprofit testing and information organization serving consumers only. Its mission is to test products, inform the public, and protect consumers. It publishes *Consumer Reports*, testifies on behalf of consumers before state and federal legislative and regulatory bodies, petitions government agencies, and files lawsuits on behalf of the consumer interest. Active areas of interest include organic standards, food contaminants, genetically modified foods, pesticides, and labeling.

Council of State and Territorial Epidemiologists

The Council of State and Territorial Epidemiologists (CSTE) grew from the ASTHO in the 1950s. It is currently a stand-alone professional organization representing public health epidemiologists. One of the key programs of CSTE is its contribution to defining the list of notifiable diseases that is used by health departments across the country. Providing competency-based training as well as position statements to support the work of epidemiologists are examples of the work of the CSTE.

Council to Improve Foodborne Outbreak Response

The Council to Improve Foodborne Outbreak Response (CIFOR) was formed in 2005 by several federal, state, and local food safety agencies for the purpose of improving foodborne outbreak investigations. Eleven organizations comprise the Council, including the AFDO, Centers for Disease Control and Prevention, and the National Environmental Health Association (NEHA). The CIFOR has developed *Guidelines for Foodborne Disease Outbreak Response* and offers training to orient food safety professionals to these guidelines. One useful feature of their web presence is the Clearinghouse, which is a searchable database of key food safety organizations and resources.

Environmental Defense

Established in 1967, Environmental Defense is an organization that brings together scientists, economists, and lawyers to formulate policies that work to support environmental rights. One food safety focus of Environmental Defense is minimizing pesticides and chemicals in foods, specifically through sustainable agriculture. Ensuring that food additives are adequately labeled and understood by the public is another project of Environmental Defense.

Environmental Health Specialists Network

The Environmental Health Specialists Network (EHS-Net) is comprised of environmental health specialists in federal governmental agencies and state and local health agencies with a common goal of addressing the environmental conditions that lead to foodborne illness. The federal government has been providing funding on five-year cycles to state and local health agencies since 2000. Funded partners investigate environmental causes of foodborne illness.

Environmental Working Group

The Environmental Working Group (EWG) was formed in 1993, and one of their main initiatives is to investigate environmental contamination of food, water, and a wide range of consumer products. In the realm of food safety, the EWG is immersed in the debate about genetically modified foods and specifically advocates labeling all foods that have been genetically modified.

Food Allergy Research and Education

FARE was formed in 2012 when the Food Allergy & Anaphylaxis Network and the Food Allergy Initiative merged. FARE works to increase food allergy and anaphylaxis awareness by contacts with media, education, advocacy, and research efforts. They host an annual conference with food allergy experts, conduct monthly webinars, influence policy makers to accommodate people with allergies through regulations, and created the Food Allergy Awareness Week.

Food Animals Concern Trust

The Food Animals Concern Trust (FACT) has been a nonprofit since 1982 with a major emphasis on humane treatment of farm animals. This treatment includes eliminating the need for and use of antibiotics in livestock. The FACT organizes campaigns that mobilize people to write to legislators in support of humane farming. In addition, the FACT provides small grants to farmers who are interested in using sustainable approaches and innovative methods to raise livestock.

Food and Water Watch

Food and Water Watch spun from Ralph Nader's Public Citizen in 2005. It is a grassroots group that organizes protests against activities that threaten the food and water supplies. Current food-related initiatives include advocating against corporate control of food. They are also involved in calling for labels on foods that contain genetically-modified organisms.

Food Marketing Institute

The Food Marketing institute represents food retail establishments. It is a membership-based organization that includes more than 1,225 members covering about 40,000 retail food stores. FMI has been an advocate for food retailers since 1977 and offers a Center for Retail Food Safety and Defense. This Center includes resources such as webinars, "backgrounders" on specific food substances, and best practice guides. The Institute also offers online training called "SafeMark" that educates food handlers and managers about the Food Code.

Food Research Institute

The Food Research Institute has been housed in the University of Wisconsin–Madison since 1966, when it moved from the University of Chicago. The Institute is interdisciplinary and includes students, faculty, and other researchers who work with industry regulators, academia, and consumers on food safety issues. The FRI provides information, expertise, and education and training in food safety. A main emphasis of the FRI is to conduct basic and applied research on food-associated illnesses caused by bacteria, molds, and viruses

Food Safety Preventive Controls Alliance

Housed at the Illinois Institute of Technology and formed in 2011, the Food Safety Preventive Controls Alliance (FSPCA) is a public-private partnership that is financially supported by the FDA. The Alliance focuses on designing and delivering training programs for the FSMA. One of their premier courses is the Preventive Controls course that focuses on many key components of the FSMA, including hazard analysis, verification, and prerequisite programs. The FSPCA also hosts regular webinars related to food safety and FSMA implementation.

Friends of the Earth

Friends of the Earth (FOE) is an international environmental organization working to preserve the health and diversity of the planet for future generations. FOE seeks to reduce or eliminate the use of pesticides, eliminate genetically modified crops, and encourage raising free-range animals instead of factory farming.

Global Resource Action Center for the Environment

Established in 1996, Global Resource Action Center for the Environment (GRACE) works with research, policy, and grassroots organizations to preserve the future of the planet and protect the quality of the environment. One of GRACE's main projects is Sustainable Table, which focuses on eliminating factory farms in favor of local sustainable food production systems that are healthful, economically viable, environmentally sound, and humane. It also provides a listing of restaurants, farms, and markets that are sources of sustainable food in their *Eat Well Guide*.

Greenpeace USA

Greenpeace is an international environmental advocacy organization working on several food-related issues. They oppose genetically modified food and support segregation and labeling of genetically engineered foods so that consumers will be able to determine whether their foods have been genetically modified. They also argue for creating a sustainable food system that relies less on chemical-laden agricultural practices and more on "ecological farming."

Grocery Manufacturer's Association

The Grocery Manufacturer's Association (GMA) is the association representing food, beverage, and consumer product companies. The GMA is active in rule making on major federal food safety legislation, including the Food Safety Modernization Act (FSMA), specifically as these regulations pertain to the industry. Trainings and educational opportunities for its members are an important component of the GMA's mission.

Institute of Food Science and Technology

The Institute of Food Science and Technology (IFST) is an independent professional group of food scientists and technologists in Europe. The Institute publishes position papers on a variety of food safety issues and promotes the application of science and technology to all aspects of the supply of safe, wholesome, nutritious, and attractive food. The IFST publishes *Food Science and Technology* and the *International Journal of Food Science and Technology*.

Institute of Food Technologists

The Institute of Food Technologists (IFT) seeks to advance the science and technology of food through the exchange of knowledge and also to be recognized as an advocate for science of food-related issues. A professional organization of food technologists, the Institute sponsors conferences and publishes four journals: *Food Technology Magazine, The Journal of Food Science, The Journal of Food Science Education,* and *Comprehensive Reviews in Food Science and Food Safety.*

Joint Institute for Food Safety and Applied Nutrition

The Joint Institute for Food Safety and Applied Nutrition (JIFSAN) is a collaboration between the FDA and the University of Maryland. Since 1996, it has been involved in multidisciplinary research and education, specifically focused on risk analysis, student engagement, and the International Food Safety Training Laboratory (IFTL). The IFTL is located at the University of Maryland research park and is a 4,600-square-foot facility that focuses extensively for training in laboratory analysis of food-related issues.

National Association of County & City Health Officials

The National Association of County & City Health Officials (NACCHO) was formed in the 1960s as an organization to represent local health departments, advocate for resources, and build capacity to protect public health. Public Health Accreditation is becoming an increasingly common goal of many local agencies, and the NACCHO is providing resources to assist in obtaining accreditation. In terms of food safety, the NACCHO has a number of demonstration projects in which they assisted local health departments in implementing innovative tools to improve their programs.

National Association of State Departments of Agriculture

Since 1916, the National Association of State Departments of Agriculture (NASDA) has represented administrators of state agriculture agencies who are the lead state regulators as well. One of the main activities of the NASDA is in their cooperative program with the National Agricultural Statistics Service in collecting data across the country related to a wide range of information that is critical to the agricultural industry. The

FSMA is a new priority of the NASDA and they are defining ways in which to help farmers comply with the prevention provisions outlined in FSMA.

National Environmental Health Association

A national professional society for environmental health practitioners, the NEHA offers credentialing programs, including the Certified Food Safety Professional. The certification requires a combination of education, experience, and passage of an exam. The association publishes the *Journal of Environmental Health.*

National Restaurant Association

The National Restaurant Association was established in 1923 to educate and represent its members and to promote the restaurant industry. Although the association has many activities, food safety is a priority. The association's education foundation created the ServSafe food safety training course in the 1970s. The program is recognized and accepted by more federal, state, and local jurisdictions than any other food safety education and training program.

Natural Resources Defense Council

The Natural Resources Defense Council (NRDC) uses law, science, and the efforts of its more than 1.2 million members to protect wildlife and open spaces and ensure a safe and healthy environment for all living things. As part of this effort, the NRDC lobbies against pesticides and supports organic farming methods, pesticide reduction, and reduction of wastes from farms into water sources.

NSF International

NSF International, formerly known as the National Sanitation Foundation, was founded in 1944 as an independent nonprofit organization to develop sanitation standards, provide education, and perform third-party conformity audits. One of its largest programs is the NSF certification program. Manufacturers can submit their products to NSF for testing. If the product meets NSF standards, the NSF mark is placed on the product. NSF enforces the standards of the mark and will take legal action against companies if the products later fail to meet NSF standards.

Organic Consumers Association

Formerly known as the Pure Food Campaign, the Organic Consumers Association claims to represent more than two million members and several thousand organic food business members. The association works to promote organic and sustainable farming worldwide. Areas of particular concern for the organization are genetically engineered food, bovine growth hormone, irradiation, and fair trade. Goals include 30 percent organic agriculture in the United States by 2015 and subsidies for organic farmers at the same rates as conventional farmers. They are also focusing on campaigns against agribusiness and in favor of raw milk.

Partnership for Food Safety Education

The Partnership for Food Safety Education was created in 1997 as a public-private partnership of industry, consumer, and government agencies concerned about food safety. The Partnership has created an educational campaign to teach children, the general public, and people at high risk for foodborne illness about ways to improve food safety. The campaign, called Fight Bac!, is divided into four elements, cook, clean, separate, and chill, with messages for different age groups.

Pesticide Action Network

The Pesticide Action Network (PAN) works to replace pesticides with ecologically sound alternatives worldwide The North American component of PAN was founded in 1982 to link to promote healthier, more effective pest management. The network uses education, media, demonstration projects, and international advocacy campaigns to promote pesticide alternatives. The PAN is involved in numerous campaigns such as reducing pesticides in McDonald's potatoes, improving school lunches, fighting against genetically modified organisms, and taking efforts to protect honeybees,

Pew Charitable Trusts—Safe Food Project

Pew Charitable Trusts is a global nonprofit that focuses on improving public policy and informing the public of important issues. The Trust was started in 1948 by heirs to the founder of Sun Oil Company and has grown into seven individual charitable funds. Research conducted by the organization in the realm of food safety includes analyzing the government's role and investigating foodborne outbreaks. It also provides grants to conduct independent research.

Produce Safety Alliance

In 2010, Cornell University entered into a Cooperative Agreement with the FDA to support implementation of the components of the FSMA related to produce safety. The Produce Safety Alliance (PSA) has provided several training programs to farmers and others who are directly affected by the FSMA. The initial cooperative agreement was set to be in place for three years; however, in 2016 the PSA is still active and offers curriculum materials, implementation resources, and guidance to produce growers.

Public Citizen

Ralph Nader founded Public Citizen in 1971 to be the consumer's eyes and ears in Washington. Public Citizen has broad interests; two of its areas of concern are food safety and food irradiation. Ensuring safe imported foods and requiring country-of-origin labeling are two of the food safety issues Public Citizen is working on.

Society for Nutrition Education and Behavior

A professional society, the Society for Nutrition Education and Behavior (SNEB) is dedicated to promoting healthy, sustainable food choices. Its members—nutrition educators—educate individuals, families, fellow professionals, and students and influence policy makers about nutrition, food, and health. The organization publishes the *Journal of Nutrition Education and Behavior.* The SNEB also developed competencies for nutrition educators.

Stone Barns Center for Food and Agriculture

The Stone Barns Center includes a farm, a restaurant, and educational facilities and programs. It is located in Pocantico Hills, New York, about an hour north of New York City. The land for the farm was donated by the Rockefeller family in 2003 and the nonprofit was formed. Stone Barns is unique in promoting sustainable agriculture because of its focus on educating farmers and the fact that it has an onsite restaurant.

STOP Foodborne Illness

STOP was founded in 1993 as a support organization for victims of foodborne illnesses and their families and has grown to be instrumental in passing legislation and educating the public about food safety. STOP changed its name to STOP Foodborne Illness and continues to fight for a wide range of food-related issues, including antibiotic use, carbon monoxide in food packaging, raw milk, and factory farming.

Union of Concerned Scientists

The Union of Concerned Scientists (UCS) is a nonprofit organization working to advance responsible public policy regarding technology. The UCS advocates sustainable agriculture policies and practices to reduce agriculture's impact on the environment and to ensure economic stability and food security. The organization's main goals include promoting agricultural practices that minimize pesticide, fertilizer, antibiotic, and energy use and researching and evaluating the risks and benefits of biotechnology in agriculture.

International Agencies and Organizations

Codex Alimentarius Commission

The Codex Alimentarius Commission was established in 1963 by the World Health Organization (WHO) and the Food and Agriculture Organization (FAO) to set international food standards aimed at enabling trade and protecting consumers. The commission has developed more than 200 standards for individual foods or groups of foods. It has also produced general standards for labeling of prepackaged foods, food hygiene, food additives, contaminants and toxins in food, irradiated food, maximum residue limits for pesticides and veterinary drugs, maximum limits for food additives and contaminants, and guidelines for nutrition labeling. Commission members include government officials, members of trade organizations, businesspeople, and representatives of consumer groups.

European Food Safety Authority

The European Food Safety Authority (EFSA) was established by the European Union in 2002 as an independent scientific body. The main focus of the EFSA is assessing risks from foods along the continuum of farm to fork. The EFSA offers guidance to EU member states about policies and legislation that could reduce risks of foodborne illness. The EFSA publishes an online, open access journal that offers scientific papers specifically related to risk assessments of food and food-related substances.

Food and Agriculture Organization

The FAO assesses and monitors the nutritional status of people all over the world and provides assistance and advice to improve nutrition for all. The FAO devotes many of its resources to helping the poor and vulnerable in developing countries. Food safety and standards, food quality, and food science are active programs of the FAO, and it sponsors research, disseminates information, and sponsors conferences in these areas. The FAO cosponsors with the WHO the Codex Alimentarius Commission, the international standards-setting body that regulates food sold internationally.

International Association for Food Protection

The International Association for Food Protection (IAFP) grew from the International Association of Milk Sanitarians, which held its first meeting in 1911. Today, the IAFP works to keep its members, food safety professionals, informed on the latest scientific, technical, and practical developments in food safety and sanitation. The association produces two publications: *Food Protection Trends*, the membership magazine with articles on applied research and current applications of technology, and *The Journal of Food Protection*, a refereed journal of food microbiology.

International Commission on Microbial Specifications for Food

The International Commission on Microbial Specifications for Food (ICMSF) is a nonprofit scientific advisory body of 20 members established under the auspices of the International Union of Microbiological Societies to address food microbiological concerns. Its main role is to serve as an objective scientific body to address international standards related to the use of microbiological methods in ensuring food safety. The commission advises national governments as well as international bodies such as Codex Alimentarius, WHO, and the United Nations Environment Program.

International Food Information Council Foundation

The International Food Information Council Foundation provides information about food safety and nutrition to consumers. It is funded by food, beverage, and agricultural companies but does not represent any product or company and does not lobby for legislative or regulatory action. Recent campaigns include debating the risks of caffeine, sugar consumption, and probiotics. The Council also conducts an annual survey about consumer attitudes toward food safety, nutrition, and health.

International Food Protection Training Institute

Even though the International Food Protection Training Institute (IFPTI) was created in 2009, helping the food industry comply with the FSMA is one of its key activities. The IFPTI offers training on several components of FSMA and partners with other organizations such as the FSPCA in training courses. The Institute is working with the FDA and other partners to develop a National Curriculum Standard based on both competencies such as leadership and communication and curriculum related to specific food safety issues.

World Health Organization

The WHO was founded in 1948. A specialized agency of the United Nations, the WHO promotes technical cooperation for health among nations and carries out programs to control and eradicate disease. The organization's safety program works to improve monitoring and control of foodborne hazards to reduce the incidence of disease. The WHO is the lead agency working to control international pandemics and has the latest information on controlling pandemic flu on its website. The WHO also cosponsors with FAO and Codex Alimentarius Commission.

U.S. Governmental Agencies

There are at least 15 federal government departments and agencies in the United States involved in food safety. The two main agencies are the USDA and the FDA. Table 4.1 summarizes the U.S. government involvement in food safety.

Table 4.1 Summary of U.S. Government Role in Food Safety

Department and/or Agency		Responsibilities
U.S. Department of Agriculture (USDA) http://www.usda.gov/	Food Safety Inspection Service (FSIS) http://www.fsis.usda.gov/wps/portal/fsis/home	Ensures safety of domestic meat, poultry, and egg products. Inspects facilities for compliance with the Federal Meat Inspection Act, Poultry Products Inspection Act, and the Egg Products Inspection Act.
	Animal and Plant Health Inspection Service (APHIS) https://www.aphis.usda.gov/aphis/home/	Protects and promotes U.S. agriculture, regulates genetically engineered organisms, administers the Animal Welfare Act, and responds to emergencies that could affect agriculture.
	Grain Inspection, Packers, and Stockyards Administration (GIPSA) https://www.gipsa.usda.gov/	Facilitates marketing of U.S. livestock, poultry, meats, cereals, oilseeds, and related agricultural products. Includes the Packers and Stockyards Program and the Federal Grain Inspection Service.
	Agricultural Marketing Service (AMS) https://www.ams.usda.gov/	Creates domestic and international marketing opportunities and sets quality standards for U.S. agricultural products. Enforces the Perishable Agricultural Commodities Act and the Seed Act.
	Agricultural Research Service (ARS) https://www.ars.usda.gov/	The scientific unit that conducts research related to agricultural products that affect public health. Facilitates technology transfer projects that propose innovative methods to solve agriculture problems.
	Economic Research Service (ERS) http://www.ers.usda.gov/	A statistical agency that provides research and economic analysis on agricultural issues. Extensively publishes reports about commodities, food safety, and global markets and trade and many others.

(continued)

Table 4.1 *(continued)*

Department and/or Agency		Responsibilities
	National Agricultural Statistics Service (NASS) https://www.nass.usda.gov/	Surveys and reports about U.S. agriculture. Produces reports by state and county level about all aspects of agriculture, including crops and livestock and offers data visualization of their reports.
	National Institute of Food and Agriculture (NIFA) https://nifa.usda.gov/	Authorized in the 2008 Farm Bill, the NIFA administers funding for scientific research. Works in collaboration with Land Grant Universities, nonprofit organizations, and private corporations.
Department of Health and Human Services (DHHS) http://www.hhs.gov/	Food and Drug Administration (FDA), Center for Food Safety and Applied Nutrition (CFSAN) http://www.fda.gov/	Primary agency for regulating veterinary drugs, food, and radiation under multiple laws. Responsible for domestic and imported foods except meat, poultry, and processed egg products. Regulations for HACCP, biotechnology, and labeling are also part of the CFSAN mandate.
	Centers for Disease Control and Prevention (CDC) http://www.cdc.gov/	A non-regulatory agency that supports food safety through research, epidemiology, and educational initiatives. Includes the epidemic intelligence service that responds to outbreaks.
Department of Commerce https://www.commerce.gov/	National Oceanic and Atmospheric Administration (NOAA) — National Marine Fisheries Service (NMFS) http://www.nmfs.noaa.gov/	Manages and regulates seafood from U.S.-managed fisheries, including setting catch limits and ensuring compliance through a permitting system. Works under the Marine Mammal Protection Act and the Endangered Species Act.

194

Environmental Protection Agency (EPA) https://www3.epa.gov/	Regulates pesticides, chemicals, and other toxins in the food supply and water supply. Operates under numerous federal laws directly and indirectly related to food safety, including animal feeding operations.
Department of the Treasury https://www.treasury.gov/	
Alcohol and Tobacco Tax Trade Bureau (TTB) https://www.ttb.gov/	Established under the Homeland Security Act of 2002. Enforces regulations for alcohol production, importation, wholesale, and labeling, and tobacco manufacturing and importing.
Department of Homeland Security (DHS) https://www.dhs.gov/	
Food, Agriculture, and Veterinary Defense Division (FAV Defense) https://www.dhs.gov/food-agriculture-and-veterinary-defense	Coordinating emergency response to threats to the U.S. food supply. Includes a Health Threats Resilience Division that operates an early warning system and coordinates the department's food, agriculture, and human and animal health programs.
Customs and Border Patrol (CBP) https://www.cbp.gov/	Inspects imports for plant pests, biological threats, select agents, and foreign diseases. Agricultural quarantine and inspection duties of imported goods were moved from APHIS to CBP in 2003.

Source: Adapted and updated from Government Accountability Office. 2014. *Federal Food Safety Oversight. Additional Actions Needed to Improve Planning and Collaboration.* GAO-15-180. http://www.gao.gov/assets/670/667656.pdf.

SANITARY INSPECTION GRADE

Card Number ___FA0031226___

Establishment Name ___PICCOLA CUCINA___

Date Issued ___2/10/2012___

Health

For additional information
or a copy of an inspection
report, call **311** or visit
nyc.gov/health

PICCOLA CUCINA

Three months ago, Sicilian brothers Philip and
Christian Guardione opened Piccola Cucina
in Soho. The infectiously positive Executive
Chef Philip oversees the menu while the
more reserved Christian keeps a low
file handling the business aspects. Among
The intimate Italian re...
focuses...

There is no shortage of information about food safety and foodborne illness available to the public. The vast amount of material creates challenges to identifying accurate, objective, and unbiased accounts of factors contributing to unsafe foods. It seems possible to find sources to validate every concern about dangerous food. In addition, some issues, such as genetically modified organisms and irradiation, are divisive pitting scientists against activists. These polarizing issues can confuse people about their safety, and this is especially the case when evidence-based research is still evolving. Nevertheless, there is evidence pinpointing the magnitude of foodborne illness; some of the data is highlighted below. Contemporary data is complemented by several pivotal documents that shaped food safety in the United States, both in the past and present.

Facts and Figures

Below are some selected facts about foodborne illness that were current as of 2016 unless otherwise noted. They are meant to provide

---

The letter "A" is shown as the Sanitary Inspection Grade for a restaurant in the SoHo neighborhood of New York, on May 28, 2012. The New York City Health Department conducts unannounced inspections of about 24,000 restaurants every year. Inspectors evaluate a range of food safety practices and assign points for compliance with regulations. The restaurant inspection score is calculated by summing the points, and lower scores indicate more compliance with regulations. The scores are converted to letter grades to inform consumers, and complete inspection results are available online. (AP Photo/Mark Lennihan)

197

a snapshot of foodborne illness. There is more detailed information on each of these subjects in Chapters 1 through 3.

1. Number of people affected by foodborne illness each year in the United States: 48 million illnesses, 300,000 hospitalizations, and 5,000 deaths.

    Source: https://www.cdc.gov/foodborneburden/

2. Most important causes of foodborne illness: *noroviruses, Campylobacter* spp., *Salmonella* spp., *E. coli* O157:H7, *Listeria monocytogenes, Staphylococcus aureus, Shigella, Toxoplasma gondii, Vibrio vulnificus.*

    Source: http://www.fightbac.org/food-poisoning/foodborne-pathogens/

3. Most common causes of foodborne illness: *noroviruses, Salmonella, Clostridium perfrigens, Campylobacter*

    Source: http://www.cdc.gov/foodsafety/foodborne-germs.html

4. Serotypes (strains) of *Salmonella*: 2,500+.

    Source: http://www.cdc.gov/salmonella/reportspubs/salmonella-atlas/serotyping-importance.html

5. Serotypes of *Salmonella* accounting for human infections: 100 or less.

    Source: http://www.cdc.gov/salmonella/reportspubs/salmonella-atlas/serotyping-importance.html

6. Number of known foodborne pathogens: 250.

    Source: http://www.cdc.gov/foodsafety/foodborne-germs.html

7. Federal agencies involved in food safety: 15.

    Source: http://www.gao.gov/key_issues/food_safety/issue_summary

8. Federal laws governing food safety: 30.

    Source: http://www.gao.gov/key_issues/food_safety/issue_summary

9. EPA-mandated inspection rate of laboratories developing pesticides for possible registration, 2009–2013: 4–6 percent of all eligible labs.

Source: http://www.gao.gov/assets/670/663236.pdf

10. Percent of foodborne illness from foods, 1998–2008:

Produce: 46 percent

Meat and poultry: 22 percent

Dairy and eggs: 20 percent

Fish and shellfish: 6.1 percent

Source: http://www.cdc.gov/foodborneburden/attribution-image.html#foodborne-illnesses

12. Percent of deaths from foodborne pathogens, 1998–2008:

Produce: 23 percent

Meat and poultry: 29 percent

Dairy and eggs: 15 percent

Fish and shellfish: 6.4 percent

Source: http://www.cdc.gov/foodborneburden/attribution-image.html#foodborne-illnesses

13. Number of foodborne outbreaks, 2010–2014: 4,163.

Source: http://www.cdc.gov/mmwr/preview/mmwrhtml/mm6443a4.htm

14. Number of multistate foodborne outbreaks, 2010–2014: 120.

Source: http://www.cdc.gov/mmwr/preview/mmwrhtml/mm6443a4.htm

15. Number of Shiga toxin *E. coli* infections every in United States: 265,000.

Source: http://www.cdc.gov/ecoli/general/

16. Percent of cases of *E. coli* O157:H7 that lead to serious kidney problems (hemolytic uremic syndrome [HUS]): 5–10 percent.

Source: http://www.cdc.gov/features/ecoliinfection/)

17. Number of farmers markets in the United States:

    1994: 1,755

    2004: 3,706

    2014: 8,284

    Source: www.ers.usda.gov/

18. Percent of human isolates of *Campylobacter jejuni* resistant to tetracycline:

    1997: 53 percent

    2002: 43 percent

    2007: 46 percent

    2013: 49 percent

    Source: http://www.fda.gov/AnimalVeterinary/SafetyHealth/AntimicrobialResistance/NationalAntimicrobialResistanceMonitoringSystem/default.htm

19. Percent of retail ground beef isolates of nontyphoidal *Salmonella* resistant to tetracycline:

    2002: 22 percent

    2007: 0 percent

    2013: 47 percent

    Source: http://www.fda.gov/AnimalVeterinary/SafetyHealth/AntimicrobialResistance/NationalAntimicrobialResistanceMonitoringSystem/default.htm

20. Estimate of medical costs associated with treating antibiotic-resistant *Salmonella* every year in the United States: $365,000,000.

    Source: http://www.cdc.gov/drugresistance/threat-report-2013/index.html

21. Percent of U.S. dairy cows treated with recombinant growth hormone:

    2002: 22 percent

    2014: 14 percent

Source: https://www.aphis.usda.gov/animal_health/nahms/
dairy/downloads/dairy14/Dairy14_dr_PartI.pdf

22. Percent of U.S. corn grown from genetically modified
    varieties in 2016: 79 percent.

    Source: http://www.ers.usda.gov/data-products/adoption-of-
    genetically-engineered-crops-in-the-us/recent-trends-in-
    ge-adoption.aspx

23. Percent of U.S. soybeans grown from genetically modified
    varieties in 2016: 94 percent.

    Source: http://www.ers.usda.gov/data-products/adoption-of-
    genetically-engineered-crops-in-the-us/recent-trends-in-
    ge-adoption.aspx

Data

*The following graph illustrates the disease trend for selected food-
borne illnesses. The relative rate is a change in incidence compared*

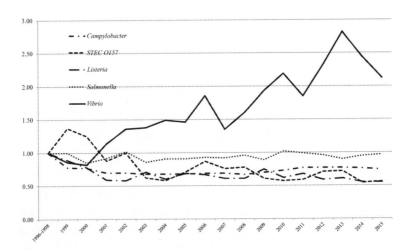

**Figure 5.1   Relative Rates of Culture-Confirmed Infections Compared to
1996–1998 Rates (CDC, www.cdc.gov/foodnet/reports/prelim-data-
2015.html)**

to the 1996–1998 period. The graph shows that rates of infections with Vibrio bacteria have increased the most, while change in incidence of other pathogens has remained relatively steady or reduced somewhat. This graphic does not suggest that Vibrio bacteria are a leading cause of foodborne illness; Salmonella and Campylobacter have higher annual incidence rates; however, it does identify Vibrio as an emerging problem.

Pesticide safety is tested in more an estimated 1,400 laboratories that are supposed to be inspected by EPA to ensure that they are following Good Laboratory Practices. Laboratory testing is a critical component of pesticide registration. However, as this table from a report of the Government Accountability Office shows, most labs are not being inspected because of resource constraints, among other factors.

Table 5.1 Summary of Pesticide-Related Activities of EPA

	2009	2010	2011	2012	2013
Number of pesticide studies submitted to EPA	7,791	10,093	8,715	8,326	7,123
Number of laboratory inspections	64	71	51	80	79
Number of lab inspectors (FTE)	8	8	5	4	4
Lab inspection budget	$1,415,000	$1,021,400	$959,5000	$734,500	$702,000

Source: GAO. 2014. *Pesticide Safety: Improvements Needed in EPA's Good Laboratory Practices Inspection Program.* GAO-14-289. http://www.gao.gov/assets/670/663236.pdf.

One of the most important ways to keep food safe is to understand the pathogens that are commonly associated with illness. Since many foodborne illnesses have similar symptoms, being aware of subtle differences and likely sources of pathogens could prevent additional cases. This table from the FDA is an excellent summary of important pathogens that commonly affect food and make people sick.

Table 5.2 Summary of Important Pathogens Affecting Food

Organism	Common Name of Illness	Onset Time after Ingesting	Signs and Symptoms	Duration	Food Sources
Bacillus cereus	B. cereus food poisoning	10–16 hours	Abdominal cramps, watery diarrhea, nausea	24–48 hours	Meats, stews, gravies, vanilla sauce
Campylobacter jejuni	Campylobacteriosis	2–5 days	Diarrhea, cramps, fever, and vomiting; diarrhea may be bloody	2–10 days	Raw and undercooked poultry, unpasteurized milk, contaminated water
Clostridium botulinum	Botulism	12–72 hours	Vomiting, diarrhea, blurred vision, double vision, difficulty in swallowing, muscle weakness. Can result in respiratory failure and death	Variable	Improperly canned foods, especially home-canned vegetables; fermented fish; baked potatoes in aluminum foil
Clostridium perfringens	Perfringens food poisoning	8–16 hours	Intense abdominal cramps, watery diarrhea	Usually 24 hours	Meats, poultry, gravy, dried or precooked foods, time and/or temperature-abused foods
Cryptosporidium	Intestinal cryptosporidiosis	2–10 days	Diarrhea (usually watery), stomach cramps, upset stomach, slight fever	May be remitting and relapsing over weeks to months	Uncooked food or food contaminated by an ill-food handler after cooking, contaminated drinking water
Cyclospora cayetanensis	Cyclosporiasis	1–14 days, usually at least 1 week	Diarrhea (usually watery), loss of appetite, substantial loss of weight, stomach cramps, nausea, vomiting, fatigue	May be remitting and relapsing over weeks to months	Various types of fresh produce (imported berries, lettuce, basil)
E. coli producing toxin	E. coli infection (common cause of "travelers' diarrhea")	1–3 days	Watery diarrhea, abdominal cramps, some vomiting	3–7 or more days	Water or food contaminated with human feces

(continued)

Table 5.2 (*continued*)

Organism	Common Name of Illness	Onset Time after Ingesting	Signs and Symptoms	Duration	Food Sources
E. coli O157:H7	Hemorrhagic colitis or *E. coli* O157:H7 infection	1–8 days	Severe (often bloody) diarrhea, abdominal pain, and vomiting. Usually, little or no fever is present. More common in children 4 years or younger. Can lead to kidney failure	5–10 days	Undercooked beef (especially hamburger), unpasteurized milk and juice, raw fruits and vegetables (e.g. sprouts), and contaminated water
Hepatitis A	Hepatitis	28 days average (15–50 days)	Diarrhea, dark urine, jaundice, and flu-like symptoms, i.e., fever, headache, nausea, and abdominal pain	Variable, 2 weeks to 3 months	Raw produce, contaminated drinking water, uncooked foods and cooked foods that are not reheated after contact with an infected food handler; shellfish from contaminated waters
Listeria monocytogenes	Listeriosis	9–48 hours for gastrointestinal symptoms, 2–6 weeks for invasive disease	Fever, muscle aches, and nausea or diarrhea. Pregnant women may have mild flu-like illness, and infection can lead to premature delivery or stillbirth. The elderly or immunocompromised patients may develop bacteremia or meningitis.	Variable	Unpasteurized milk, soft cheeses made with unpasteurized milk, ready-to-eat deli meats
Noroviruses	Variously called viral gastroenteritis, winter diarrhea, acute non-bacterial gastroenteritis, food poisoning, and food infection	12–48 hours	Nausea, vomiting, abdominal cramping, diarrhea, fever, headache. Diarrhea is more prevalent in adults; vomiting more common in children	12–60 hours	Raw produce, contaminated drinking water, uncooked foods and cooked foods that are not reheated after contact with an infected-food handler; shellfish from contaminated waters

Organism	Illness	Onset	Symptoms	Duration	Sources
Salmonella	Salmonellosis	6–48 hours	Diarrhea, fever, abdominal cramps, vomiting	4–7 days	Eggs, poultry, meat, unpasteurized milk or juice, cheese, contaminated raw fruits and vegetables
Shigella	Shigellosis or Bacillary dysentery	4–7 days	Abdominal cramps, fever, and diarrhea. Stools may contain blood and mucus.	24–48 hours	Raw produce, contaminated drinking water, uncooked foods and cooked foods that are not reheated after contact with an infected food handler
Staphylococcus aureus	Staphylococcal food poisoning	1–6 hours	Sudden onset of severe nausea and vomiting, abdominal cramps. Diarrhea and fever may be present.	24–48 hours	Unrefrigerated or improperly refrigerated meats, potato and egg salads, cream pastries
Vibrio parahaemolyticus	*V. parahaemolyticus* infection	4–96 hours	Watery (occasionally bloody) diarrhea, abdominal cramps, nausea, vomiting, fever	2–5 days	Undercooked or raw seafood, such as shellfish
Vibrio vulnificus	*V. vulnificus* infection	1–7 days	Vomiting, diarrhea, abdominal pain, blood-borne infection. Fever, bleeding within the skin, ulcers requiring surgical removal. Can be fatal to persons with liver disease or weakened immune systems	2–8 days	Undercooked or raw seafood, such as shellfish (especially oysters)

Source: http://www.fda.gov/Food/FoodborneIllnessContaminants/FoodborneIllnessesNeedToKnow/default.htm.

205

Documents

Upton Sinclair's *The Jungle* (1906)

In 1906, Upton Sinclair was a young socialist who set out to write a novel exposing the abuses of the meat-packing industry committed against immigrant workers. In the process of telling Americans about the horrible conditions under which the workers suffered, he also revealed the disgusting practices in Chicago's meat processing plants. He included stories of grinding up rats and sometimes workers' fingers with the sausage. The book became an immediate best-seller. Theodore Roosevelt was so sickened by what he read that he demanded and got the passage of a federal meat inspection bill.

The carcass hog was scooped out of the vat by machinery, and then it fell to the second floor, passing on the way through a wonderful machine with numerous scrapers, which adjusted themselves to the size and shape of the animal, and sent it out at the other end with nearly all of its bristles removed. It was then again strung up by machinery, and sent upon another trolley ride; this time passing between two lines of men, who sat upon a raised platform, each doing a certain single thing to the carcass as it came to him. One scraped the outside of a leg; another scraped the inside of the same leg. One with a swift stroke cut the throat; another with two swift strokes severed the head, which fell to the floor and vanished through a hole. Another made a slit down the body; a second opened the body wider; a third with a saw cut the breastbone; a fourth loosened the entrails; a fifth pulled them out—and they also slid through a hole in the floor. There were men to scrape each side and men to scrape the back; there were men to clean the carcass inside, to trim it and wash it. Looking down this room, one saw, creeping slowly, a line of dangling hogs a hundred yards in length; and for every yard there was a man, working as if a demon were after him. At the end of this hog's progress every inch of the carcass had been gone over several times, and then it was rolled into the chilling room, where it stayed for twenty-four hours, and where a stranger might lose himself in a forest of freezing hogs.

Before the carcass was admitted here, however, it had to pass a government inspector, who sat in the doorway and felt of the glands in the neck for tuberculosis. This government inspector did not have the manner of a man who was worked to death; he was apparently not haunted by a fear that the hog might get by him before he had finished his testing. If you were a sociable person, he was quite willing to enter into conversation with you, and to explain to you the deadly nature of the ptomaines which are found in tubercular pork; and while he was talking with you you could hardly be so ungrateful as to notice that a dozen carcasses were passing him untouched. This inspector wore an imposing silver badge, and he gave an atmosphere of authority to the scene, and, as it were, put the stamp of official approval upon the things which were done in Durham's.

Source: Upton Sinclair. *The Jungle.* New York: Doubleday, Page & Company, 1906.

Pure Food and Drug Act (1906)

Passed on June 30, 1906, the Pure Food and Drug Act was enacted in response to widespread public outrage over the lack of sanitation standards in the food and drug industry. It is considered the first federal food safety law and the basis for all subsequent legislation.

An Act for preventing the manufacture, sale, or transportation of adulterated or misbranded or poisonous or deleterious foods, drugs, medicines, and liquors, and for regulating traffic therein, and for other purposes.

Be it enacted by the Senate and House of Representatives of the United States of America in Congress assembled, That it shall be unlawful for any person to manufacture within any Territory or the District of Columbia any article of food or drug which is adulterated or misbranded, within the meaning of this Act; and any person who shall violate any penalty of the provisions of this section shall be guilty of a misdemeanor, and for each offense shall, upon conviction thereof, be fined not to exceed five hundred dollars or shall be sentenced to one year's imprisonment, or both such fine and imprisonment, in the discretion of the court, and for each subsequent offense and conviction thereof shall be fined not less than one thousand dollars or sentenced to one year's imprisonment, or both such fine and imprisonment, in the discretion of the court, Interstate, etc. . . .

SEC. 2. That the introduction into any State or Territory or the Disperce of adulterated or misbranded goods from any other State or Territory or the District of Columbia, or from any foreign country, or shipment to any foreign country of any article of food or drugs which is adulterated or misbranded, within the meaning of this Act, is hereby prohibited; and any person who shall ship or deliver for shipment from any State or Territory or the District of Columbia to any other State or Territory or the District of Columbia, or to a foreign country, or who shall receive in any State or Territory or the District of Columbia from any other State or Territory or the District of Columbia, or foreign country, and having so received, shall deliver, in original unbroken packages, for pay or otherwise, or offer to deliver to any other, person, any such article so adulterated or misbranded within the meaning of this Act, or any person who shall sell or offer for sale in the District of Columbia or the Territories of the United States any such adulterated or misbranded foods or drugs, or export or offer to export the same to any foreign country, shall be guilty of a misdemeanor, and for such offense be fined not exceeding two hundred dollars for title first offense, and upon conviction for each subsequent offense not exceeding three hundred dollars or be imprisoned not exceeding one year, or both, in the discretion of the court, provided that no article shall be deemed misbranded or adulterated within the provisions of this Act when intended for export to any foreign country and prepared or packed according to the specifications or directions of the foreign purchaser when no substance is used in the preparation or packing thereof in conflict with the laws of the foreign country to which said article is intended to be shipped; but if said article shall be in fact sold or offered for sale for domestic use or consumption, then this proviso shall not exempt said article from the operation of any of the other provisions of this Act.

SEC. 3. That the Secretary of the Treasury, the Secretary of Agriculture, and the Secretary of Commerce and Labor shall make uniform rules and regulations for carrying out the provisions of this Act, including the collection and examination of specimens of foods and drugs manufactured or offered for sale in the District of Columbia, or in any Territory of the United States or which shall be offered for sale in unbroken packages in any State other than that in which they shall have been respectively manufactured or produced, or which shall be received from any foreign country, or intended for shipment to any foreign country, or which may be submitted for examination by the chief health, food, or drug officer of any State, Territory, or the District of Columbia, or at any domestic or foreign port through which such product is offered for interstate commerce, or for export or import between the United States and any foreign port or country.

SEC. 4. That the examinations of specimens of foods and drugs shall Chemical examinations be made in the Bureau of Chemistry of the Department of Agriculture, or under the direction and supervision of such Bureau, for the purpose of determining from such examinations whether such articles are adulterated or misbranded within the meaning of this Act; and if Notice of result shall appear from any such examination that any of such specimens is adulterated or misbranded within the meaning of this Act, the Secretary of Agriculture shall cause notice thereof to be given to the party from whom such sample was obtained. Any party so notified shall be given opportunity to be heard, under such rules and regulations as may be prescribed as aforesaid, and if it appears that any of the provisions of this Act have been violated by such party, then the Secretary of Agriculture shall at once certify the facts to the proper United States district attorney, with a copy of the results of the analysis, the examination of such article duly authenticated by the analyst or officer making such examination, under the oath of such officer. After judgement of the court, notice shall be given by publication in such manner as may be prescribed by the rules and regulations aforesaid.

SEC. 5. That it shall be the duty of each district attorney to whom Legal proceedings. the Secretary of Agriculture shall report any violation of this Act, or to whom any health or food or drug officer or agent of any State, Territory, or the District of Columbia shall present satisfactory evidence of any such violation, to cause appropriate proceedings to be commenced and prosecuted in the proper courts of the United States, without delay, for the enforcement of the penalties as in such case herein provided.

SEC. 6. That the term "drug," as used in this Act, shall include all medicines and preparations recognized in the United States Pharmacopoeia or National Formulary for internal or external use, and any substance or mixture of substances intended to be used for the cure, mitigation, or prevention of disease of either man or other animals. The term "food," as used herein, shall include all articles used for food, drink, confectionery, or condiment by man or other animals, whether simple, mixed, or compound.

SEC. 7. That for the purposes of this Act an article shall be deemed to be adulterated: First. If, when a drug is sold under or by a name recognized or from recognized standards. . . . If it differs from the standard of strength, quality, or purity, as determined by the test laid down in the United States Pharmacopoeia or National Formulary official at the time of investigation: Provided, That no drug defined in the United States

Pharmacopoeia or National Formulary shall be deemed to be adulterated under this provision if the standard of strength, quality, or purity be plainly stated upon the bottle, box, or other container thereof although the standard may differ from that determined by the test laid down in the United States Pharmacopoeia or National Formulary.

Second. If its strength or purity fall below the professed standard of quality under which it is sold. In the Case of confectionery: If it contain terra alba; barytes, talc, chrome yellow, or other mineral narcotics, etc. Substance or poisorfous color or flavor, or other ingredient deleterious or detrimental to health, or any vinous, malt or spirituous liquor or compound or narcotic drug.

In the case of food: First. If any substance has been mixed and packed with it so as to reduce or lower or injuriously affect its quality or strength. Second. If any substance has been substituted wholly or in part for the article. Third. If any valuable constituent of the article has been Wholly or in part abstracted. Fourth. If it be mixed, colored, powdered, coated, or stained in a sealed manner whereby damage or inferiority is concealed. Fifth. If it contain any added poisonous or other added deleterious ingredient which may render such article injurious to health:

Provided, That when in the preparation of food products for shipment they are preserved by any external application applied in such manner that the preservative is necessarily removed mechanically, or bv maceration in water, or otherwise, and directions for the removal of said preservative shall be printed on the covering or the package, the provisions of this Act shall be construed as applying only when said products are ready for consumption.

Sixth. If it consists in whole or in part of a filthy decomposed or putrid animal or vegetable substance, or any portion of an animal unfit for food, whether manufactured or not, or if it is the product of a diseased animal, or one that has died otherwise than by slaughter.

SEC. 8. That the term "misbranded," as used herein, shall apply to all drugs, or articles of food, or articles which enter into the composition of food, the package or label of which shall bear any statement, design, or device regarding such article or the ingredients or substances contained therein which shall be false or misleading in any particular, and to any food or drug product which is falsely branded as to the State, Territory, or country in which it is manufactured or produced. That for the purposes of this Act an article shall also be deemed to be misbranded drugs. (In case of drugs: False name). First. If it be an imitation of or offered for sale under the name of another article: False contents. Second, If the contents of the package as originally put up shall have been removed, in whole or in part, and other contents shall have Failure to state narcotics been placed in such package, or if the package fail to bear a statement on the label of the quantity or proportion of any alcohol, morphine, opium, cocaine, heroin, alpha or beta eucain, chloroform, cannabis, chloral hydrate, or acetanilide, or any derivative or preparation of any such substances contained therein.

In the case of food: First. If it be an imitation of or offered for sale under the distinctive name of another article. Second. If it be labeled or branded so as to deceive or mislead the purchaser, or purport to be a foreign product when not so, or if the contents of the package as originally put up shall have been removed in whole or in part and other contents shall have been placed in such. Failure to state package, or if it fail to bear a statement on the label of the quantity narcotics, etc., used or proportion of any morphine, opium, cocaine, heroin, alpha or beta eucane, chloroform, cannabis indica, chloral hydrate, or acetanilide, or any derivative or preparation of any of such substances contained therein. Third. If in package formal and the contents are stated in terms of Incorrect weight or measure, they are not plainly and correctly stated on the outside of the package. Fourth. If the package containing it or its label shall bear any state leading in easiment, design, or device regarding the ingredients or the substances contained therein, which statement, design, or device shall be false or misleading in any particular: Preluded, That an article of food which does not contain any added poisonous or deleterious ingredients shall not be deemed to be adulterated or misbranded in the following cases:

First, In the case of mixtures or compounds which may be now or Compounds under from time to time hereafter known, as articles of food, under their own distinctive names, and not an imitation of or offered for sale under the distinctive name of another article, if the name be accompanied on the same label or brand with statement of the place where said article has been manufactured or produced. Second. In the case of articles labeled, branded, or tagged so as to plainly indicate that they are compounds, imitations, or blends, and plainly stated the word "compound," "imitation," or "blend," as the case may be, is plainly stated on the package in which it is offered for sale:

Provided, That the term blend as used herein shall be construed to mean a mixture of like substances, not excluding harmless coloring or flavoring ingredients used for the purpose of coloring and flavoring only: And provided, That nothing in this Act shall be construed as require compelling proprietors or manufacturers of proprietary foods which contain no unwholesome added ingredient to disclose their trade formulas, except in so far as the provisions of this Act may require to secure freedom from adulteration or misbranding.

SEC. 9. That no dealer shall be prosecuted under the provisions manufacturer Guarantee this Act when he can establish a guaranty signed by the wholesaler, jobber, manufacturer, or other party residing in the United States, from whom he purchases such articles, to the effect that the same is not adulterated or misbranded within the meaning of this Act, designating it. Said guarantee, to afford protection, shall contain the name and address of the party or parties making the sale of such articles to such dealer, and in such case said party or parties shall be amenable to the prosecutions, fines, and other penalties which would attach, in due course, to the dealer under the provisions of this Act.

SEC. 10. That any article of food, drug, or liquor that is adulterated or misbranded within the meaning of this Act, and is being transported from one State, Territory, District, or insular possession to another mercy for sale, or, having been transported, remains unloaded, unsold, or in original unbroken packages, or if it be sold or offered for sale in the District of Columbia or the Territories, or insular possessions of the United States, or if it be imported from a foreign country for sale, or if it is intended for export to a foreign country, shall be liable to be proceeded against in any district court of the United States within the district where the same is found, and seized for confiscation by a process of libel for condemnation. And if such article is condemned as being adulterated or misbranded, or of a poisonous or deleterious character, within the meaning of this Act, the same shall be disposed of by destruction or sale, as the said court say direct, and the proceeds thereof, if sold, less the legal costs and charges, shall be paid into the Treasury of the United States, but such goods shall not be sold in any jurisdiction contrary to the provisions of this Act or the laws of that jurisdiction: Provided, however, That upon the payment of the costs sufficient bond to the effect that such articles shall not be sold or otherwise disposed of contrary to the provisions of this Act, or the laws of any State, Territory, District, or insular possession, the court may by direct that such articles be delivered to the owner thereof.

SEC. 11. The Secretary of the Treasury shall deliver to the Secretary of Agriculture, upon his request from time to time, samples of foods and drugs which are being imported into the United States or offered for import, giving notice thereof to the owner or consignee, who may appear before the Secretary of Agriculture, and have the right to introduce testimony, and if it appear from the examination of such samples that any article of food or drug offered to be imported into the United States is adulterated or misbranded within the meaning of this Act, or is otherwise dangerous to the health of the people of the United States, or is of a kind forbidden entry into, or forbidden to be sold or restricted in sale in the country in which it is made or from which it is exported, or is otherwise falsely labeled, in any respect, the said article shall be reused admission, and the Secretary of the Treasury shall refuse delivery to the consignee and shall cause the destruction of any goods refused delivery which shall not be exported by the consignee within three months from the date of notice of such refusal under such regulations as the Secretary of the Treasury may prescribe: Provided, That the Secretary of the Treasury may deliver to the consignee such goods pending examination and decision in the matter on execution of a penal bond for the amount of the full invoice value of such goods, together with the duty thereon, and on refusal to return such goods for any cause to the custody of the Secretary of the Treasury, when demanded, for the purpose of excluding them from the country, or for any other purpose, said consignee shall forfeit the full amount of the bond. And provided further, That all charges for storage, cartage, and labor on goods which are refused admission or delivery shall be paid by the owner or consignee, and in default of such payment shall constitute a lien against any future importation made by such owner or consignee.

Source: Federal Food and Drugs Act of 1906. U.S. Statutes at Large 34 (1906): 768.

Rachel Carson's Testimony on Pesticide Use (1963)

Environmentalist Rachel Carson of Springdale, Pennsylvania, began researching the effects of chlorinated hydrocarbons in 1957 and published her findings in a classic book Silent Spring *in 1962. Her lectures to the Audubon Society and the Women's Press Club gained the attention of President John F. Kennedy. Her address to Congress proposed specific solutions to chemical spraying, specifically, the registration and control of pesticides. She crusaded for environmental health in the final months of her treatment for breast and liver cancer. She died without knowing the impact she had on government scrutiny of poisonous chemicals. From her testimony evolved a public demand for a ban on DDT and, in 1967 during the Johnson administration, the formation of the Environmental Defense Fund.*

Contamination of various kinds has now invaded all of the physical environment that supports us—water, soil, air, and vegetation. It has even penetrated that internal environment within the bodies of animals and of men. It comes from many sources—radioactive wastes from reactors, laboratories and hospitals, fallout from nuclear explosions, domestic wastes from cities and towns, chemical wastes from factories, detergents from homes and industries. When we review the history of mankind in relation to the earth we cannot help feeling somewhat discouraged, for that history is for the most part that of the blind or shortsighted despoiling of the soil, forests, waters, and all the rest of the earth's resources. We have acquired technical skills on a scale undreamed of even a generation ago. We can do dramatic things and we can do them quickly. By the time damaging side effects are apparent it is often too late or impossible to reverse our actions. . . .

There are several other recommendations I would like to suggest, bearing on various specific aspects of the immensely complex pesticide problem. These are as follows:

1. I hope this committee will give serious consideration to a much neglected problem—that of the right of the citizen to be secure in his own home against the intrusion of poisons applied by other persons. I speak not as a lawyer but as a biologist and as a human being, but I strongly feel that this is or should be one of the basic human rights. I am afraid however that it has little or no existence in practice.

I have countless letters in my files describing situations in which a person has been subject to personal injury or to the loss of pets or valuable horses or other domestic animals because poisons from a neighbor's spraying invaded his property. Residents of Norfolk, Virginia, have informed me that they were told last winter that the state had the authority to apply poisons to their land but assumed no responsibility for injury that might result. It is a matter of record that dairy farmers in New York State suffered contamination of their land by federal-state spraying for gypsy moths with the inevitable result that their milk later contained illegal residues and was condemned by the state as unfit for market. . . .

As a minimum protection, I suggest a legal requirement of adequate advance notice of all community, state, or federal spraying programs so that all interests involved may receive hearing and consideration before any spraying is done. I suggest further that machinery be established so that the private citizen inconvenienced or damaged by the intrusion of his neighbor's sprays may seek appropriate redress.

2. In another area, I hope this committee will give its support to new programs of medical research and education in the field of pesticides. I have long felt that the medical profession, with of course notable individual exceptions, was inadequately informed on this very important environmental health hazard. It was sobering to have the President's science advisors confirm this view by saying, "Physicians are generally unaware of the wide distribution of pesticides, their toxicity, and their possible effects on human health." The panel also found a complete lack of any federally sponsored research to develop methods of diagnosing pesticide poisoning, especially when this takes the form of chronic, rather than acute illness. I am told that in the medical schools today, because of the many subjects to be taught, the attention given the whole field of toxicology is greatly reduced. Yet this is happening at a time when toxic substances are being introduced into the environment at a rate never before approached.

The plight of the person affected by these poisons is pitiful. Many case histories have come to me in letters. As a rule these people can find no physician who understands their problem. Indeed, I remember several cases in current medical literature in which the physician, even though told of the patient's exposure to such relatively common insecticides as malathion or lindane, had never heard of the chemical and did not know the appropriate treatment. . . .

3. I should also like to see legislation, possibly at the state level, restricting the sale and use of pesticides at least to those capable of understanding the hazards and of following directions. To me, it is shocking that these chemicals can be bought and applied by illiterate and even by mentally deficient persons. We place much more stringent restrictions on the sale of drugs—which at least are not sprayed from powerful machines! Someone wrote me recently about a man who was thought to have contracted hepatitis from a spray he had been using, making the pertinent observation that the man could buy the chemicals that made him ill with no restrictions but had to have prescriptions to buy the drugs to cure him.

4. I should like to see the registration of chemicals made a function of all agencies concerned rather than of the Department of Agriculture alone. The deficiency in the present law has been pointed out in the report of the President's Science Advisory Committee. Many of the miscellaneous uses of chemicals, as in mothproofing, floor waxes, household sprays, and garden pesticides, have a direct relation to human health. It seems not only logical but necessary that the Department of Health, Education and Welfare should participate in decisions regarding the registration of chemicals so used. Similarly, many, probably the majority, of pesticides are used at some time in such a manner that they affect wildlife and commercial and recreational fishery resources. The Department of the Interior needs to have a voice in the registration and labeling of such chemicals. . . .

5. It seems to me that our troubles are unnecessarily compounded by the fantastic number of chemical compounds in use as pesticides. As matters stand, it is quite impossible for research into the effect of these chemicals on the physical

environment, on wildlife, and on man to keep pace with their introduction and use. It is hard to escape the conclusion that the great proliferation of new chemicals is dictated by the facts of competition within the industry rather than by actual need. I should like to see the day when new pesticides will be approved for use only when no existing chemical or other method will do the job.

6. In conclusion, I hope you will give full support to research on new methods of pest control in which chemicals will be minimized or entirely eliminated. You have heard from Secretary Freeman what some of this work is. One of the outstanding values of biological controls is that they are specifically adapted to a particular species or groups of species. Therefore, since our problems of pest control are numerous and varied, we must search not for one super-weapon that will solve all our problems, but for a great diversity of armaments, each precisely adjusted to its task. To accomplish this end requires ingenuity, persistence, and dedication, but the rewards to be gained are great.

Source: Rachel Carson. Interagency Coordination in Environmental Hazards (Pesticides), June 4, 1963, 88th Congress (1st session). Washington, D.C.: Government Printing Office, 1964.

Local Food Systems: Concepts, Impacts, and Issues (2010)

The tremendous increase in the number of farmers' markets in recent years is one outcome of a growing consumer preference for local foods. However, there is no uniformly accepted definition of the meaning of "local." As this report indicates, "local" can mean more than geography; "local" foods can be defined by cultural and environmental production techniques. There are multiple reasons that local foods are becoming increasingly prominent, including a rising interest in environmental, social, and health impacts of food production. This report summarizes the local foods movement from multiple perspectives, including the economic impact of direct-to-consumer or direct-to-retail sales. The report also identifies barriers that may constrain the expansion of local foods in some areas. The safety of local foods is discussed in the context of the ability to conduct trace-back investigations, train farmers, and address regulatory issues with farmers' markets. In addition to an overview of the current regulatory system relevant to local foods, the report provides a literature review that should be helpful to anyone examining the issue. The excerpt below is from the summary of the report.

What Did the Study Find?

There is no generally accepted definition of "local" food

Though "local" has a geographic connotation, there is no consensus on a definition in terms of the distance between production and consumption. Definitions related to geographic distance between production and sales vary by regions, companies, consumers, and local food markets. According to the definition adopted by the U.S. Congress in the 2008 Food, Conservation, and Energy Act, the total distance that a product can be transported and still be considered a "locally or regionally produced agricultural food product" is less than 400 miles from its origin, or within the State in which it is produced. Definitions based on market arrangements, including direct-to-consumer arrangements such as regional farmers' markets, or direct-to-retail/foodservice arrangements such as farm sales to schools, are well-recognized categories and are used in this report to provide statistics on the market development of local foods.

Local food markets account for a small but growing share of total U.S. agricultural sales

- Direct-to-consumer marketing amounted to $1.2 billion in current dollar sales in 2007, according to the 2007 Census of Agriculture, compared with $551 million in 1997.
- Direct-to-consumer sales accounted for 0.4 percent of total agricultural sales in 2007, up from 0.3 percent in 1997.

If nonedible products are excluded from total agricultural sales, direct-to-consumer sales accounted for 0.8 percent of agricultural sales in 2007.

- The number of farmers' markets rose to 5,274 in 2009, up from 2,756 in 1998 and 1,755 in 1994, according to USDA's Agricultural Marketing Service.

- In 2005, there were 1,144 community-supported agriculture organizations, up from 400 in 2001 and 2 in 1986, according to a study by the National Center for Appropriate Technology. In early 2010, estimates exceeded 1,400, but the number could be much larger.

- The number of farm to school programs, which use local farms as food suppliers for school meals programs and promote relationships between schools and farms, increased to 2,095 in 2009, up from 400 in 2004 and 2 in the 1996–97 school year, according to the National Farm to School Network. Data from the 2005 School Nutrition and Dietary Assessment Survey, sponsored by USDA's Food and Nutrition Service, showed that 14 percent of school districts participated in Farm to School programs, and 16 percent reported having guidelines for purchasing locally grown produce.

Production of locally marketed food is more
likely to occur on small farms located in or
near metropolitan counties

Local food markets typically involve small farmers, heterogeneous products, and short supply chains in which farmers also perform marketing functions, including storage, packaging, transportation, distribution, and advertising. According to the 2007 U.S. Census of Agriculture, most farms that sell directly to consumers are small farms with less than $50,000 in total farm sales, located in urban corridors of the Northeast and the West Coast. In 2007, direct-to-consumer sales accounted for a larger share of sales for small farms, as defined above, than for medium-sized farms (total farm sales of $50,000 to $499,999) and large farms (total farm sales of $500,000 or more). Produce farms engaged in local marketing made 56 percent of total agricultural direct sales to consumers, while accounting for 26 percent of all farms engaged in direct-to-consumer marketing. Direct-to-consumer sales are higher for the farms engaged in other entrepreneurial activities, such as organic production, tourism, and customwork (planting, plowing, harvesting, etc. for others), than for other farms.

In 2007, direct sales by all U.S. farms surpassed customwork to become the leading on-farm entrepreneurial activity in terms of farm household participation. Barriers to local food-market entry and expansion include: capacity constraints for small farms and lack of distribution systems for moving local food into mainstream markets; limited research, education, and training for marketing local food; and uncertainties related to regulations that may affect local food production, such as food safety requirements.

Consumers who value high-quality foods produced with low environmental impact are willing to pay more for locally produced food

Several studies have explored consumer preferences for locally produced food. Motives for "buying local" include perceived quality and freshness of local food and support for the local economy. Consumers who are willing to pay higher prices for locally produced foods place importance on product quality, nutritional value, methods of raising a product and those methods' effects on the environment, and support for local farmers.

Federal, State, and local government programs increasingly support local food systems

Many existing government programs and policies support local food initiatives, and the number of such programs is growing. Federal policies have grown over time to include the Community Food Project Grants Program, the WIC Farmers' Market

Nutrition Program, Senior Farmers' Market Nutrition Program, Federal State Marketing Improvement Program, National Farmers' Market Promotion Program, Specialty Crop Block Grant Program, and the Community Facilities Program. State and local policies include those related to farm-to-institution procurement, promotion of local food markets, incentives for low-income consumers to shop at farmers' markets, and creation of State Food Policy Councils to discuss opportunities and potential impact of government intervention. (WIC is the acronym for the Special Supplemental Nutrition Program for Women, Infants, and Children.)

As of early 2010, there were few studies on the impact of local food markets on economic development, health, or environmental quality

- Empirical research has found that expanding local food systems in a community can increase employment and income in that community.

- Empirical evidence is insufficient to determine whether local food availability improves diet quality or food security.

- Life-cycle assessments—analyses of energy use at all stages of the food system including consumption and disposal—suggest that localization can but does not necessarily reduce energy use or greenhouse gas emissions.

How was the study conducted?

Existing analyses of local food markets by universities, government agencies, national nonprofit organizations, and others of local food markets were synthesized to evaluate the definition of local foods and the effects of local food systems on economic development, health and nutrition, food security, and energy use and greenhouse gas emissions. The report's content relies on data collected through the 2007 Census of Agriculture, as well as other surveys by USDA's Agricultural Marketing Service, the National Farm to School Network, university extension departments, and others, to provide a comprehensive picture of types of local food markets, their characteristics, and their importance over time.

Source: S. Martinez, et al. 2010. Local Food Systems: Concepts, Impacts, and Issues. Economic Research Service, U.S. Department of Agriculture. http://www.ers.usda.gov/webdocs/publica tions/err97/7054_err97_1_.pdf

Food Safety Modernization Act (2010)

The 2010 Food Safety Modernization Act was the most sweeping food safety legislation enacted by the U.S. government in more than 70 years. The law focuses on preventing foodborne illness rather than responding to illness that has already occurred. The regulations pertaining to the act are under development by federal agencies and will take years to adopt and implement. Implementation is dependent on budget resources that are under control of U.S. Congress. The Table of Contents, showing the wide range of topics covered, is included here, along with sections from Title II on inspection and reporting; the full bill is available online.

Title I—Improving Capacity To Prevent Food Safety Problems

Sec. 101. Inspections of records.

Sec. 102. Registration of food facilities.

Sec. 103. Hazard analysis and risk-based preventive controls.

Sec. 104. Performance standards.

Sec. 105. Standards for produce safety.

Sec. 106. Protection against intentional adulteration.

Sec. 107. Authority to collect fees.

Sec. 108. National agriculture and food defense strategy.

Sec. 109. Food and Agriculture Coordinating Councils.

Sec. 110. Building domestic capacity.

Sec. 111. Sanitary transportation of food.

Sec. 112. Food allergy and anaphylaxis management.

Sec. 113. New dietary ingredients.

Sec. 114. Requirement for guidance relating to post harvest processing of raw oysters.

Sec. 115. Port shopping.

Sec. 116. Alcohol-related facilities.

Title II—Improving Capacity to Detect and Respond to Food Safety Problems

Sec. 201. Targeting of inspection resources for domestic facilities, foreign facilities, and ports of entry; annual report.

Sec. 202. Laboratory accreditation for analyses of foods.

Sec. 203. Integrated consortium of laboratory networks.

Sec. 204. Enhancing tracking and tracing of food and recordkeeping.

Sec. 205. Surveillance.

Sec. 206. Mandatory recall authority.

Sec. 207. Administrative detention of food.

Sec. 208. Decontamination and disposal standards and plans.

Sec. 209. Improving the training of State, local, territorial, and tribal food safety officials.

Sec. 210. Enhancing food safety.

Sec. 211. Improving the reportable food registry.

Title III—Improving the Safety of Imported Food

Sec. 301. Foreign supplier verification program.

Sec. 302. Voluntary qualified importer program.

Sec. 303. Authority to require import certifications for food.

. . .

Sec. 201. Targeting of Inspection Resources for Domestic Facilities, Foreign Facilities, and Ports of Entry; Annual Report

(a) Identification and Inspection of Facilities.—

(1) Identification.—The Secretary shall identify high-risk facilities and shall allocate resources to inspect facilities according to the known safety risks of the facilities, which shall be based on the following factors:

(A) The known safety risks of the food manufactured, processed, packed, or held at the facility.

(B) The compliance history of a facility, including with regard to food recalls, outbreaks of foodborne illness, and violations of food safety standards.

(C) The rigor and effectiveness of the facility's hazard analysis and risk-based preventive controls.

(D) Whether the food manufactured, processed, packed, or held at the facility meets the criteria for priority under section 801(h)(1).

(E) Whether the food or the facility that manufactured, processed, packed, or held such food has received a certification as described in section 801(q) or 806, as appropriate.

(F) Any other criteria deemed necessary and appropriate by the Secretary for purposes of allocating inspection resources.

(2) Inspections.—

(A) In general.—Beginning on the date of enactment of the FDA Food Safety Modernization Act, the Secretary shall increase the frequency of inspection of all facilities.

(B) Domestic high-risk facilities.—The Secretary shall increase the frequency of inspection of domestic facilities identified under paragraph (1) as high-risk facilities such that each such facility is inspected—

(i) not less often than once in the 5-year period following the date of enactment of the FDA Food Safety Modernization Act; and

(ii) not less often than once every 3 years thereafter.

(C) Domestic non-high-risk facilities.—The Secretary shall ensure that each domestic facility that is not identified under paragraph (1) as a high-risk facility is inspected—

(i) not less often than once in the 7-year period following the date of enactment of the FDA Food Safety Modernization Act; and

(ii) not less often than once every 5 years thereafter.

(D) Foreign facilities.—

    (i) Year 1.—In the 1-year period following the date of enactment of the FDA Food Safety Modernization Act, the Secretary shall inspect not fewer than 600 foreign facilities.

    (ii) Subsequent years.—In each of the 5 years following the 1-year period described in clause (i), the Secretary shall inspect not fewer than twice the number of foreign facilities inspected by the Secretary during the previous year.

(E) Reliance on federal, state, or local inspections.— In meeting the inspection requirements under this subsection for domestic facilities, the Secretary may rely on inspections conducted by other Federal, State, or local agencies under interagency agreement, contract, memoranda of understanding, or other obligation.

. . .

(h) Annual Report Regarding Food.—Not later than February 1 of each year, the Secretary shall submit to Congress a report, including efforts to coordinate and cooperate with other Federal agencies with responsibilities for food inspections, regarding—

    (1) information about food facilities including—

        (A) the appropriations used to inspect facilities registered pursuant to section 415 in the previous fiscal year;

        (B) the average cost of both a non-high-risk food facility inspection and a high-risk food facility inspection, if such a difference exists, in the previous fiscal year;

        (C) the number of domestic facilities and the number of foreign facilities registered pursuant to section 415 that the Secretary inspected in the previous fiscal year;

(D) the number of domestic facilities and the number of foreign facilities registered pursuant to section 415 that were scheduled for inspection in the previous fiscal year and which the Secretary did not inspect in such year;

(E) the number of high-risk facilities identified pursuant to section 421 that the Secretary inspected in the previous fiscal year; and

(F) the number of high-risk facilities identified pursuant to section 421 that were scheduled for inspection in the previous fiscal year and which the Secretary did not inspect in such year.

(2) information about food imports including—

(A) the number of lines of food imported into the United States that the Secretary physically inspected or sampled in the previous fiscal year;

(B) the number of lines of food imported into the United States that the Secretary did not physically inspect or sample in the previous fiscal year; and

(C) the average cost of physically inspecting or sampling a line of food subject to this Act that is imported or offered for import into the United States; and

(3) information on the foreign offices of the Food and Drug Administration including—

(A) the number of foreign offices established; and

(B) the number of personnel permanently stationed in each foreign office.

Source: 111th Congress, 2nd Session. H.R. 2751 (EAS). December 10, 2010. Available online at https://www.govinfo.gov/content/pkg/BILLS-111hr2751eas/html/BILLS-111hr2751eas.htm

New York City's Restaurant Grading System (2012)

Local health departments are the main players in ensuring food safety in retail establishments, especially restaurants. A trend has developed recently to make the inspection process more transparent in order to inform consumers and encourage operators to comply with regulations. Restaurant grading systems are emerging in many places; the following is an example of the system used in New York City. Grades are typically posted in places for easy viewing by customers and may contribute to dining choices.

How We Score and Grade

The Health Department inspects about 24,000 restaurants a year to monitor compliance with City and State food safety regulations. Since July 2010, the Health Department has required restaurants to post letter grades showing sanitary inspection results. Restaurants with a score between 0 and 13 points earn an A, those with 14 to 27 points receive a B and those with 28 or more a C. Inspection results are posted on the Health Department's website.

Food Safety Inspections: What's Behind the Score?

A restaurant's score depends on how well it follows City and State food safety requirements. Inspectors check for food handling, food temperature, personal hygiene, facility and equipment maintenance and vermin control. Each violation earns a certain number of points. At the end of the inspection, the inspector totals the points and this number is the restaurant's inspection score; the lower the score, the better.

The points for a particular violation depend on the health risk it poses to the public. Violations fall into three categories:

- A **public health hazard**, such as failing to keep food at the right temperature, triggers a minimum of 7 points. If the violation can't be corrected before the inspection ends, the Health Department may close the restaurant until it's fixed.

- A **critical violation**, for example, serving raw food such as a salad without properly washing it first, carries a minimum of 5 points.

- A **general violation**, such as not properly sanitizing cooking utensils, receives at least 2 points. Inspectors assign additional points to reflect the extent of the violation. A violation's condition level can range from 1 (least extensive) to 5 (most extensive). For example, the presence of one contaminated food item is a condition level 1 violation, generating 7 points. Four or more contaminated food items is a condition level 4 violation, resulting in 10 points.

When Is a Score Converted to a Grade?

Two types of inspections result in a letter grade: initial inspections for which the restaurant earns an A and re-inspections that result in an A, B or C. A restaurant has two chances to earn an A in every inspection cycle. If it doesn't earn an A on the first inspection, it's scored but ungraded. An inspector goes back to the restaurant unannounced, typically within a month, to inspect it again and the re-inspection is graded. If the grade is a B or C, the restaurant will receive a grade card and a grade pending card. It can post either card until it has an opportunity to be heard at the Office of Administrative Trials and Hearings Health Tribunal. Until a restaurant has a graded inspection, it is listed as Not Yet Graded on the Health Department website.

Which Inspections Are Not Graded?

The following are scored but not graded:

- Initial inspections that result in a score of 14 points or higher
- Monitoring inspections at a restaurant that has performed very poorly on its re-inspection. The Health Department may continue to inspect the restaurant roughly once a month until it scores below 28 or the Department closes it for serious and persistent violations.

- Inspections at new restaurants not yet open to the public
- An inspection at a restaurant seeking to reopen after the Department closed it
- Some inspections in response to complaints
- Inspections before July 27, 2010

Source: NYC Health. How We Score and Grade. http://www1 .nyc.gov/site/doh/services/restaurant-grades.page

The FDA Food Code (2013)

The Food Code is a guidance document prepared by the FDA and is updated every four years; it is not a law or regulation, meaning that complying with it is voluntary, not mandatory. However, state and local governments can adopt the code in whole or in part to serve as food safety regulations. The table of contents and excerpts from the preface are included below.

Table of Contents

Preface

1. Foodborne illness estimates, risk factors, and interventions

2. PHS Model Codes history, purpose and authority

3. Public health and consumer expectations

4. Advantages of uniform standards

5. Modifications and improvements in this edition

6. Discussion of the Food Code as a HACCP model and the intention to incorporate other models

7. Code adoption/Certified copies

8. Information to assist the user

9. The code revisions process

10. Acknowledgements

Preface

Foodborne illness in the United States is a major cause of personal distress, preventable illness and death, and avoidable economic burden. Scallan et al. (2011) estimated that foodborne diseases cause approximately 48 million illnesses, 128,000 hospitalizations, and 3,000 deaths in the United States each year. The occurrence of approximately 1,000 reported disease outbreaks (local, regional, and national) each year highlights the challenges of preventing these infections.

Most foodborne illnesses occur in persons who are not part of recognized outbreaks. For many victims, foodborne illness results only in discomfort or lost time from the job. For some, especially preschool age children, older adults in health care facilities, and those with impaired immune systems, foodborne illness is more serious and may be life threatening.

The annual cost of foodborne illness in terms of pain and suffering, reduced productivity, and medical costs are estimated to be $10–$83 billion. As stated by Meade et al., the nature of food and foodborne illness has changed dramatically in the United States over the last century. While technological advances such as pasteurization and proper canning have all but eliminated some disease, new causes of foodborne illness have been identified. Surveillance of foodborne illness is complicated by several factors. The first is underreporting. Although foodborne illnesses can be severe or even fatal, milder cases are often not detected through routine surveillance. Second, many pathogens transmitted through food are also spread through water or from person to person, thus obscuring the role of foodborne transmission. Finally, pathogens or agents that have not yet been identified and thus cannot be diagnosed cause some proportion of foodborne illness.

Epidemiological outbreak data repeatedly identify five major risk factors related to employee behaviors and preparation practices in retail and food service establishments as contributing to foodborne illness:

• Improper holding temperatures,
• Inadequate cooking, such as undercooking raw shell eggs,
• Contaminated equipment,
• Food from unsafe sources, and
• Poor personal hygiene

The Food Code addresses controls for risk factors and further establishes 5 key public health interventions to protect consumer health. Specifically, these interventions are: demonstration of knowledge, employee health controls, controlling hands as a vehicle of contamination, time and temperature parameters for controlling pathogens, and the consumer advisory. The first two interventions are found in Chapter 2 and the last three in Chapter 3.

The Food and Drug Administration (FDA) endeavors to assist the approximately 75 state and territorial agencies and more than 3,000 local departments that assume primary responsibility for preventing foodborne illness and for licensing and inspecting establishments within the retail segment of the food industry. This industry segment consists of more than one million establishments and employs a work force of over 16 million.

PHS Model Codes History, Purpose, and Authority

History and Purpose

U.S. Public Health Service (PHS) activities in the area of food protection began at the turn of the 20th century with studies on the role of milk in the spread of disease. These studies led to the conclusion that effective disease prevention requires the application of comprehensive food sanitation measures from production to consumption. Additional studies identified and evaluated measures which would most effectively control disease, including work which led to improved processes for pasteurization.

Next, model codes were developed to assist state and local governments in initiating and maintaining effective programs for prevention of foodborne illness. The first of these, which is now titled *Grade A Pasteurized Milk Ordinance—Recommendations of the PHS/FDA*, was initially published in 1924. Subsequently, the PHS published recommended model food codes that address the various components of the retail segment of the food industry. These code editions are listed chronologically on pp. iii and iv. Through the years all states, hundreds of local jurisdictions, and many federal agencies have adopted some edition of model food codes recommended by the PHS.

Today, FDA's purpose in maintaining an updated model food code is to assist food control jurisdictions at all levels of government by providing them with a scientifically sound technical and legal basis for regulating the retail segment of the food industry. The retail segment includes those establishments or locations in the food distribution chain where the consumer takes possession of the food.

The model Food Code is neither federal law nor federal regulation and is not preemptive. Rather, it represents FDA's best advice for a uniform system of regulation to ensure that food at retail is safe and properly protected and presented. Although not federal requirements (until adopted by federal bodies for use within federal jurisdictions), the model Food Code provisions are designed to be consistent with federal food laws and regulations, and are written for ease of legal adoption at all levels of government. A list of jurisdictions that have reported to FDA their status in adopting the Food Code is available on the FDA CFSAN Web Page at: http://www.fda.gov/Retail FoodProtection. The list is self-reported and FDA has not yet evaluated whether all the adopted codes are equivalent to the model Food Code.

Providing model food codes and model code interpretations and opinions is the mechanism through which FDA, as a lead federal food control agency, promotes uniform implementation of national food regulatory policy among the several thousand federal, state, and local agencies and tribes that have primary responsibility for the regulation or oversight of retail level food operations.

Source: The full text of the current Food Code and past versions can be found at http://www.fda.gov/Food/GuidanceRegulation/ RetailFoodProtection/FoodCode/default.htm

Voluntary National Retail Food Regulatory Program Standards (2015)

The FDA refers to these standards as the "Retail Program Standards." They were designed to provide guidance to state and local agencies that regulate food retail establishments. These agencies can

choose to enroll in the Retail Food Standards program and make a commitment to completing self-assessments of nine standards corresponding with the current Food Code: (1) regulatory foundation; (2) trained regulatory staff; (3) inspection program based on HACCP principles; (4) uniform inspection program; (5) foodborne illness and food defense preparedness and response; (6) compliance and enforcement; (7) industry and community relations; (8) program support and resources; and (9) program assessment. The introduction, which provides an overview and the definitions used in the standards, is reproduced below.

Introduction

Achieving national uniformity among regulatory programs responsible for retail food protection in the United States has long been a subject of debate among the industry, regulators and consumers. Adoption of the *FDA Food Code* at the state, local and tribal level has been a keystone in the effort to promote greater uniformity. However, a missing piece has been a set of widely recognized standards for regulatory programs that administer the *Food Code.* To meet this need FDA has developed the "Voluntary National Retail Food Regulatory Program Standards" (Retail Program Standards) through ideas and input from federal, state, and local regulatory officials, industry, trade and professional associations, academia and consumers on what constitutes a highly effective and responsive retail food regulatory program.

In March of 1996, the FDA hosted a meeting to explore ways in which its retail food protection program could be improved. Participants in the meeting included FDA Retail Food Specialists, FDA headquarters personnel, state and local regulatory officials from the six FDA regions, the president of the Association of Food & Drug Officials, and industry representatives. Following that meeting, FDA established a National Retail Food Team comprised of the Regional Retail Food Specialists, CFSAN personnel and other FDA personnel directly involved in retail food protection. A Retail Food Program Steering Committee was established and tasked with leading the team to respond to the direction given by the participants in the meeting, i.e. providing national leadership, being equal partners, being responsive, providing communication and promoting uniformity.

The Steering Committee was charged with developing a five-year operational plan for FDA's retail food program. The Steering Committee was also charged with ensuring the operational plan was in keeping with the goals and mission of the President's Food Safety Initiative. FDA solicited input from the regulatory community, industry and consumers in developing the plan. The resulting Operational Plan charted the future of the National Retail Food Program and prompted a reassessment of the respective roles of all stakeholders and how best to achieve program uniformity.

From the goals established in that first Operational Plan, two basic principles emerged on which to build a new foundation for the retail program:

- Promote active managerial control of the risk factors most commonly associated with foodborne illness in food establishments, and
- Establish a recommended framework for retail food regulatory programs within which the active managerial control of the risk factors can best be realized.

These principles led to the drafting of standards that encourage voluntary participation by the regulatory agencies at the state, local, and tribal level. The Program Standards were developed with input obtained through a series of meetings over a two-year period including: the 1996 stakeholders meeting, FDA Regional Seminars, meetings with state officials hosted by the Retail Food Specialists, and six Grassroots Meetings held around the country in 1997. Valuable input from industry associations, associations of regulatory officials, and others was also obtained. The Retail Program Standards were provided to the Conference for Food Protection for further input and to achieve broad consensus among all stakeholders.

In developing the Retail Program Standards, FDA recognized that the ultimate goal of all retail food regulatory programs is to reduce or eliminate the occurrence of illnesses and deaths from food produced at the retail level and that there are different approaches toward achieving that goal. Federal, state, local, and tribal agencies continue to employ a variety of mechanisms with differing levels of sophistication in their attempt to ensure food safety at retail.

While the Retail Program Standards represent the effective, focused food safety program to which we ultimately aspire, they begin by providing a foundation and system upon which all regulatory programs can build through a continuous improvement process. The Standards encourage regulatory agencies to improve and build upon existing programs. Further, the Standards provide a framework designed to accommodate both traditional and emerging approaches to food safety. The Retail Program Standards are intended to reinforce proper sanitation (good retail practices) and operational and environmental prerequisite programs while encouraging regulatory agencies and industry to focus on the factors that cause and contribute to foodborne illness, with the ultimate goal of reducing the occurrence of those factors.

Purpose

The Retail Program Standards serve as a guide to regulatory retail food program managers in the design and management of a retail food regulatory program and provide a means of recognition for those programs that meet these standards. Program managers and administrators may establish additional requirements to meet individual program needs.

The Retail Program Standards are designed to help food regulatory programs enhance the services they provide to the public. When applied in the intended manner, the Program Standards should:

- Identify program areas where an agency can have the greatest impact on retail food safety
- Promote wider application of effective risk-factor intervention strategies
- Assist in identifying program areas most in need of additional attention
- Provide information needed to justify maintenance or increase in program budgets
- Lead to innovations in program implementation and administration
- Improve industry and consumer confidence in food protection programs by enhancing uniformity within and between regulatory agencies

Each Standard has one or more corresponding worksheets, forms and guidance documents. Regulatory agencies may use existing, available records or may choose to develop and use alternate forms and worksheets that capture the same information.

Scope

The Retail Program Standards apply to the operation and management of a retail food regulatory program that is focused on the reduction of risk factors known to cause or contribute to foodborne illness and to the promotion of active managerial control of these risk factors. The results of a self-assessment against the Standards may be used to evaluate the effectiveness of food safety interventions implemented within a jurisdiction. The Standards also provide a procedure for establishing a database on the occurrence of risk factors that may be used to track the results of regulatory and industry efforts over time.

History

The Retail Program Standards were pilot tested in each of the five FDA regions in 1999. Each regulatory participant reported the results at the 2000 Conference for Food Protection. Improvements to the Standards were incorporated into the January 2001 version based on input from the pilot participants. Further refinements to the Standards were made in subsequent drafts leading up to the endorsement of the March 2002 version of the Retail Program Standards by the 2002 Conference for Food Protection. Subsequent changes and enhancements have been made following concurrence of the stakeholders at the biennial meetings of the Conference for Food Protection.

In maintaining these standards, FDA intends to allow for and encourage new and innovative approaches to the reduction of factors that are known to cause foodborne illness. Program managers and other health professionals participating in this voluntary program who have demonstrated means or methods other than those described here may submit those to FDA for consideration and inclusion in the Retail Program Standards. Improvements to future versions of the Standards will be made through a process that includes the Conference for Food Protection to allow for constant program enhancement and promotion of national uniformity.

Impact on Program Resources

During pilot testing of the Retail Program Standards in 1998, some jurisdictions reported that the self-assessment process was time consuming and could significantly impact an agency's resources. Collection, analysis, and management of information for the database Occurrence of Risk Factor Studies were of special concern. However, participating jurisdictions also indicated that the resource commitment was worthwhile and that the results of the self-assessment were expected to benefit their retail food protection program. Advance planning is recommended before beginning the data collection process in order to use resources efficiently. In addition, changes to the Standards now allow jurisdictions to use routine inspection data for analysis on the occurrence of risk factors, significantly reducing the resource requirements for separate data collection.

It is further recommended that jurisdictions not attempt to make program enhancements during the self-assessment process. A better approach is to use the self-assessment to identify program needs and then establish program priorities and plans to address those needs as resources become available.

Definitions

The following definitions apply in the interpretation and application of these Standards.

1. **Active Managerial Control**—The purposeful incorporation of specific actions or procedures by industry management into the operation of a business to attain control over foodborne illness risk factors.

2. **Auditor**—Any authorized city, county, district, state, federal, tribal or other third party person who has no responsibilities for the day-to-day operations of that jurisdiction and is charged with conducting a verification audit, which confirms the accuracy of the self-assessment.

3. **Baseline Survey**—See Risk Factor Study.

4. **Candidate**—A regulatory officer whose duties include the inspection of retail food establishments.

5. **Compliance and Enforcement**—Compliance includes all voluntary or involuntary conformity with provisions set forth by the regulatory authority to safeguard public health and ensure that food is safe. Enforcement includes any legal and/or administrative procedures taken by the regulatory authority to gain compliance.

6. **Confirmed Foodborne Disease Outbreak**—means a foodborne disease outbreak in which laboratory analysis of appropriate specimens identifies a causative agent and epidemiologic analysis implicates the food as the source of the illness or epidemiological analysis alone implicates the food as the source of the illness.

7. **Direct Regulatory Authority (DRA)**—The organizational level of government that is immediately responsible for the management of the retail program. This may be at the city, county, district, state, federal, territorial, or tribal level.

8. **Enforcement Actions**—Actions taken by the regulatory authority such as, but not limited to, warning letters, revocation or suspension of permit, court actions, monetary fines, hold orders, destruction of food, etc., to correct a violation found during an inspection.

9. **Follow-up Inspection**—An inspection conducted after the initial routine inspection to confirm the correction of a violation(s).

10. **Food Code Interventions**—the preventive measures to protect consumer health stated below:

    1. management's demonstration of knowledge;
    2. employee health controls;
    3. controlling hands as a vehicle of contamination;
    4. time/temperature parameters for controlling pathogens; and
    5. consumer advisory.

11. **Food-Related Injury**—Means an injury from ingesting food containing a physical hazard such as bone, glass, or wood.

12. **Foodborne Disease Outbreak**—The occurrence of two or more cases of a similar illness resulting from the ingestion of a common food.

13. **Good Retail Practices (GRP's)**—Preventive measures that include practices and procedures to effectively control the

introduction of pathogens, chemicals, and physical objects into food, that are prerequisites to instituting a HACCP or Risk Control Plan and are not addressed by the *FDA Food Code* interventions or risk factors.

14. **Hazard**—A biological, chemical or physical property that may cause food to be unsafe for human consumption.

15. **National Registry of Retail Food Protection Programs (National Registry)**—A listing of retail food safety programs that have voluntarily enrolled as participants in the *Voluntary National Retail Food Regulatory Program Standards*.

16. **Person in charge (PIC)**—The individual present at a food establishment who is responsible for the operation at the time of inspection.

17. **Program Element**—One of the program areas for which a National Standard has been established such as regulations, training, inspection system, quality assurance, foodborne illness investigation, compliance and enforcement, industry and consumer relations, and program resources.

18. **Program Manager**—The individual responsible for the oversight and management of a retail food regulatory program.

19. **Quality Records**—Documentation of specific elements of program compliance with the National Standards as specified in each Standard.

20. **Risk Control Plan (RCP)**—a concisely written management plan developed by the retail or food service operator with input from the health inspector that describes a management system for controlling specific out-of-control risk factors.

21. **Risk Factors**—the improper employee behaviors or improper practices or procedures in retail food and food service establishments stated below which are most frequently

identified by epidemiological investigation as contributing to foodborne illness or injury:

1. improper holding temperature;
2. inadequate cooking;
3. contaminated equipment;
4. food from unsafe source; and
5. poor personal hygiene.

22. **Risk Factor Study** (formerly Baseline Survey)—A study on the occurrence of foodborne illness risk factors within institutional, foodservice, restaurants, and retail food facility types under a jurisdiction's regulatory authority. Criteria for a Risk Factor Study are detailed in Standard 9, including at a minimum:

    1. Data Collection, analysis, and a written report;
    2. A collection instrument with data items pertaining to the five foodborne illness risk factors;
    3. A collection instrument that uses the convention of IN, OUT, NA and NO to document observations;
    4. All facility types identified by FDA's national study that are under the jurisdiction's regulatory authority; and
    5. Studies subsequent to the initial study repeated at 5-year intervals.

23. **Routine Inspection**—A full review and evaluation of a food establishment's operations and facilities to assess its compliance with Food Safety Law, at a planned frequency determined by the regulatory authority. This does not include re-inspections and other follow-up or special investigations.

24. **Self-Assessment**—An internal review by program management to determine whether the existing retail food safety program meets the *Voluntary National Retail Food Regulatory Program Standards*.

25. **Self-Assessment Update**—Comparison of one or more program elements against the *Voluntary National Retail Food Regulatory Program Standards* between the required 60-month periodic self-assessment.

26. **Standardization Inspection**—An inspection used to demonstrate a candidate's knowledge, communication skills, and ability to identify violations of all regulatory requirements and to develop a risk control plan for identified, uncontrolled risk factors.

27. **Suspect Foodborne Outbreak**—Means an incident in which two or more persons experience a similar illness after ingestion of a common food or eating at a common food establishment/gathering.

28. **Trainer**—An individual who has successfully completed the following training elements as outlined in Steps 1–3, Standard 2, and is recognized by the program manager as having the field experience and communication skills necessary to train new employees.

    1. Satisfactory completion of the prerequisite curriculum;

    2. Completion of a field training process similar to that contained in Appendix B-2; and

    3. Completion of a minimum of 25 independent inspections and satisfactory completion of the remaining course curriculum.

29. **Training Standard**—An individual who has successfully completed the following training elements AND standardization elements in Standard 2 and is recognized by the program manager as having the field experience and communication skills necessary to train new employees. The training and standardization elements include:

    1. Satisfactory completion of the prerequisite curriculum;

    2. Completion of a field training process similar to that contained in Appendix B-2;

3. Completion of a minimum of 25 independent inspections and satisfactory completion of the remaining course curriculum; and

4. Successful completion of a standardization process based on a minimum of eight inspections that includes development of HACCP flow charts, completion of a risk control plan, and verification of a HACCP plan, similar to the FDA standardization procedures.

30. **Verification Audit**—A systematic, independent examination by an external party to confirm the accuracy of the Self-Assessment.

Source: The complete National Voluntary Retail Food Regulatory Program Standards including self-assessment and audit worksheets can be found at http://www.fda.gov/Food/Guidance Regulation/RetailFoodProtection/ProgramStandards/ucm 245409.htm

There is an immense amount of information available to aid in understanding food safety issues. Much of the most compelling information is found online and is publicly available, free of charge. This chapter identifies some of these common, influential, and interesting resources. These resources range from databases where people can look up information about specific pathogens or illnesses, to textbooks that are seminal works in food microbiology, to journals that published peer-reviewed scientific research. In addition, it is becoming increasingly common to find data visualization tools for creating maps and graphics.

Online Databases, Reports, and Libraries

Foodborne Pathogenic Microorganisms and Natural Toxins Handbook (Bad Bug Book)

http://www.fda.gov/Food/FoodborneIllnessContaminants/
CausesOfIllnessBadBugBook/default.htm

Compiled and maintained by the U.S. Food and Drug Administration's (U.S. FDA's) Center for Food Safety and

A Chipotle Mexican Grill employee prepares a burrito for a customer in Seattle on December 15, 2015. Chipotle has been implicated in a series of foodborne illness outbreaks. The company addressed public concern with an open letter from co-CEO Steve Ells and an online video outlining the steps it has taken to improve food safety practices. Chipotle's stock lost more than one-third of its value immediately following an *E. coli* outbreak in 2015. (AP Photo/Stephen Brashear)

Applied Nutrition, this is a comprehensive resource on the causes of foodborne illnesses. Each disease entry contains links to the Centers for Disease Control and Prevention's *Morbidity and Mortality Weekly Report*, which contains current outbreak information, and to the National Institute of Health's Medline database, which supplies current abstracts about the disease from medical journals. Each entry includes the nature of the disease, infective dose, associated foods, relative frequency of the disease, possible complications, target populations, and selected outbreaks.

Government Accountability Office

http://www.gao.gov/

The Government Accountability Office (GAO) is a non-partisan organization that conducts research in answer to questions raised by Congress. Their reports cover a wide range of food safety issues, including law and policy, government oversight, and health concerns. All of their reports are available free online.

National Academies Press

http://www.nap.edu/

The National Academies Press (NAP) publishes more than 200 books annually from work of the National Academy of Sciences. All of their publications are available to purchase or free for downloading. The NAP has more than 5,000 publications available in PDF, including many related to food safety and food issues in general.

National Food Safety Database

http://www.foodsafety.gov

Supported by the U.S. Department of Agriculture (USDA) and the Food Research Institute, this database has comprehensive information about a range of food safety topics, such as storing and handling food such as wild game; canning, drying, and freezing; people at high risk for foodborne illness; how foods can cause illness;

microwave safety; product recalls; seafood safety; food safety for children; and additives and chemical residues. It also includes a compilation of state experts and agencies.

Pesticide Residues in Food 2015

http://www.fao.org/3/a-i5186e.pdf

This is an annual report from the Joint Food and Agriculture Organization/World Health Organization (FAO/WHO) meetings of a panel of international experts on pesticides in food. The panel reviews specific pesticides and recommends acceptable daily intakes and acute references doses. The annual reports are used by Codex Alimentarius in setting maximum residue levels in foods. Reports from the work of this committee since 1991 are available online at http://www.fao.org/agriculture/crops/thematic-sitemap/theme/pests/jmpr/jmpr-rep/en/

Publications.USA.gov

http://publications.usa.gov/USAPubs.php

This is an online library operated by the Federal Citizen Information Center that includes access to hundreds of government publications sorted into categories. Many of the publications can be downloaded from the website if available, or print copies will be shipped free within the United States.

United States Food Code 2013

http://www.fda.gov/Food/GuidanceRegulation/Retail FoodProtection/FoodCode/

The complete *United States Food Code* is updated every four years by the FDA, Food Safety Inspection Service of the U.S. Department of Agriculture, and the Centers for Disease Control and Prevention in collaboration with the Conference for Food Protection, state and local officials, consumers, industry representatives, and academics. The code includes guidelines for a wide range of food safety issues, including facilities, personnel, time and tempera-ture, and model regulations.

Data and Visualization Tools

Foodborne Outbreak Online Database (FOOD Tool)

http://wwwn.cdc.gov/foodborneoutbreaks/
Searchable map providing information on foodborne out-breaks since 1998. Includes capacity to filter search by year, state, location of preparation, food/ingredient, and etiology.

National Environmental Assessment Reporting System (NEARS)

http://www.cdc.gov/nceh/ehs/nears/index.htm
This system compiles information from environmental assessment conducted during outbreak investigations. Ac-cess is available only to eligible public health programs.

National Outbreak Reporting System (NORS)

http://wwwn.cdc.gov/foodborneoutbreaks/
A web-based platform for health departments to report outbreak information. Not available to the general public.

National Pesticide Information Retrieval System (NPIRS)

http://npirspublic.ceris.purdue.edu/npirs.html
A subscription-based online system compiling informa-tion from several pesticide databases at the federal and state levels. The NPIRS only includes information about active ingredients in pesticides and is updated weekly.

Food Safety Training

EHS e-Learning

http://www.cdc.gov/nceh/ehs/elearn/
Online trainings offered by the governmental agencies in-cluding the CDC and Agency for Toxic Substances and

Disease Registry. The website provides links to courses in environmental assessment of foodborne illness outbreaks, integrated pest management, and essential environmental health services. This website also includes links to training programs available outside of government agencies and offered by trade groups, local and state agencies, and academia.

ServeSafe

https://www.servsafe.com/home
A common food safety training program from the National Restaurant Association. This training covers the basics of food safety for managers and food handlers. Students take a test and earn a certificate.

StateFoodSafety.com

https://www.statefoodsafety.com/
StateFoodSafety creates and offers online courses for food safety handlers and managers. The courses are location specific so students select their state and then enroll in specific training modules. Their Health Department Solutions customizes training for regulatory agencies.

Journals, Periodicals, Newsletters, and Blogs

Online Consumer and Trade Publications

Environmental Health News

http://www.environmentalhealthnews.org/
A daily publication that covers a wide range of environmental health issues, including food safety. Includes some original reporting, but mainly offers links to stories from other news sources. Free.

FDA Consumer Updates

http://www.fda.gov/fdac/
Informs the public about the activities of the FDA; includes information about food safety issues. Free.

Food and Environmental Protection Newsletter

http://www-pub.iaea.org

Newsletter from the Joint Food and Agriculture Organization of the United Nations and International Atomic Energy Agency focusing on international food safety and security issues with a specific emphasis on nuclear technologies such as irradiation. Free.

Food Chemical News

https://www.agra-net.com/agra/food-chemical-news/

Trade publication providing current information about government regulation of food and food additives. Subscription required.

Food Safety News

http://www.foodsafetynews.com/

Daily news covering a wide range of food safety issues, including policy, outbreaks, management, and opinions. Published by food safety attorney Bill Marler. Free.

Morbidity and Mortality Weekly Report

http://www.cdc.gov/mmwr/

Weekly periodical reporting current foodborne disease outbreaks, pathogens, and studies about foodborne disease. Published by the Centers for Disease Control and Prevention. Free.

Pesticide & Chemical Policy

https://www.agra-net.com/agra/agrow/pesticide-and-chemical-policy/

Targeted to the agriculture industry, this periodical covers tolerances, administrative guidelines, and exemptions for pesticide residues in food and feed as well as genetically modified organisms (GMOs). Subscription required.

World Food Regulation Review

http://www.researchinformation.co.uk/wfrr.php

Publication for public health labs, hospitals, environmental health officers, and food industry professionals covering legal and regulatory developments affecting the food industry as well as current international news on food pathogens and food safety. Subscription required.

Refereed Journals

Food and Chemical Toxicology

http://www.journals.elsevier.com/food-and-chemical-toxicology

Includes original research on the toxic effects of chemicals in foods, food additives, and other consumer products as well as new approaches to toxicology; includes open access articles.

Journal of Food Protection

http://www.foodprotection.org/publications/journal-of-food-protection/

A refereed monthly journal about food science published by the International Association for Food Protection and directed toward food safety professionals.

Journal of Food Quality

http://onlinelibrary.wiley.com/journal/10.1111/(ISSN) 1745–4557

Scientific journal that covers methods for improving food quality, shelf-life testing, environmental factors that affect food quality, and many other issues.

Journal of Food Safety

http://onlinelibrary.wiley.com/journal/10.1111/(ISSN) 1745–4565

Technical journal presenting chemical and microbiological coverage of food safety, including the toxicology, metabolism, and environmental conversion of materials entering the food supply. Open access options available.

Journal of Food Science

http://www.ift.org/knowledge-center/read-ift-publications/
journal-of-food-science.aspx

This journal is a publication of the Institute of Food
Technologists and includes original research related to
food chemistry, microbiology, safety, toxicology, and
engineering.

General Public/Consumer Interest

Consumer Reports

http://www.consumerreports.org

A magazine targeted to the general public and known for
test reports on consumer goods; also provides regular coverage of food safety.

Nutrition Action

https://cspinet.org/

Nutrition, food policy, and food safety issues information
for consumers from the Center for Science in the Public
Interest. Subscription required.

Books

There are hundreds of books on the subject of food and the
many issues related to it. The books below were chosen to be
representative of some of those that cover a broad range of food
issues. This list is not the definitive source of books; rather, it
is a starting point for learning more about specific issues as
outlined below. Prices are provided as found at the publisher's
website or online bookstores and noted for print versions of the
book; in most cases an eBook is available as well.

The books are categorized according to their major focus
or audience, and for each category, two to three of the most
relevant or popular books are noted. In most cases, books are

listed because they discuss food safety in the context of a solid scientific foundation. In cases of contemporary and sometimes controversial issues, such as GMOs, books expressing differing viewpoints are noted.

- Reference Works: Books that compile food safety information in an encyclopedic way and can be a source of information for a wide range of audiences.

- Bioterrorism: How food production and agriculture might be targets for terrorist attacks, and how attacks might be defended against.

- Consumer Resources: Consumer information about safe food handling, storing, cooking, and avoiding foodborne illness.

- Epidemiology: Texts explaining the basics of epidemiology, the study of how diseases spread among populations.

- Farming/Agriculture: Discussions of modern farming methods and how methods affect food safety.

- Food Additives, Toxins, and Contaminants: Listings of chemicals, including pesticides, added to foods and the science to evaluate their safety.

- Food Safety in Commercial Applications: Practical methods for food safety in restaurants, processing facilities, and other food service industry establishments.

- Food Safety Law and Policy: The legal basis for food safety and examination of the food safety system.

- Genetically Modified Foods: Discussions of the effects of biotechnology on the way many foods are produced.

- History: Works describing how food safety legislation came about.

- Microbiology of Foods: The role microorganisms play in food spoilage, food production, food preservation, and foodborne disease.

Reference Works

Batt, Carl A., ed. 2014. *Encyclopedia of Food Microbiology.* 2nd ed. 3 vols. San Diego, CA: Academic Press. 2372 pp. eBook ISBN: 9780123847331. $1,750.00.

> The more than 400 entries in this book cover important groups of bacteria, fungi, parasites, and viruses; methods for their detection in foods; factors that govern the behavior of these organisms; and likely outcomes of microbial growth or metabolism in terms of disease and/or spoilage. This work also covers beneficial microorganisms for industrial fermentation, including traditional food fermentations from the Middle and Far East and production of fermented foods like bread, cheese, and yogurt. The book includes contributions by dozens of leading scientists and is organized alphabetically by pathogen and food products. It is available as an eBook only.

Igoe, Robert S. 2011. *Dictionary of Food Ingredients.* 5th ed. New York: Springer. 234 pp. eBook ISBN: 978-1-4419-9713-5. $39.99.

> More than 1,000 food ingredients and additives are summarized in this reference. The first part of the book is organized alphabetically by ingredient, including both natural and artificial ingredients. Part 2 organizes ingredients by categories such as antioxidants, flavors, gums, and starch, Food definitions for items such as dressing, processed cheese, and yogurt are summarized in Part 3; the fourth part of the book discusses additives that are covered by U.S. regulations. The final part of the book covers food additives in the European Union.

Lawley, Richard, Laurie Curtis, and Judy Davis. 2012. *The Food Safety Hazard Guidebook.* 2nd ed. London: Royal Society of Chemistry. 546 pp. ISBN: 978-1849733816. $125.00.

> This book is promoted as a guidebook rather than an encyclopedia, even though it lays out information in an

encyclopedic way. The book provides information on bacteria, viruses, parasites, prions, and biological and chemical toxins. This edition also covers food allergens, including control options and legislation. Food safety legislation and food management systems are also discussed in the book. The work is designed as a reference for food safety professionals but could be an important book for consumers as well.

Bioterrorism

Bari, Md. Latiful and Dike O. Ukuku, eds. 2015. *Foodborne Pathogens and Food Safety.* Boca Raton, FL: CRC Press. 318 pp. ISBN: 978-0-313-34975-1. $149.95.

This collection of essays offers perspectives on food safety from developed and developing countries. Topics include drug resistance, emerging foodborne pathogens, climate change, and foodborne pathogens and how consumer demand affects food safety. Chapters also offer strategies to control and prevent foodborne diseases. This book is included under the bioterrorism category because of discussions of biosecurity issues and global food safety.

Chalk, Peter. 2004. *Hitting America's Soft Underbelly: The Potential Threat of Deliberate Biological Attacks against the U.S. Agricultural and Food Industry.* Santa Monica, CA: RAND Corporation. 68 pp. ISBN: 0-833-03522-3. $18.

This thorough report assesses the vulnerabilities of the agricultural sector and the food industry in general to biological terror threats. It discusses the results of a RAND Corporation study with methods used for analysis, the state of research on threats to agricultural livestock and produce, agriculture's importance to the U.S. economy, how the vulnerabilities in the general food industry might be exploited by terrorists, and likely outcomes of a successful attack. It also considers why terrorists might choose to target agriculture and makes policy recommendations for the future.

Rasco, Barbara, and Gleyn E. Bledsoe. 2004. *Bioterrorism and Food Safety.* Boca Raton, FL: CRC Press. 432 pp. ISBN: 0-849-32787-3. $220.00

> Barbara Rasco, a scientist and attorney, and Gleyn Bledsoe, a certified public accountant specializing in management advisory services to fishery, agricultural, and food-processing companies, bring a business perspective to bioterrorism issues. Besides terrorist threats from foreign organizations, the authors consider eco-terrorism perpetrated on biotechnology targets. They discuss the nature of bioterrorist threats; potential biological and toxic chemical agents; bioterrorism regulations and their impact on the safety of the food supply and trade; food security strategies and plans for agricultural and food-processing concerns; security improvements by tracking food; operational risk management approach to food safety; Food Safety and Inspection Service (FSIS) safety and security guidelines for distribution of meat, poultry, and eggs; emergency preparedness competence; terrorist threats to food, including guidelines for prevention; and public health response to biological and chemical terror.

Consumer Resources

Booth, Michael and Jennifer Brown. 2014. *Eating Dangerously: Why the Government Can't Keep Your Food Safe . . . and How You Can.* Lanham, MD: Rowman & Littlefield. 200 pp. ISBN: 978-1442222663. $17.98.

> This book is written by two journalists, which make it a readable account of the food safety system in the United States. The authors discuss food safety in the context of outbreaks that have involved hundreds of Americans. The book is divided into two sections: the first section focuses on explaining how the government regulates food safety in the United States and highlights significant weaknesses in their efforts. The second part of the book offers suggestions for consumers to avoid foodborne illness.

Specifically, the authors offer information that might go against some common perceptions of dangerous foods and guides people to taking steps to make safe eating as important as healthy eating.

Morrone, Michele. 2008. *Poisons on Our Plates: The Real Food Safety Problem in the United States.* Santa Barbara, CA: ABC-CLIO. 192 pp. ISBN: 978-0-313-34975-1. $64.00.
Common foodborne illnesses are presented in the context of outbreaks with popular foods in this book. Readers are provided an overview of food microbiology; then, in-depth discussions of some key microbes, including Salmonella and *E. coli*, are offered. Overall, this book attempts to convince consumers that they should be most concerned about microbial contamination of foods because these are the leading cause of illness and are entirely preventable.

Satin, Morton. 2008. *Food Alert: The Ultimate Sourcebook for Food Safety.* 2nd ed. New York: Checkmark Books. 350 pp. ISBN: 978-0816069699. $39.95.
This food safety book includes numerous charts, tables, checklists, and quizzes. Historical background, antibiotic resistance, and the 20 most common causes of foodborne illness in the kitchen comprise the first part of the book. Several chapters are divided by food type: poultry, beef, dairy products, fish and shellfish, and fruits and vegetables. These chapters tell what kinds of hazards exist and how to avoid them. A helpful appendix lists disease causes and symptoms, safe food storage procedures, and information sources on foodborne diseases.

Epidemiology and Outbreak Investigation
Bhopal, Raj. 2008. *Concepts of Epidemiology: An Integrated Introduction to the Ideas, Theories, Principles, and Methods of Epidemiology.* 2nd ed. New York: Oxford University Press. 472 pp. ISBN: 9780199543144. $58.00.

Written by a professor of epidemiology at the University of Edinburgh, this text assumes a basic understanding of biology but is not highly mathematical. Topics include how populations are defined; how diseases vary by time, place, and person; the role of bias and error; confounding in measurement; cause and effect from an epidemiological point of view; the natural history of disease; risk and measurement of disease frequency; and study design and evaluation.

Gertsman, B. Burt. 2013. *Epidemiology Kept Simple: An Introduction to Traditional and Modern Epidemiology.* 3rd ed. Hoboken, NJ: Wiley-Blackwell. 478 pp. ISBN: 978-1-4443-3608-5. $75.95.

This introductory text on epidemiology designed for non-epidemiologists presents history, causation, incidence, and prevalence of disease; outbreak investigation; study design evaluation; and error analysis. Many mathematical methods of analysis are included. Examples, charts, and exercises with answers are included throughout the text. The third edition is designed for use in academic institutions affiliated with the Association of Schools and Programs of Public Health.

Soon, Jan Mei, Louise Mannaing, and Carol A. Wallace, eds. 2016. *Foodborne Diseases: Case Studies of Outbreaks in the Agri-Food Industries.* Boca Raton, FL: CRC Press. 418 pp. ISBN: 9781482208276. $239.95. eBook, $167.97.

Outbreak investigations involve surveillance, epidemiology, lab analysis, and trace-backs, and no two outbreaks are alike. This book provides case studies of specific outbreaks that include fresh produce, dairy, eggs, animal feed, and wild game. In addition, a chapter on the melamine scandal is included. A unique aspect of the book is a chapter on risk communication during an outbreak, making this book appropriate as a textbook in higher-level food safety or graduate public health classes.

Agriculture

Pollan, Michael. 2007. *The Omnivore's Dilemma: A Natural History of Four Meals.* New York: Penguin Press. 450 pp. ISBN: 978-0143038580. $18.00.

In this account, Michael Pollan explores modern agricultural methods, from growing feed-grade corn in Iowa to fattening cattle on a feedlot, to a meal in a fast food chain, and then compares the methods to organic farming techniques, starting with grass to finding his own food as a forager and hunter.

Striffler, Steve. 2007. *Chicken: The Dangerous Transformation of America's Favorite Food.* New Haven, CT: Yale University Press. 195 pp. ISBN: 9780300123678. $23.00.

Steve Striffler worked in a processing plant before writing this book about the chicken industry, in which he describes how it is representative of the American food industry in general. He includes a popular history of chicken from a consumption perspective, development of the poultry industry during and after World War II, how the change to large processing plants affected rural areas, the loss of family farms to corporation-run farms, the dependence on an immigrant labor force, and healthier ways chicken farming could be conducted.

Torrence, Mary E., and Richard E. Isaacson, eds. 2003. *Microbial Food Safety in Animal Agriculture: Current Topics.* Ames, IA: Iowa State Press. 420 pp. ISBN: 9780813814957. $169.95.

This collection of articles deals with pre-harvest aspects of food safety and related microorganisms in food animals. It includes an overview of food safety, antimicrobial resistance in foodborne organisms, *Salmonella*, *E. coli*,

Campylobacter, Listeria, bovine spongiform encephalopathy, risk assessment, caliciviruses and other potential foodborne viruses, paratuberculosis, and *Toxiplasma gondii.*

Food Additives and Toxins

Ash, Michael, and Irene Ash. 2008. *Handbook of Food Additives.* 3rd ed. Endicott, NY: Synapse Information Resources. 1263 pp. ISBN: 978-1-934764-00-8. $375.00.

Worldwide in scope, this handbook of food additives has entries for more than 5,500 trade names and 4,000 generic chemicals. Each entry contains a chemical description, analysis, uses, properties, storage, use level (percentage), regulatory information, toxicology, precautions, hazardous decomposition products, and names of manufacturers and distributors. The handbook also has a directory of manufacturers, Chemical Abstracts Service number index, a name index, and a function index (e.g., antioxidants, fat replacers, anticaking agents, suspension agents, propellants).

Püssa, Tõna. 2013. *Principles of Food Toxicology.* 2nd ed. Boca Rotan, FL: CRC Press. 414 pp. ISBN: 9781466504103. $85.95.

Toxicology is a critical component of food science, and this textbook starts with an in-depth synopsis of toxicology and an explanation of toxicants. A significant portion of the book is a summary of foodborne toxicants that includes those found in plants, the soil, pesticides, and veterinary drugs, among many others. The book also covers food additives and vitamins and offers a discussion on food adulteration.

Food Safety in Commercial Applications

International Commission on Microbiological Specifications for Foods. 2011. *Microorganisms in Foods 8: Use of Data for*

Assessing Process Control and Product Acceptance. Springer. 400 pp. ISBN: 978-1-4419-9373-1. $269.00.

This book presents a detailed account of methods for enhancing the safety of food and protecting foods from microbiological organisms. The book includes 26 chapters that cover meat and poultry products, fish and seafood, pet foods, produce, dairy and egg products, and processed foods. The book, and all of the books in this series, is not intended for a general public audience; rather, its audience is food scientists in industry, regulatory agencies, and academia. It is also geared toward upper-level microbiology classes.

Mortimore, Sara, and Carol Wallace. 2013. *HACCP: A Practical Approach.* 3rd ed. 475 pp. Springer. ISBN: 978-1-4614-5027-6. $79.95.

This book is intended to be a guide for food professionals developing or currently implementing Hazard Analysis and Critical Control Points (HACCP) systems. The book includes guidance on all of the HACCP principles and case studies to demonstrate the application of HACCP. A new addition also includes updated information on pathogen characteristics. The book covers planning effective food safety management, prerequisite programs, and how to implement HACCP.

Varzakas, Theodoros, and Constantina Tsai, eds. 2015. *Handbook of Food Processing: Food Safety, Quality, and Manufacturing Processes.* Boca Raton, FL. CRC Press. 659 pp. ISBN: 1498721776. $189.95.

This is an in-depth reference for understanding and applying techniques for food processing that will ensure safety and quality. The book includes case studies on ISO 22000, HACCP, and food waste management from the perspective of food processors and manufacturers. Specific processing methods discussed in detail include chocolate manufacturing, alcoholic and nonalcoholic beverages, poultry and meat products, and snack foods.

Food Safety Law and Policy

Roberts, Michael. 2016. *Food Law in the United States.* Oxford: Cambridge University Press. 470 pp. ISBN: 978-1107545762. $74.99.

This comprehensive legal reference examines food regulations in the context of commerce, safety, marketing, nutrition, and food systems. The book summarizes the major laws with citations and presents case studies on how the laws have been applied. The legal definitions of food-related issues are presented. The book is intended for students and legal scholars but could also serve as a reference for practitioners and consumers.

Neff, Roni, ed. 2014. *Introduction to the US Food System: Public Health, Environment, and Equity.* 576 pp. ISBN: 978-1-118-06338-5. $85.00.

This collection of essays comes from the Johns Hopkins Center for a Livable Future. The perspectives in the book include discussion of how the U.S. food system affects food security, community health, and social justice. The contributors frame their topics in the context of public health and the environmental impacts of the food system. The book is designed as a textbook and includes chapter objectives and discussion questions.

Nesheim, Malden C., Maria Oria, and Peggy Tsai Yih, eds. 2015. *A Framework for Assessing Effects of the Food System.* Washington, DC: National Academies Press. 477 pp. ISBN: 13: 978-0-309-30780-2. $78.00. Available free online: http://www.nap.edu/catalog/18846/a-framework-for-assessing-effects-of-the-food-system

This book is the result of work by a committee formed by the Institute of Medicine and the National Research

Council, which was charged with evaluating all aspects of the U.S. food system. The idea for a framework document came from a 2012 workshop called Exploring the True Costs of Food. The report begins with an overview of the U.S. food system, and then offers details on the health, environmental, social, and economic effects of the system. The main focus of the work is a proposed framework for assessing the impacts of the food system that includes four principles. Examples of how the framework can be applied are provided.

Genetically Modified Foods

Elderidge, Sarah, ed. 2003. *Food Biotechnology: Current Issues and Perspectives.* New York: Nova Science Publishers. 151 pp. ISBN: 1590338480. $59.

Writers with different viewpoints present information on the basic science and regulation of food biotechnology, the Starlink corn controversy, labeling of genetically modified foods, consumer adoption of genetically modified agricultural products, the terminator gene and other genetic-use-restriction technologies in crops, biosafety protocols for genetically modified foods, acceptance and intellectual property rights and issues in South America, and the introduction of U.S. agricultural biotechnology products in global markets.

Mphil, Claire Robinson, Michael Antoniou, and John Fagan. 2016. *GMO Myths and Truths: A Citizen's Guide to the Evidence on the Safety and Efficacy of Genetically Modified Crops and Foods.* 3rd ed. London: Earth Open Source. 164 pp. ISBN: 978-0993436703. $19.95.

In this book, the authors present the science related to GMOs to argue that GMOs are harmful to people and the environment. This is the third edition of a very popular book, and this edition is intended as a handbook for those interested in the subject, rather than an in-depth discussion, as was the case in the 330-page second edition. The book is promoted as a paperback that can be a pocket reference on the subject.

Ronald, Pamela C., and R.W. Adamchak. 2010. *Tomorrow's Table: Organic Farming, Genetics, and the Future of Food.* Oxford University Press. 232 pp. ISBN: 978–0195393576. $19.95.

The married authors are a geneticist and an organic farmer, and this book is a somewhat personal account of how organic farming and genetic engineering could work together to solve food security issues of the future. The book is written as sort of a memoir as the authors explain genetic engineering and organic farming and the potential environmental and health impacts of both. There are also some recipes included in the book, inspired by the farm that is the home of the authors.

History

Coppin, Clayton, and Jack High. 1999. *Politics of Purity: Harvey Washington Wiley and the Origins of Federal Food Policy.* Ann Arbor: University of Michigan Press. 232 pp. ISBN: 0-472-10984-7. $85.

The authors examine the economics and politics behind the 1906 pure food law. They conclude that Harvey Wiley, the principal regulator behind the pure food law, acted to nationalize regulation in order to concentrate his own power, and his actions gave competitive advantage to national brands over local ones. Uniform national labels and regulations favored national brands that could prepare food and label it to one standard rather than having to make separate labels for each state. The authors argue that the national food concerns supported national food legislation because it was a strategic use of public policy.

Goodwin, Lorine. 1999. *Pure Food and Drink Crusaders, 1879–1914.* Jefferson, NC: McFarland and Co. 359 pp. ISBN: 0-786-42742-6. $39.95.

Lorine Goodwin discusses the women and women's groups that became concerned about the food, drink, and drugs affecting their families and what they did about their concerns. The author argues that the crusaders were instrumental in mobilizing government to enact pure food laws and that without consumer pressure the laws would not have been enacted.

Microbiology of Foods

Doyle, Michael P., Larry R. Beuchat, and Thomas J. Montville, eds. 2012. *Food Microbiology: Fundamentals and Frontiers.* 4th ed. Washington, D.C.: ASM Press. ISBN: 978-1555816261. $199.95.

This work contains specialized vocabulary that may require a companion text on microbiology. It includes molecular and mechanistic aspects of food microbiology; description of the basic factors affecting growth, survival, and death of microbes; coverage of spores and molds; principles of spoilage; spoilage patterns for meats, dairy products, grains, fruits, and vegetables; specific foodborne pathogens; epidemiology of foodborne diseases; foodborne viruses; parasites; preservatives and preservation methods; food fermentation; and techniques in food microbiology, including conventional, rapid, automated, genetic, and immunological methods, modeling, and HACCP principles.

Erkman, Osman, and T. Faruk Bozoglu. 2016. *Food Microbiology: Principles into Practice.* 2 vols. New York: Wiley & Sons. 944 pp. ISBN: 978-1-119-23776-1. $275.00.

These two volumes are a comprehensive reference for those studying and working in food microbiology. The books cover microbiology in detail and focus on types of microbes in foods. A section of how foods become contaminated with microbes covers water sources, food handlers, sewage, and food ingredients and many others. Foodborne diseases caused by microorganisms are categorized according to the types of health effects associated with them and discussed in detail. The textbooks also cover laboratory testing methods and food spoilage.

Montville, Thomas J., Karl R. Matthews, and Kalmia E. Kniel. 2012. *Food Microbiology: An Introduction.* 3rd ed. Washington, DC: ASM Press. 570 pp. ISBN: 978-1555816360. $109.95.

Intended for undergraduates with one semester of microbiology and limited exposure to biochemistry, this adaptation of *Food Microbiology: Fundamentals and Frontiers* (see earlier) is a primer for the study of food microbiology. It includes methods of culturing bacteria for study and for determining microbial contamination. The book explains how food processing can inhibit or encourage microbial growth, disease outbreaks, spoilage organisms, molds, viruses, and prions. Chapters on specific foodborne microbes cover the characteristics of the organism and profiles of the disease and describe how the microbe is affected by chemical and physical treatments.

Ray, Bibek, and Arun Bhunia. 2013. *Fundamental Food Microbiology.* 5th ed. Boca Raton, FL: CRC Press. 608 pp. ISBN: 978-1466564435. $91.95.

This text is designed to accompany introductory food microbiology courses. It covers the history of food microbiology, characteristics of microorganisms important in food, significance of microbial sublethal injury and bacterial sporulation in foods, beneficial uses of microorganisms (e.g., starter cultures), bioprocessing, biopreservation, probiotics, spoilage of foods by microorganisms and their enzymes, methods of determining food spoilage, and emerging spoilage bacteria in refrigerated foods.

Audiovisual Resources

Top Documentary Films (www.topdocumentaryfilms.com) is a website offering access to hundreds of videos free of charge.

The documentaries are categorized according to the main topics covered. Films about food can be found under the "health" and "environment" categories.

All Hands on Deck! True Confessions of a Filthy, Rotten, Disgusting Germ

Year: 2006

Length: 10 minutes per segment

Price: $35

Source: Brevis

https://www.brevis.com/products/755493/hwsdvd-hand wash-dvd

A germ wearing a sweatshirt that says "SOAP KILLS" tells the family secrets by explaining how and where germs linger in public restrooms. Thorough hand-washing techniques are demonstrated, including how to avoid reinfection while turning off the water faucet and leaving the restroom. This material is presented in three versions: health care, food service, and young people, in both English and Spanish.

Antibiotic Resistance

Year: 2016

Length: 29 minutes

Source: Australian Broadcasting Corporation

According to this documentary, Australia is the world's largest consumer of antibiotics. The film begins with an overview of the importance of bacteria and antibiotics and walks through the current situation with pathogens that have evolved to be resistant to them.

Digital Food

Year: 2015

Length: 47 minutes

Source: VPRO Backlight

In the context of projections for a world population of nine billion people, this film explores options for ensuring food security in the future. The role of the local foods movement is discussed, as is sustainable energy use in farming. An innovative approach to using solar energy in grow houses is presented as one possible solution. Organic chef Dan Barber talks about the impact of local food and minimizing waste in restaurant dining.

Dr. X and the Quest for Food Safety

Year: 2006

Length: 45 minutes

Source: National Science Teachers Association

https://www.youtube.com/watch?v=j8YfUEzBQ20

This video is part of a curriculum package sponsored by the National Science Teachers Association and the FDA. Designed for middle and high school students, the video features Dr. X, a food scientist, and Tracy, a student, who learns about how emerging microbes live, grow, and spread. The video also talks about how the latest food safety technologies affect the foods we eat and features interviews with scientists working at food science careers.

Food Fight: The Debate over GMO Labels

Year: 2013

Length: 58 minutes

Source: http://wafoodfight.com/

The film opens at Pike Place Market in Seattle and talks about genetically engineered Salmon. The arguments for and against GMOs are presented from scientists, farmers, and activists. The film attempts to present all sides of the issue to raise awareness of the state of the science and policy on GMOs.

Food Inc.

Year: 2009

Length: 91 minutes

Price: $24.99

Source: http://www.takepart.com/foodinc

Examines the food industry in the United States, specifically focusing on factory farms, and includes footage inside an animal-processing facility. Discusses how the food industry has affected consumer preferences and several controversies surrounding large-scale food production. Highlights sustainable agriculture as a solution.

Food Safety, It's Up to You

Year: 2005

Length: 30 minutes

Source: Seattle King County Department of Public Health

https://www.youtube.com/watch?v=90BSHxWgTHM

Recorded to train food service workers in Washington State, this video's commonsense approach makes it valuable to food service workers everywhere. Covers hand washing, avoiding cross-contamination, and proper food handling.

Frontline: The Trouble with Chicken

Year: 2015

Length: 60 minutes

Price: $19.99

Source: PBS Home Video

http://www.shoppbs.org

Explores the persistence of *Salmonella* in poultry production in the context of a major outbreak that made more than 600 people sick. Compares governmental response to *E. coli* with efforts to curb *Salmonella*.

Our Chemical Lives

Year: 2015

Length: 29 minutes

Source: Australian Broadcasting Corporation

Presents a case against the insidious use of chemicals and daily human exposure. Discusses mercury, lead, and endocrine-disrupting chemicals. Includes interviews with U.S. public health officials.

A Place at the Table

Year: 2012

Length: 84 minutes

Source: http://www.takepart.com/place-at-the-tablePrice: $9.99

http://www.takepart.com/place-at-the-table/film

This film follows families in America who are struggling with hunger and food security. It raises important questions about food policy in the United States and is a reminder that even rich developed countries have many people who cannot put healthy food on the table.

Revolution: Food

Year: 2015

Length: 1 hour 10 minutes

Price: $12.99

Source: Idee Films

http://www.revolutionfoodmovie.com/#main

This documentary examines a positive approach to changing the way we eat and solving some of the inherent problems with food distribution systems.

State Contacts

State Food Regulators

http://dslo.afdo.org/
> The Association of Food and Drug Officials compiles and maintains a comprehensive listing of state regulatory agencies and officials. This list includes state epidemiologists, food emergency response coordinators, and contacts for specific foods such as dairy and shellfish, among others.

State HACCP Contacts

http://www.fsis.usda.gov/wps/portal/informational/contactus/
state-haccp-contacts-and-coordinators
> The list of contacts in states is maintained by the USDA Food Safety Inspection Service. These individuals provide technical assistance and guidance on implementing HACCP.

WORLD HEADQUARTERS

ConAgra Foo

Food you love

There is a long history of activities and events that have shaped contemporary food safety. The listing below identifies some of the more prominent items and includes legislative and political actions as well as scientific discoveries. In addition, some of the unusual events, such as scandals and litigation, are noted to contextualize the importance of food safety.

6000 BC   Neolithic man is growing crops and keeping food animals captive. Food is salted and cooled to preserve it for later consumption.

ca. 750–687 BC   Old Testament's book of Leviticus offers a whole series of food and hygiene rules to protect the Israelites. (The kosher dietary laws prevent mixing of meat and milk. If these are mixed at warm temperatures, it creates an idyllic culture medium for potentially lethal bacteria. It is unknown whether these rules were based on food safety knowledge or were adopted for other reasons.)

Flags fly over ConAgra Foods world headquarters in Omaha, Nebraska, on June 30, 2015. Nearly a decade after hundreds of Americans got sick after eating Peter Pan peanut butter tainted with *Salmonella*, ConAgra Foods appears close to settling a federal criminal case stemming from the outbreak. In 2014, federal prosecutors announced that Chicago-based ConAgra had agreed to pay $11.2 million, a sum that includes the highest fine ever in a U.S. food safety case, and pled guilty to a single misdemeanor charge in the 2007 outbreak. (AP Photo/Nati Harnik)

AD **1206**   King John of England prohibits adulteration of bread.

1265   Assize of Bread and Ale of 1265 prohibits British merchants from using chalk instead of flour and watering down beer.

1266   English law enacted that prohibits the practice of short-weighting customers and selling unsound meat.

1822   Frederick C. Marcus, a German chemist living in London, publishes *A Treatise on Adulteration of Food and Culinary Poisons*. A pirated version appearing in the United States reveals that many common foodstuffs are adulterated.

1862   Charles M. Wetherhill, the first chemist of the USDA, conducted experiments to determine if adding sugar to increase the alcohol content of wine was considered adulteration. The first report about food adulteration was published by the Food and Drug Administration (FDA), which also discussed food preservation.

1866   Corn syrup is discovered. Acid is used to break down cornstarch into glucose. Corn syrup becomes the first inexpensive domestic substitute for cane sugar.

1872   England enacts the Adulteration of Food or Drink Act with stiff penalties for violations, including six months hard labor for the second offense. This act is not modernized until 1955, when the Food and Drug Act is passed.

1880s   Women's groups around the United States begin to organize for pure food, drink, and drugs. In 1884, 15 Beekman Hill women declare war on New York City's slaughterhouse district, a tangle of 55 broken-down wooden sheds that reek with filth from accumulated refuse and slaughter. Through the women's persistence, lawsuits, and negotiations with the Health Department, the slaughterhouses are cleaned up in the early 1890s. Also in 1884, the Women's Christian Temperance Union teaches classes to delegates at its national convention in Battle Creek, Michigan, on how to rid American homes of dangerous and adulterated food, drink, and drugs.

1883   The U.S. Tea Act of 1883 attempts to prevent sale of adulterated teas. The law proves to be useless because it sets no standards and no method of enforcement.

Robert Koch discovers the cholera bacterium and determined that it was transmitted through water and food.

1890   The first American food inspection law is enacted. Although this act benefits consumers, it is established by merchants trying to convince foreign companies that American foods are safe.

1895   Henri Becquerel discovers radioactivity, and suggestions for using it to kill pathogens in food are made immediately.

1897   The Tea Importation Act of 1897 makes it illegal to import tea that is inferior in purity, quality, and fitness for consumption.

1898   The Committee on Food Standards within the Association of Official Agricultural Chemists is established. The Committee is headed by Dr. Harvey Wiley.

1902   Harvey Wiley, director of the Bureau of Chemistry, starts a "poison squad" to test common food additives. Volunteer testers are fed a carefully controlled diet to test for adverse effects. One at a time, a different additive is incorporated into the diet in high quantities.

The Food Standards Committee is formed as the first advisory committee to the FDA. This committee met regularly to debate national food regulations.

1905   The first U.S. and British patents are issued for using ionizing radiation to kill bacteria in foods.

1906   *The Jungle* by Upton Sinclair is published. The book details the unsanitary practices of the meat-packing industry. Six months after publication, the Pure Food and Drug Act and the Meat Inspection Act are passed.

The Pure Food and Drug Act of 1906, administered by the U.S. Department of Agriculture's (USDA's) Bureau of Chemistry, provides the basic legal and institutional frameworks for latter-day food safety laws. Laws prohibit the shipment in interstate commerce of foods that are adulterated by any of several definitions, including food that is spoiled, is contaminated with filth, is derived from diseased animals, or contains unsafe substances.

The Federal Meat Inspection Act, administered by the USDA, requires continuous, on-site factory inspection by government inspectors using sight, smell, and touch to detect unsafe meat.

1908 The first Inspector's Manual was written by Walter G. Campbell and published by the FDA. Campbell eventually became the first commissioner of the FDA in 1940.

1910 The Insecticide Act marks the federal government's first attempt to regulate pesticides.

1913 The Gould Amendment of the Food and Drug Act requires that net contents be stated on the label.

1914 The Federal Trade Commission Act establishes the Federal Trade Commission and empowers it to monitor food advertising.

1918 The influenza virus emerges and spreads around the world, killing more people than any other outbreak of disease in human history. Epidemiologists believe 675,000 U.S. deaths occurred; total U.S. population at the time was 105 million. Estimates of worldwide deaths range from 21 to 100 million. The virus, H1N1, is currently found in swine.

1923 The Filled Milk Act prohibits the sale of milk to which fats or oils, other that milk fats, have been added.

Mrs. Cecile Steele, a resident of the Delmarva region of eastern Maryland, mistakenly receives a shipment of 500 chicks instead of the 50 she ordered and raises them, selling the meat for a hefty profit. News of her success spreads quickly, positioning the region to be a center of U.S. broiler production until just after World War II.

1924 Oysters contaminated with *Salmonella* Typhi kills 150 people in New York and makes at least 1,500 sick.

1927   The Federal Milk Importation Act establishes regulations on importation of milk and cream into the United States to protect public health.

The USDA's Bureau of Chemistry is renamed the Food, Drug and Insecticide Administration.

1931   The Food, Drug, and Insecticide Administration renamed the Food and Drug Administration.

1934   The U.S. Public Health Services proposes *Restaurant Sanitation Regulations.*

1935   The *Ordinance and Code Regulating Eating and Drinking Establishments* recommended by U.S. Public Health Service.

1936   John Tyson (founder of Tyson Foods) picks up a load of 500 chickens and drives them 600 miles north to Chicago, bypassing the local slaughterhouses and thus breaking the tight bond between local farmers and slaughterhouses. From now on, slaughterhouses don't have to buy the birds closest to them to get the best prices.

1938   The Federal Food, Drug and Cosmetic Act gives the FDA authority to perform food-processing facility inspections, establish standards of identity for individual food products, and certify colors. (Colors are divided into categories based on whether they can be used in food, drugs, and cosmetics [F, D, and C colors], or just drugs and cosmetics, or cosmetics only.) The act also grants the FDA the right to seek injunctions in federal court against violators of the law.

1939   Swiss chemist Paul Muller recognizes the value of dichlorodiphenyltrichloroethane (DDT) as a potent nerve poison that will work on insects, ushering in a new era in agricultural pesticides. DDT is successfully used during World War II to kill malaria-causing insects. Muller wins the Nobel Prize for his work in 1948 but realizes the harm DDT can do to the environment, to wildlife, and to humans because of its persistence.

1940s   The U.S. Army begins testing irradiation of common foods.

1940   The FDA becomes part of the U.S. Federal Security Agency.

1944   The Public Health Service Act is passed, creating the U.S Public Health Service and addressing the control of biological and communicable diseases.

1946   The Agricultural Marking Act provides USDA with authority to inspect and classify the quality of agricultural products.

1947   The Federal Insecticide, Fungicide, and Rodenticide Act (FIFRA) establishes criteria to evaluate the safety of pesticides. Pesticides must now be licensed and proven effective and hazards must be accurately labeled. This law is primarily a labeling law and only applies to pesticides used to produce goods sold in interstate commerce.

Radiation is proven to be effective in sterilizing meats and other foods, an important discovery for military use.

1949   Dr. Thomas Jukes, then director of nutrition and physiology research at Lederle Laboratories, a division of American Cyanamid, discovers that animals fed small doses of antibiotics gain weight faster.

The FDA publishes guidance to industry for the first time. This guidance, "Procedures for the Appraisal of the Toxicity of Chemicals in Food," came to be known as the "black book."

Early 1950s   Farmers begin feeding livestock antibiotics subtherapeutically to prevent and treat subclinical disease (diseases that don't cause evident symptoms but are nonetheless taxing to the animal) and to promote growth. By 1954, American farmers are using 245 tons of antibiotics each year in livestock feed.

1950   The Delaney Committee starts congressional investigation of the safety of chemicals in foods and cosmetics, laying the foundation for the 1954 Miller Pesticide Amendment, the 1958 Food Additives Amendment, and the 1960 Color Additive Amendment.

1953   The FDA becomes a separate entity in the U.S. Department of Health, Education, and Welfare. This department is later renamed the Department of Health and Human Services.

1954   The Miller Amendment to the Federal Drug and Cosmetic Act allows the FDA to establish tolerances for "economic poisons," or pesticides, on agricultural products like fruit, vegetables, and grains.

1956   The Chicago Board of Trade institutes a grading system for corn, making corn a commodity.

Late 1950s   The Pillsbury Corporation, under contract from the National Aeronautics and Space Administration (NASA), develops the Hazard Analysis and Critical Control Points (HACCP) system to protect astronauts from foodborne illness. HACCP, as originally conceived by Pillsbury, included (1) identification and assessment of hazards associated with growing/harvesting to marketing/preparation; (2) determination of the critical control points to control any identifiable hazard; and (3) establishment of systems to monitor critical control points.

1957   The Poultry Products Inspection Act of 1957 requires that poultry products be wholesome, unadulterated, properly marked, labeled, and packaged. Poultry is now subject to the same inspection criteria as beef; it must be continuously monitored and inspected in the factory.

The first commercial use of irradiation takes place in Stuttgart, Germany, where the process is used to preserve spices.

Asian flu, caused by the H2N2 virus, creates a violent pandemic.

1958   The Food Additives Amendment to the Federal Food, Drug, and Cosmetics Act empowers the FDA to prohibit additives to food that have not been adequately tested to establish safety. In effect, the FDA also has premarket review and approval authority over chemical additives in foods. This amendment includes the Delaney Clause (after the congressman responsible for its inclusion), which states that no additive will be deemed safe if any quantity of the additive is found to cause cancer in humans or any animal species. As part of this amendment, irradiation is regulated as a food additive rather than a preservation process. Therefore, irradiation must meet a higher standard of proof before it will be declared safe.

The Humane Slaughter Act requires cattle and pigs to be rendered senseless to pain before being shackled, hoisted, thrown, cast, or cut. The act only applies to animals whose meat is sold to the federal government, but in practice the act is applied in all commercial plants.

The FDA publishes first list of nearly 200 substances Generally Recognized as Safe.

The former Soviet Union becomes the first country to allow human consumption of irradiated foods when they cleared it for use in potato farming.

1959   Germany passes a law banning irradiation, and the machine used to process spices in Stuttgart is dismantled.

A massive recall of cranberries right before Thanksgiving, after it was discovered to be contaminated with a carcinogenic weed killer, is considered to be the first major food scare in the United States.

1960s   Scientists working at Keio University's School of Medicine in Japan, including Tsutomo Watanabe and Stuart Levy, discover that antibiotic drug resistance is a transferable trait between different strains of bacteria. For example, a strain of *Salmonella* that is resistant to penicillin can pass on this resistance to a strain of *Campylobacter.*

The "Green Revolution" increases crop yields due to use of chemical fertilizers and pesticides around the world.

Pigs and cows begin to be raised on factory farms.

1960   The Color Additives Amendment creates uniform pretesting requirements for food. Previously, the FDA could not set limits on the amounts of color that could be used. This act requires the FDA to consider the probable consumption levels of the color, cumulative effects, substances formed as a result of consumption of the color, safety factors, and potential carcinogenicity.

1961 The Food and Agriculture Organization (FAO) and the World Health Organization (WHO), both agencies of the United Nations, establish the Codex Alimentarius Commission to set standards for food production, including technical specifications and good manufacturing practices. The purpose of the standards is to facilitate trade between nations and ensure safe food.

1962 *Silent Spring* by Rachel Carson is published. Carson, a marine biologist, describes the environmental damage caused by DDT in the environment.

The *Food Service Sanitation Manual Including a Model Food Service Sanitation Ordinance and Code is* published by the Public Health Service.

1963 Irradiation is approved by the FDA to control insects in wheat and wheat powder.

1964 The FDA approves irradiation to extend the shelf-life of white potatoes.

The first meeting of the United Nations' Joint Expert Committee on Food Irradiation takes place.

1966 The Fair Packaging and Labeling Act stipulates that all food labels contain the same basic information, including the common or usual name of the product, the name and address of the manufacturer, ingredients in order of weight, net weight, and a statement that the product contains artificial color or flavor if any.

1967 A complete revision of the 1906 act, the Wholesome Meat Act, requires meat be wholesome, unadulterated, properly marked, labeled, and packaged. All cattle, sheep, swine, and goats must be inspected prior to slaughter. Previous legislation applied to meat sold in interstate commerce only; now state inspection standards must be at least equal to federal standards. Additionally, the USDA has the power to seize unsafe meat, and federal regulators may examine company records.

1968   The Poultry Products Act extends federal poultry inspection standards to poultry produced and sold within the same state. In 1968, 87 percent of poultry was federally inspected. This act extends inspection to the remaining 13 percent.

The Hong Kong flu, the H3N2 virus, spreads worldwide with large numbers of infection but low rates of death.

1969   The FDA begins administering Sanitation Programs for milk, shellfish, food service, and interstate travel facilities and for preventing poisoning and accidents. These responsibilities were transferred from other units of the Public Health Service.

The first Good Manufacturing Practices for food establishments are issued.

1970s   NASA adopts irradiation to sterilize food for astronauts.

The Livestock Revolution, similar to Green Revolution of the 1960s, increases meat production through factory farming techniques around the world.

1970   The Egg Products Inspection Act stipulates that eggs be wholesome, not adulterated, and properly labeled and packaged. Egg products must be continuously monitored and inspected in the factory.

The International Atomic Energy Agency (IAEA), FAO, WHO, and the Organization for Economic Cooperation and Development (OECD) create the International Project in the Field of Food Irradiation to sponsor a worldwide research program on the wholesomeness of irradiated foods.

The Environmental Protection Agency (EPA) is created. Regulation of pesticides is transferred from the USDA to the new agency.

Cyclamate, a type of artificial sweetener, is banned by the FDA. At the time, it was thought to cause bladder cancer and damage to the testes. Later research suggests that it does not cause cancer directly but increases the potency of other carcinogens.

1971   The HACCP concept is presented to the public for the first time, at the 1971 National Conference on Food Protection.

1972   The Federal Environmental Pesticide Control Act (revised FIFRA) requires that all pesticides be registered with the EPA. This includes pesticides that were previously excluded because they were not used on foodstuffs sold across state lines. This legislation makes it easier to ban hazardous pesticides and imposes penalties for improper use. The law divides pesticides into two categories: general use and restricted use. Restricted-use pesticides must be clearly labeled and can only be used by certified applicators.

DDT is banned in the United States except for use in extreme health emergencies.

1973   About 1 ton of polybrominated biphenyl, a closely related but much more toxic chemical than polychlorinated biphenyl, is mistakenly added to cattle feed in Michigan. It is estimated that virtually all the citizens of Michigan and some of the citizens of other states consumed the substance either in dairy products or meat.

Earl Butz, President Nixon's second Secretary of Agriculture and an agricultural economist from Purdue, restructures the agriculture support program from a system of loans to direct payments to farmers. This has the effect of encouraging farmers to grow as much corn as possible on their land, while stabilizing corn prices for corn used in corn products and in animal feeds.

The first major recall of a food product in the United States occurs as millions of cans of mushrooms are recalled because of botulism.

1974   The Safe Drinking Water Act directs the EPA to establish national standards setting the maximum allowable levels for certain chemical and bacteriological pollutants for water systems serving more than 25 customers.

1976   Red dye number one and number two are banned by the FDA. Red dye number one is found to cause liver cancer, and red dye number two is found to be a possible carcinogen.

The *Food Service Sanitation Manual Including a Model Food Service Sanitation Ordinance*, the 1976 Recommendations of the FDA, is published.

1977   The FDA bans saccharin because many animal studies show that it causes cancer of the bladder. Other studies show it may also cause other cancers. In 1977, saccharin is the primary sweetener in diet soft drinks and a number of other artificially sweetened products, and the American public is outraged at the ban. However, before the ban can take effect, Congress intervenes. Saccharin continues to be available but must carry a warning notice.

The Food Safety and Quality Service is created and is involved in grading and inspections.

1979   Diethylstilbestrol is banned for use in cattle. Other growth hormones may still be used.

The Surgeon General's report *Healthy People: The Surgeon General's Report on Health Promotion and Disease Prevention* is the precursor to the Healthy People objectives for improving health.

1980   The Joint IAEA, FAO, WHO, and OECD Expert Committee on the Wholesomeness of Irradiated Foods concludes that the irradiation of any food commodity up to an overall dose of 10 kilograys (kGy) (a measure of the absorbed dose) presents no toxicological hazard. Therefore, toxicological testing of foods so treated is no longer required and the report suggests a maximum does for irradiated foods.

The National Academy of Sciences issues a report entitled *The Effects on Human Health of Subtherapeutic Use of Antibiotics in Animal Feed*. The report states that almost half of the antibiotics manufactured in the United States are fed to animals but the Academy is unable to determine from existing research whether antibiotics in animal feed harms human health.

1981   Aspartame, the artificial sweetener marketed under the names NutraSweet and Equal, is approved by the FDA for use in drinks, mixes, desserts, and cold cereals. It is 200 times sweeter than sugar, and one teaspoon has one-tenth of a calorie.

The Food Quality and Safety Service is renamed the Food Safety and Inspection Service (FSIS).

1982   The *Retail Food Store Sanitation Code*, 1982 (Recommendations of the Association of Food and Drug Officials and U.S. Department of Health and Human Services, Public Health Service, FDA), is published.

1983   The FDA approves irradiation for spices and dry vegetable seasonings to kill insects and bacteria.

1984   The EPA asks the National Academy of Sciences to explore the level of protection that law and regulation provide against cancer risks from pesticide residues in food. The academy forms the Delaney Committee to address this question.

Food-related bioterrorism occurs in The Dalles, Oregon, when followers of Bhagwan Shree Rajneesh intentionally poison local salad bars with *Salmonella* to keep people from voting in a local election.

Pulsed-field gel electrophoresis, the current gold standard for DNA fingerprinting, is developed.

1985   The largest-ever *Salmonella* outbreak occurs in Illinois. The source is traced to a milk plant where one day's output was incorrectly pasteurized. More than 200,000 people are affected and 4 die.

Nearly 1,000 people in several western states and Canada are poisoned by residues from the pesticide Temik in watermelons. Symptoms include nausea, vomiting, blurred vision, and muscle weakness. Some become gravely ill and suffer grand mal seizures and cardiac irregularities. At least two stillbirths result from the poisoning.

A subcommittee of the Food Protection Committee of the National Academy of Sciences issues a report on microbiological criteria strongly endorsing HACCP. The report recommends that both regulators and industry use HACCP because it is the most effective and efficient means of assuring the safety of the food supply.

The FDA approves low-dose irradiation to control *Trichinella* in pork.

1986 The first cases of bovine spongiform encephalopathy (BSE) are confirmed in the United Kingdom. The disease is nicknamed "mad cow disease" because the cows stagger around as if drunk, become belligerent, and die.

The FDA approves irradiation for fruits and vegetables. It is used both to control insects and to slow the ripening of fruits and vegetables.

1987 The National Academy of Sciences issues a report on pesticides entitled Regulating Pesticides: The Delaney Paradox. The Delaney Committee finds that nearly all registrations for pesticide use on food crops are set using a risk-benefit balancing standard contained within the FIFRA. Using this standard does not protect the public from significant health risk. The higher Delaney standard, which requires that strict limits be placed on pesticides suspected of inducing cancer, are used in only 3 percent of cases. Using this data, it is estimated that there will be an additional 1 million cancer cases over a 70-year period.

1988 The Pesticide Monitoring and Improvements Act requires a computerized monitoring system for the FDA to record, summarize, and evaluate results of its program for monitoring food products for pesticide residues.

An expert scientific advisory panel to the secretaries of Agriculture, Commerce, Defense, and Health and Human Services, the National Advisory Committee on Microbiological Criteria for Foods (NACMCF), is convened. Part of the mission of NACMCF is to promote adoption of HACCP principles.

The British government appoints a committee to assess any possible risk to human health from BSE in cattle. At the committee's recommendation, a ban is placed on feeding animal-derived protein to ruminants like cattle, and farmers must report suspected cases of BSE. Over 2,000 confirmed cases of BSE are reported in 1988.

1989   CBS broadcasts "A is for Apple" on the news magazine *60 Minutes*. The broadcast publicizes the Natural Resources Defense Council report Intolerable Risk: Pesticides in Our Children's Food. The report and news story focus on the dangers, particularly to children, of the pesticide Alar, a growth regulator used on apples. Uniroyal, the maker of Alar, voluntarily withdraws the pesticide from the U.S. market, and the EPA bans the pesticide.

Over 7,000 cows are confirmed with BSE in the United Kingdom.

Two grapes in a shipment from Chile are discovered with cyanide. The cyanide was injected into the grapes at too small a dose to cause any harm, even to a small child. The FDA imposes a ban on Chilean fruit that lasts for five days.

The European Union fully implements a ban on imported meat and meat products that are from animals treated with hormones.

1990s   As many as one-third of all wells in the chicken-producing region along Maryland's lower Eastern Shore and in southern Delaware exceed the EPA's safe drinking water standards for nitrate, according to a study by the U.S. Geological Survey.

1990   The Sanitary Food Transportation Act prohibits the practice of shipping food in trucks or railcars that had earlier been used to transport potentially hazardous materials.

The Nutrition Labeling and Education Act mandates the nutrition facts label on food products, which must include standardized serving size, servings per container, calories from fat, and amounts of other food nutrients.

Healthy People 1990 is published by the U.S. Surgeon General, including goals for food safety.

The Organic Production Act defines what is meant by the term "organic" and sets standards for what can be labeled "organic" in the United States.

Over 14,000 cows are confirmed with BSE in the United Kingdom. Twenty-six countries ban the import of British cattle and beef.

1991   Over 25,000 new cases of BSE confirmed in British cows.

1992   The first industrial irradiation facility designed exclusively for food processing opens in Tampa, Florida, and the FDA approves irradiation for poultry.

BSE is successfully transmitted by injection to animals from seven mammalian species, including pigs and monkeys. Over 35,000 new cases of BSE are confirmed in the United Kingdom.

1993   A widespread outbreak of *Escherichia coli* O157:H7 bacteria is traced to tainted beef served primarily at Jack-in-the-Box restaurants. Some 732 people become ill; 195 are hospitalized and 4 children die.

The FDA approves recombinant bovine growth hormone (rBGH) marketed under the name Posilac. The drug, made by Monsanto, boosts milk production by 5 to 20 percent.

Two British farmers, whose herds were infected with BSE, die of Creutzfeldt-Jakob disease.

The National Academy of Sciences releases the report Pesticides in the Diets of Infants and Children. The academy concludes that fetuses, infants, and children are more susceptible than adults to toxic pesticides because their internal organs are still developing and their enzymatic, metabolic, and immune systems may provide less natural protection than those of adults.

The first version of the *Food Code* is published, to be used by state and local governments that regulate the food industry.

1994   Vermont becomes the first state in the nation to mandate labeling for dairy products from cows injected with rBGH. The International Dairy Foods Association sues Vermont, stating that "the mandatory labeling of milk products derived from supplemented cows will have the inherent effect of causing consumers to believe that such products are different from and inferior to milk products from unsupplemented cows." Although Vermont wins in District Court, the Circuit Court suspends the state law on appeal.

1995   The FDA adopts the HACCP approach to seafood inspection.

The Ninth Circuit of the U.S. Court of Appeals dismisses a lawsuit against CBS by apple growers claiming that the 1989 *60 Minutes* broadcast warning of potential health hazards was false.

The wall of an artificial waste lagoon gives way at a pig farm in North Carolina, spilling 24 million gallons of putrefying urine and feces into the New River. Millions of fish and other aquatic organisms die. A few weeks later, 9 million gallons of poultry waste flow down a North Carolina creek into the Northeast Cape Fear River. A few months later, 1 million gallons of pig waste trickle through a network of tidal creeks into the Cape Fear Estuary.

PulseNet conducts its initial project to demonstrate its effectiveness.

1996   A group of cattlemen from Texas sue Oprah Winfrey and Howard Lyman for food disparagement. The cattlemen claim that the two disparaged beef on the *Oprah Winfrey Show.*

After 10 people under the age of 42 die of Creutzfeldt-Jakob disease, a disease that generally strikes much older adults, the UK Secretary of State for Health, Stephen Dorell, tells the House of Commons that the most likely cause of these cases is exposure to BSE from eating beef.

The FDA approves olestra (Olean), Procter & Gamble's controversial indigestible fat for use in salty foods. Olestra has been proven to cause diarrhea, cramps, and other adverse effects.

New USDA regulations require microbial testing for beef and poultry products. The regulations reduce the allowable levels of various bacteria.

The Animal Medicinal Drug Use Clarification Act gives veterinarians the authority to prescribe medications intended for use in other species. Although the American Veterinary Medical Association supports the bill, Food Animals Concerns Trust opposes, citing concerns that untested drugs used in food animals could harm humans in the form of drug residues. Regulations require well-established veterinarian-client-patient relationships, documentation, and accountability when medications are prescribed under this act.

The Food Quality Protection Act repeals the Delaney Clause, which stated that any substance that increased cancer risk must not be in the food supply. The new law sets tolerance levels for chemical residues provided they do not cause more than one additional cancer case for each 1 million people. In addition, all exposures to pesticides must be shown to be safe for infants and children.

The CDC launches the National Molecular Surveillance Network (PulseNet), which is a national laboratory network that allows pathogens to be identified using DNA fingerprinting. Taking advantage of technology that allows subtyping of *E. coli* O157:H7, PulseNet traces and detects routes of pathogen transmission up to five times faster than earlier epidemiological surveillance methods.

FSIS issues the HACCP rule, which focuses on preventing pathogens in raw products.

1997 Sixteen people become ill from eating hamburger patties containing *E. coli* O157:H7. Some 25 million pounds of hamburger are recalled.

Food Safety: From Farm to Table, A National Food Safety Initiative, A Report to the President is released. It calls for an interagency response to food safety issues, declares foodborne illness a significant public health problem, and calls for a new early warning surveillance system.

As part of the initiative, the Active Foodborne Disease Surveillance System, or FoodNet, is established. An interagency network of the CDC, USDA, FDA, and states participating in CDC's Emerging Infections program, the network conducts population-based active surveillance of nine foodborne pathogens (*Salmonella, Campylobacter, Cyclospora, E. coli* O157:H7 and non-O157, *Listeria, Yersinia, Cryptosporidium, Shigella,* and *Vibrio*). Using surveys of laboratories, physicians, and the population, the network aims to determine the magnitude of diarrheal illnesses and the proportion attributable to food.

Stanley Prusiner, the developer of the prion theory, receives the Nobel Prize in Medicine or Physiology. According to Prusiner, prions are protein strands that can distort other protein strands, causing certain types of neurological diseases. Prions are a completely different type of infectious agent from bacteria, fungi, viruses, and parasites. Prusiner believes prions are the transmission agents for Creutzfeldt-Jakob disease, kuru, scrapie in sheep, BSE, and perhaps Alzheimer's disease.

An FDA ban on ruminant-to-ruminant feeding goes into effect. Cattle can no longer be fed rendered sheep or goats. However, cattle can still eat rendered horse, dog, cat, pig, chicken, turkey, or blood or fecal material from cows or chickens.

The FDA approves irradiation of beef and more intensive use of irradiation for pork and poultry.

The Canadian government consolidates all federally mandated food inspection and quarantine services into a single food inspection agency, the Canadian Food Inspection Agency. The goal of the new agency is to harmonize standards among federal, provincial, and municipal governments and make the process more efficient.

The USDA completes implementation of HACCP for meat and poultry.

Ben and Jerry's, Stonyfield Farm, Whole Foods Market, and Organic Valley Foods reach a settlement with the state of Illinois allowing food producers to state on their labels that their dairy products are rBGH free.

Avian influenza H5N1 jumps the species barrier from chickens to humans in Hong Kong, killing 6 of the 18 people infected. Public health officials order all 1.2 million chickens in Hong Kong to be slaughtered.

1998   The jury finds in favor of Howard Lyman and Oprah Winfrey in the suit filed against them by a group of Texas cattlemen claiming that the two disparaged beef on the *Oprah Winfrey Show* in 1996.

The CDC develops a web-based platform called FOOD, Foodborne Outbreak Online Database, that allows the public direct access to information about foodborne outbreaks.

Mandatory seafood HACCP controls begin. The juice HACCP rule is passed, requiring HACCP for processing and importing juices. Unpasteurized juice is required to contain a warning label.

1999   Twenty-one people die, 5 women miscarry, and 70 others are sickened when a Sara Lee–owned meat plant becomes contaminated with *Listeria*. Fifteen million pounds of hot dogs and cold cuts are recalled.

The National Academy of Sciences warns that use of antibiotics in food animals, particularly for subtherapeutic use, increases antibiotic-resistant bacteria, making it more difficult to treat disease in humans. The academy calculates that eliminating the use of these drugs would cost consumers about $10 each per year.

2000   Irradiated beef becomes available in the United States.

Foods that have been genetically modified, grown with sewage sludge, or treated with irradiation can no longer be labeled organic.

Over 1,000 people become ill and four die from *E. coli* O1547:H7 when the municipal water system in Walkerton,

Ontario, Canada, becomes contaminated with runoff from a nearby feedlot.

2001   The WHO cites antibiotic resistance as one of three major public health threats of the 21st century and develops a global action plan to contain antibiotic resistance. The General Assembly of 125 nations pledges efforts to contain the problem.

Japan requires all cattle to be tested for BSE before slaughter.

The World Trade Center is bombed, killing more than 2,700 people. Bioterrorism affecting the food and agriculture sectors becomes a subject of speculation.

2002   The Public Health Security and Bioterrorism Preparedness and Response Act of 2002 is ratified and includes mandates for ensuring the safety of domestic and imported foods from bioterrorism.

2003   Influenza virus H7N7 appears in poultry farms in the Netherlands, Belgium, and Germany. It infects 82 people and kills 1. Nearly 30 million poultry and some swine are killed to halt the spread of infection.

The first U.S. cow infected with BSE is discovered in Washington State, causing meat to be pulled from key markets and costing the U.S. beef industry $3.2 to $4.7 billion in 2004 alone, according to a study at Kansas State University.

Japan bans U.S. beef imports to protect consumers from exposure to cows infected with BSE.

A Hepatitis A outbreak is linked to green onions imported from Mexico. Chi Chi's restaurant in Pennsylvania was implicated in more than 600 cases of illness and 4 deaths. Chi Chi's never recovered and eventually declared bankruptcy in 2004.

The FDA requires nutrition labels to include information on trans fat.

2004   The FDA implements recordkeeping requirements for all foods and items that come in contact with food so that should a bioterrorism incident occur, the source can be traced.

The Food Allergy Labeling and Consumer Protection Act is passed, requiring labels to include information related to peanuts, soybeans, dairy, and other food allergens.

2005   French researchers discover that a goat slaughtered in 2002 tested positive for BSE.

A second U.S. cow that was slaughtered in 2004 is found to have been infected with BSE. This cow never entered the human or animal food supply.

The United States begins using the more accurate Western Blot test for BSE.

Vietnam imposes a ban on live poultry markets and begins requiring farms to convert to factory-style farming methods in 15 cities and provinces in an effort to control avian influenza.

The FAO and OIE (Office International des Epizooties or World Organization for Animal Health), finding that culling the chicken population is ineffective for controlling the spread of avian influenza, recommend not using culling as a primary means of control but instead recommend vaccination of chickens, which is effective but also expensive.

2006   Bagged spinach from California contaminated with *E. coli* O157:H7 kills 3 and sickens over 200 in a multistate outbreak. The outbreak is traced to cattle living in an adjacent field.

Prepackaged lettuce from California, used at Taco Bell and Taco John restaurants, causes another *E. coli* O157:H7 outbreak, sickening more than 150 people.

A bacteriophage (a virus that attacks bacteria) that kills the bacteria *Listeria monocytogenes* is approved for use in packaged foods to prevent contaminated packages from causing disease.

2007   A multistate outbreak of *Salmonella* in Tennessee is linked to peanut butter from a single facility in Georgia. There were 425 cases reported with 71 hospitalizations.

2009   The CDC launches the National Outbreak Reporting System, allowing local and state health departments to report food and waterborne outbreaks.

More than 700 people are sickened with *Salmonella* Typhimurium linked to peanut butter.

The final rule for Egg Safety is issued requiring control for *Salmonella* Enteritidis in eggs from production to distribution.

2010   The Egg Safety Rule implementation begins for large producers.

2011   The Food Safety Modernization Act is signed by President Obama, enhancing enforcement, education, and preventive activities. This is the first major food safety legislation in more than 70 years. It includes components that focus on training food safety professionals, enhancing regulatory authority at all governmental levels, and improving the safety of food imports.

2013   Twenty-nine states are involved in an outbreak of *Salmonella* Heidelberg linked to Foster Farms Chicken. A total of 634 people confirmed ill.

2015   Cucumbers imported from Mexico are implicated in an outbreak of *Salmonella* Poona that makes 907 ill.

ConAgra, which was implicated in the 2007 *Salmonella* outbreak in peanut butter, agrees to pay more than $8 million in fines and pleads guilty to a misdemeanor.

The former executive of Peanut Corporation of America receives the toughest sentence possible for his role in a *Salmonella* outbreak that sickened hundreds and killed nine people. He is sentenced to 28 years in prison for knowingly providing an unsafe product to consumers and processors and for adulterating food.

active ingredient   Substance in a product that performs the function of the product.

acute toxicity   A toxic reaction that occurs shortly after exposure to a toxin (usually within a few hours or days).

additive   Any substance the intended use of which results or may reasonably be expected to result—directly or indirectly—in its becoming a component or otherwise affecting the characteristics of any food.

adulterant   Contaminant to a product added either intentionally or unintentionally; poisonous or deleterious substance.

aerobic   Process that requires oxygen.

aerobic bacteria   Bacteria that multiply in oxygenated environments.

anaerobic   Absence of oxygen.

anaerobic bacteria   Bacteria that multiply in an oxygen-free environment.

antigen   Substance that stimulates an immune response when introduced to the body.

assay   Laboratory test or analysis.

bacteremia   Blood disease caused when bacteria enters the bloodstream.

bacteria   Single-celled organisms that multiply by dividing in two.

bioaccumulation   The process by which a pesticide or other contaminant concentrates in higher amounts as it makes its way up the food chain.

bovine spongiform encephalopathy (BSE)   A fatal neurological disease of cows also known as mad cow disease.

cancer   Unregulated cell growth, which causes malignant tumors.

carbamates   A class of synthetic pesticides that work by disrupting nerve function.

carcinogen   A substance that causes cancer.

codex Alimentarius   International body that sets food standards to facilitate international trade and promote food safety.

colonization   Proliferation of bacteria in the gut.

competitive exclusion   A system that introduces enough harmless bacteria into the gut of an animal to prevent bacteria harmful to humans from thriving.

concentrated animal feeding operation (CAFO)   A livestock operation in which the animals are confined at least 45 days in a given year and are raised in larger numbers.

contaminant   Any substance, object, or germ that is in food and should not be.

cross-contamination   Occurs when disease-causing organisms from one food (usually uncooked animal product) get onto another food. Usually occurs when foods are prepared on the same surface, or transferred by sponges, utensils, or aprons.

danger zone   Temperature most conducive to bacterial growth in food; 41 degrees Fahrenheit to 135 degrees Fahrenheit; established in the Food Code.

dose-response   Occurs when there is a correlation between the amount of drug or toxin and its effect on health.

dysentery   A diarrheal infection.

enteric infections   Infections of the digestive system.

environmental assessment In-depth, multidisciplinary, systems-based approach to determining how food was contaminated.

epidemiology The study of the incidence and distribution of disease or toxicity in human populations.

fecal-oral route Transfer of microorganisms from infected fecal matter to the digestive tract via the mouth. Usually occurs as a result of inadequate hand washing.

food and agriculture organization (FAO) United Nations agency that works to improve agricultural practices, facilitate trade between nations, and improve the quality and quantity of the food supply.

food poisoning An illness that occurs from eating a harmful food. Illness can be caused by chemicals, germs, or naturally occurring substances in the food.

foodborne illness An infectious disease caused by pathogens in food.

foodborne infection Foodborne disease occurring when ingested pathogen grows in intestinal tract.

foodborne intoxication Illness that results from eating a toxin.

foodborne outbreak Incident in which two or more persons experience similar illness resulting from ingestion of a common food.

fungicide Chemicals used to kill or suppress fungi.

gamma radiation A type of radiation emitted from radioactive isotopes; used to irradiate food.

gastroenteritis An inflammation of the stomach and intestinal tract that usually causes diarrhea.

genetically modified food Food developed by manipulating DNA.

gram negative Bacteria that do not take on the Gram stain, do not form spores, and are generally a fecal source.

hazard analysis and critical control point (HACCP) A science-based system for improving food safety. Potential trouble spots are identified and products tested at various production points to ensure safety. This system is required for many food industries and is widely used in most others.

hemolytic uremic syndrome (HUS) A serious complication of some foodborne illnesses, including poisoning by *E. coli* O157:H7. The syndrome causes destruction of blood cells and then kidney damage when the shredded blood cells clog the kidneys.

herbicide Chemicals used to kill or suppress weeds.

immune-compromised Person with a weakened immune system.

in vitro Literally, *in glass.* Studies or procedures carried out on cells or tissues in a test tube.

in vivo Literally, *in life.* Studies or procedures carried out on living animals or plants.

incubation period Length of time it takes to contract a disease after exposure.

infectious dose Number of bacteria, virus, or protozoa needed to cause disease.

insecticide Chemical used to kill insects.

integrated pest management (IPM) Use of two or more methods to control or prevent damage from pests. May include cultural practices (such as rotating crops), use of biological control agents (such as using beneficial insects to eat undesirable ones), and selective use of pesticides.

irradiation Treatment of food with low doses of radiation to kill or stop microorganisms from reproducing.

kuru A fatal form of dementia caused by cannibalism. Specifically, a transmissible spongiform encephalopathy of the Fore people of New Guinea.

metabolite   A compound derived by a chemical, biological, or physical action on a pesticide within a living organism. Metabolites can be more than, less than, or equally toxic as the original compound. Metabolites may also be produced by the action of environmental factors like sunlight and changing temperatures.

microbe   Life form only visible through a microscope, for example, bacteria, viruses, and protozoa.

microbial contamination   In the case of food, food tainted with disease-carrying bacteria, parasites, or viruses.

microorganisms   Life forms only visible through a microscope, for example, bacteria, viruses, and protozoa.

mutagen   A substance that causes changes (mutations) in the genetic traits passed from parent to offspring.

mycotoxins   Toxins produced by fungi.

nematodes   Wormlike organisms that inhabit the soil. They may also be a parasite on fish.

neurotoxins   Chemicals that affect the nervous system. Severe reactions can include visual problems, muscle twitching, weakness, abnormalities of brain function, and behavioral changes.

offal   Internal organs and soft tissue that are removed from a carcass when an animal is butchered.

oocyst   Egg of a protozoa.

organochlorines   Class of pesticides made by adding chlorine atoms to hydrocarbons. Examples are DDT, dieldrin, and endrin. Used as insecticides, these pesticides are persistent in the environment.

organophosphates   Class of pesticides containing phosphorus. Kill insects by disrupting nerve function.

parasite   An organism that lives off another.

pasteurization   Process for treating food by raising the temperature to a specific level and maintaining it for a set time to destroy microorganisms.

pathogen   A microorganism that causes disease.

persistence   The ability to remain in the environment for months or years without degrading into inert substances.

persistent pesticides   Pesticides that remain in the environment for months or years without degrading into inert substances.

postmortem   After-death examination of a body: autopsy.

protozoa   Single-celled animals that live in soil or water.

radiolytic products   Substances produced when food is irradiated.

rendered animal protein   Unused animal parts from slaughtering plants and euthanized pets boiled (sometimes using vacuum technology at low temperatures), dried, and used in animal feed.

residue   Substance remaining in or on the surface of a food.

rodenticide   Chemical used to kill rodents such as mice, rats, and gophers.

ruminant-to-ruminant feeding   Process of feeding herbivores, like cows, animal products from a rendering plant.

serotype   A group of closely related microorganisms.

shelf life   Length of time a product is safe to eat as determined by the manufacturer and marked on the label.

shiga toxin   A poison released by certain types of bacteria, including *E. coli* O157:H7.

strain   A variant of a species member.

systemic pesticide   Pesticide that migrates to a different part of a plant or animal from which it was applied.

time and temperature control for safety (TCS) foods   Foods that require time and temperature controls to prevent the growth of microorganisms.

tolerance   Maximum amount of a substance legally allowed to contaminate a food.

toxicant   Poisons produced by human-made activities such as pesticides.

toxin-mediated infection   Illness caused by bacteria that produces toxin in the intestinal tract.

toxins   Poisons produced by natural organisms such as pathogenic bacteria.

trace-back/trace-forward   Process to identify the origin of contaminated food.

verotoxins   Powerful toxins produced by some types of *E. coli*.

virulence   Degree to which bacteria can cause illness.

virus   A microbe smaller than bacteria which needs a host cell to replicate.

zoonosis   Disease communicable from animals to humans.

Acronyms

APHIS:	Animal and Plant Health Inspection Service
BPA:	Bisphenol A
BSE:	Bovine Spongiform Encephalopathy
CAFO:	Concentrated Animal Feeding Operation
CFIA:	Canadian Food Inspection Agency
CFSAN:	Center for Food Safety and Applied Nutrition (of the FDA)
CJD:	Creutzfeldt-Jakob Disease
CSPI:	Center for Science in the Public Interest
EFSA:	European Food Safety Authority
EPA:	U.S. Environmental Protection Agency
EWG:	Environmental Working Group
FAO:	Food and Agriculture Organization of the United Nations
FDA:	U.S. Food and Drug Administration
FFDCA:	Federal Food, Drug, and Cosmetic Act

FIFRA: Federal Insecticide, Fungicide, and
                Rodenticide Act

FSIS: Food Safety Inspection Service

FSMA: Food Safety Modernization Act

GMO: Genetically Modified Organism

GRAS: Generally Recognized as Safe

LFTB: Lean Finely Textured Beef

MAP: Modified Atmosphere Packaging

NACMCF: National Advisory Committee on
                Microbiological Criteria for Foods

NIEHS: National Institute of Environmental
                Health Science

NTP: National Toxicology Program

PFGE: Pulsed-Field Gel Electrophoresis

rBGH: Recombinant Bovine Growth Hormone

RTE: Ready to Eat

TCS: Time and Temperature Control for Safety

TDS: Total Dietary Study

USDA: U.S. Department of Agriculture

WHO: World Health Organization

About the Authors

Nina E. Redman, MLIS, RD, is a registered dietitian working with HIV-positive patients in Sonoma County, California. She is a former librarian, and has worked in academic, public, and corporate libraries. She is the author of the first two editions of *Food Safety: A Reference Handbook*, and also co-wrote the second edition of *Human Rights: A Reference Handbook*, all part of the Contemporary World Issues series from ABC-CLIO.

Michele Morrone is professor of Environmental Health, coordinator of the nationally accredited Environmental Health Science program, and director of the Appalachian Rural Health Institute at Ohio University in Athens, Ohio. She has degrees from the Ohio State University and the University of New Hampshire. She is an award-winning teacher, offering courses in food safety, vector control, risk communication, built environment and health, and climate change and public health. Dr. Morrone previously served as the chief of the Office of Environmental Education at Ohio Environmental Protection Agency. She has authored or coauthored numerous papers on a variety of environmental issues and has published three books: *Sound Science, Junk Policy: Environmental Health Science and the Decision Making Process* (2002), *Poisons on Our Plates: The Real Food Safety Problem in the United States* (2008), and *Mountains of Injustice: Case Studies in Environmental Equity* (2011). She is working on her next book: *Ailing in Place: Environmental and Public Health in Appalachia*. She was the 2012 Fulbright Research Scholar in Science and the Environment at McMaster University in Hamilton, Ontario, Canada.